William Ralston Shedden Ralston

The Songs of the Russian People,

as illustrative of Slavonic mythology and Russian social life

William Ralston Shedden Ralston

The Songs of the Russian People,
as illustrative of Slavonic mythology and Russian social life

ISBN/EAN: 9783337412913

Printed in Europe, USA, Canada, Australia, Japan

Cover: Foto ©Thomas Meinert / pixelio.de

More available books at **www.hansebooks.com**

THE SONGS
OF THE RUSSIAN PEOPLE,

AS ILLUSTRATIVE OF SLAVONIC MYTHOLOGY
AND RUSSIAN SOCIAL LIFE.

BY

W. R. S. RALSTON, M.A.

OF THE BRITISH MUSEUM,

AUTHOR OF "KRILOF AND HIS FABLES."

SECOND EDITION.

London:

ELLIS & GREEN,
33, KING STREET, COVENT GARDEN.
1872.
[*All rights reserved.*]

PREFACE.

When the present volume was originally planned it was intended to contain an account of Russian folk-lore in general—of the stories, legends, riddles, proverbs, and epic as well as lyric poems, which oral tradition has preserved among the Russian peasantry. But I soon found that the subject was one which, if treated at all in detail, would require more time and space than I had expected. So I thought it best to restrict myself for the present to a part of it only, leaving the rest to be described afterwards. In this first instalment of the work, therefore, I have dealt chiefly, though not exclusively, with the lyric poetry of the peasantry; the next will be mainly devoted to their Popular Tales and their Metrical Romances.

In order to render intelligible the songs I have quoted, it has been necessary to give some slight account of the religious ideas attributed to the ancient

Slavonians and the superstitions current among their descendants, as well as of some of the manners and customs of the Russian peasantry, especially with regard to marriages and funerals. But my book can make no pretence to any thing like a satisfactory grappling with the difficult problems—mythological, ethnological, philological, historical—suggested by the study of Slavonic antiquities. Perhaps the best excuse I can offer for my shortcomings with respect to those questions is this. A great part of the ground over which I have hastily skimmed has been explored by a scholar who is far better qualified for the task than I am. And so to Mr. Morfill's forthcoming work on "The Slaves" I refer, at all events for a time, all who wish for fuller information on the subject.

In the translations contained in the present volume I have attempted to give, in every case, as literal a version of the original as possible. My rule has been to translate the songs into prose, line for line and word for word, and this rule has scarcely ever been broken. Only here and there, in the introductory chapter and in that on Marriage, I have been sometimes almost unconsciously led into following, to some slight extent, the rhythmical flow of the Russian. Rhyme, as my readers are probably aware, very rarely appears in any but modern Russian Songs, and upon recent poetry I have not touched.

For inconsistency in the use of accents I have only this excuse to offer. On my "copy" I had marked every accented syllable, but typographical difficulties prevented me from carrying out my original idea. After having begun to print, however, I found that certain words were specially liable to be mispronounced, so I inserted a few marks here and there, where they seemed to be most needed, in order to show on which syllable the accent ought to fall.

With respect to the authorities I have consulted, it may be as well to say a few words. My chief aim has been to render available to such students of mythology and folk-lore as may happen not to read Russian, some part, at least, of the evidence bearing upon those subjects which has been collected in Russia, but which has not been hitherto rendered into generally intelligible speech, and therefore I have not thought it necessary to make more than occasional reference to books written in, or translated into, the languages of Western Europe [1]. Of the

---

[1] A long list of books in various languages on Slavonic Antiquities is given by Dr. I. J. Hanusch. See *Die Wissenschaft des slawischen Mythus*, pp. 48—71. A number of Russian Songs have been faithfully translated by P. Von Goetze, under the title of *Stimmen des russischen Volks in Liedern*. Stuttgart, 1828. A

Russian authorities on which I have principally relied a full list will be given at the end of the book. The Songs contained in the present volume have been taken, for the most part, from the rich collections made by Sakharof and Shein; the descriptions of popular manners and customs have been mainly borrowed from the valuable works of Snegiref and Tereshchenko; the greater part of the chapter on Funeral Songs I have extracted from the erudite treatise by Kotlyarevsky, "On the Funeral Rites of the Heathen Slavonians;" and for the arrangement and much of the contents of the chapter on Mythic and Ritual Songs I am indebted to Orest Miller's "Historical Survey of Russian Literature."

But it is to Alexander Nikolaevich Afanasief, whose recent and premature death cannot sufficiently be deplored, that I am under the deepest obligations. His great work, "On the Poetic Views of the Old Slavonians about Nature" is a rich storehouse to which I have had constant recourse in the present volume; on his excellent collections of Russian Popular Tales and Legends the next volume will be based; and from his writings in general I have derived frequent assistance while studying the Builinas,

---

few occur also in the collection entitled *Balalaika. Eine Sammlung slawischer Lieder von W. von Waldbrühl.* Leipzig, 1848.

or Metrical Romances—with respect to which the special books of reference are the collections of Ruibnikof and Kiryeevsky[2], and the critical works of Buslaef, Bezsonof, Maikof, Orest Miller, Schiefner, Stasof, and many others. There is one other Russian scholar to whom I wish to render hearty acknowledgments for aid constantly received. Were it not for the great dictionary " of the living Russian language " by Vladimir Dahl, a foreigner would be hopelessly bewildered when trying to make his way through the difficult field of Russian folk-lore.

Finally, let me offer cordial thanks for the assistance personally tendered to me by many Russian friends, as well upon other occasions as on those of my visits to Russia in 1868 and 1870. To them I dedicate my book, trusting that, imperfect as it is, they will recognize in it such traces of honest work as may render them lenient towards its sins both of omission and of commission.

January, 1872.

---

[2] A new collection of *builinas* is now in the press, containing the poems written down from the dictation of the Olonets "rhapsodists" by the editor, A. F. Hilferding. They will not be arranged according to their subjects, nor chronologically; but they will be grouped in relation to their reciters—all the poems dictated by each rhapsodist being kept together.

PREFACE TO THE SECOND EDITION.

A WORK has recently been published, to which, had I seen it before my book went to press, I should have made frequent reference—Professor Bernhard Schmidt's *Das Volksleben der Neugriechen und das hellenische Alterthum*. The similarity between the folk-lore of the modern Greeks, as described in it,[3] and that of the Russians, is most striking—so much so, that it seems to point to something more than a common origin ages ago. Professor Schmidt utterly repudiates Fallmerayer's doctrine with respect to the preponderance of the Slavonic element in the population of modern Greece, and he will not allow that Slavonic myths have at all seriously affected those of Hellenic descent. However this may be, many of the customs and songs which I have quoted

[3] And in the works of Wachsmuth, Ulrichs, Passow, Kind, Fauriel, Firmenich-Richartz, and many others, of most of which an account is given in the "Notes on the ballads, tales, and classical superstitions of the modern Greeks," contained in chapters 21 and 28—30 of the Rev. H. F. Tozer's "Researches in the Highlands of Turkey."

in the present book offer a singular resemblance to those of the modern Greeks, one which is often far closer than that which can be traced between them and the rest of their kin in other lands. It may be worth while in this Preface to mention a few of the details in which Slavonic and Hellenic folk-life and folk-lore seem most alike.

The Russian Khorovod—the circling dance to song often of a serious or even sad nature, which Kavelin traces back to heathen rites performed in circle around an idol—appears to be closely akin to the dances which in Greece still retain much of their old religious character. The Russian *Kaliki*, or blind psalm-singers, and the reciters of the *builinas*, find their exact counterpart in Greece. Such ideas as are held by the Slavonians about the demoniacal character of mid-day, and which are common to many countries, exercise special influence on the Greeks. The Slavonic nymphs—Rusalkas, Vilas, Mavkas etc.—bear a much closer resemblance to the *Neraides* of modern Greece than they do to their sisters in other European lands. A similar resemblance is to be found between the Greek Lamia and the Russian Baba Yaga. The ideas about vampires are identical among the Greeks and Slavonians, the name for a vampire being one of the very few words of Slavonic origin in modern Greek. The ceremonies, also, attendant on the building of a new house are almost the same, whether the builders be Greeks or Slavonians. The three Baba Yagas of Russian Storyland are very like the three *Moirais* who in Greece have succeeded to the old Fates. And the Slavonic folk-beliefs with respect to the life beyond the grave, like as they are to those held in Latin, Teutonic, and Celtic lands, yet still more closely resemble those of the modern Greeks.

Since the Preface to the first edition was printed I have read Professor Hilferding's most interesting account (in the March number of the *Vyestnik Evropui*) of his recent expedition to the home of the "Rhapsodists" described by Ruibnikof. I have, for the present, availed myself in a few instances only of his criticisms, but they will be of the utmost value to me when I am dealing with the "metrical romances" in detail.

It may be as well to observe that, throughout the following chapters, I have generally confined myself to stating, without criticizing, the opinions held by the Russian Mythologists whom I have quoted.

April, 1872.

CONTENTS.

CHAPTER I.

INTRODUCTORY.

	PAGE
Khorovod, or Choral, Songs	1
The Posidyélka, or Social Gathering	32
The Besyéda	36
Divisions of Songs	39
Cossack and Robber Songs	42
Soldier Songs	51
The Builínas, or Metrical Romances	55
Story of Svyatogor	58
Story of Sukhman	64
Ruibnikof's Researches	67

CHAPTER II.

MYTHOLOGY.

SECTION I.—THE OLD GODS.

Old Slavonic Mythology	80
Perun	86
Other Slavonic Deities	103

SECTION II.—DEMIGODS AND FAIRIES.

Ideas about the Soul	107
The Domovoy, or House-spirit	120

xiv CONTENTS.

	PAGE
House-changing Ceremonies	136
The Rusálka, or Naiad	139
The Vodyany, or Water-sprite	148
The Lyeshy, or Wood-demon	153

SECTION III.—STORYLAND BEINGS.

The Bába Yagá, or Ogress	161
Koshchei the Immortal	164
The Witch	168
The Snake	172
The Water-king	178
Swan Maidens	179
Tom Thumb	183

CHAPTER III.

MYTHIC AND RITUAL SONGS.

Kolyádki, or Christmas Songs	186
Gadániya, or Guessings	195
Ovsen and New Year Songs	202
Feast of the Epiphany	207
Death of Winter	210
Reception of the Spring	211
Cuckoo Christening	214
Eastertide	219
Krasnaya Gorka	222
Dodola Songs	227
St. George Songs	229
Semik and Whitsuntide Songs	233
Midsummer Rites	239
Kupálo	241
Funeral of Kostroma, or Yarilo	244
Harvest Rites	247

		PAGE
Volos, the Cattle-God	.	251
September Customs	.	254
The Ovín, or Corn-kiln	.	257
Dmitry's Saturday	.	260

CHAPTER IV.

MARRIAGE SONGS.

A modern Peasant Wedding	263
Old Slavonian ideas about Marriage	282
Purchase of the Bride	283
Bride's Sorrow at leaving her Home	287
Her affection towards her Parents	292
Mitigation of Patriarchal Severity	293
Love Songs	295
A Bride's Complaint	303
Songs of Married Life	305
Mythical Wedding Guests	306

CHAPTER V.

FUNERAL SONGS.

Death Weddings	309
The Rádunitsa	310
Modern Funeral Rites	313
Funeral Banquets	320
Ghost Banquets	321
Ancient Funeral Rites	322
Human Sacrifices	327
Strava and Trizna	331

xvi   CONTENTS.

	PAGE
Lament of Orphans	334
A Widow's Lament	338
Wailings at Graves	343

CHAPTER VI.

SORCERY AND WITCHCRAFT.

Zagádkas, or Enigmas	346
Zagovórs, or Spells	357
Buyan, the Elysian Isle	374
The stone Alatuir	376
Wizards and Witches	378
Amulets	387
Cattle-spells	389
Poisoners	393
Cattle-plague Spells	395
Cholera and Small-pox	402
Werewolves	404
Vampires	409
History of Russian Witchcraft	417
Mythological Explanations	427
Conclusion	433

APPENDICES.

(A.) List of Authorities	437
(B.) Note on Metres	440

THE SONGS
OF THE RUSSIAN PEOPLE.

CHAPTER I.

INTRODUCTORY.

BEFORE entering upon the consideration of the more important features of the poetical folk-lore of Russia —the relics of mythic and ritual song, the remains of a wide-spread system of sorcery which have drifted down to our days in the form of truncated spells, exorcisms, and incantations, and the fragmentary epics or metrical romances called Builinas—before endeavouring to fix the fleeting images they offer of the past, it may be as well to tarry awhile in the present; to trace a rapid outline of the general aspect of Russian popular poetry; to give some brief account of the songs which are sung on ordinary occasions by the peasantry, of the times and places when and where they are usually to be heard, and of what manner of persons they are who sing them. And perhaps the simplest method of conveying this information will be to describe in a few words what are, so far at least as the younger members of the peasantry are concerned, two of the most popular institutions of Russia—the Khorovod, or choral dance, and the Posidyelka, or social gathering.

As soon as the long winter has fully passed away, and the spring has made its welcome influence felt, the thoughts of the younger members of every village community in Russia begin to turn towards the blended dance and song of the Khorovod. Before long, what are called the vernal Khorovods are making their voices heard all over the land, to pass successively into those of summer and autumn, before they disappear at the approach of wintry weather. Whence were derived these circling dances to the sound of song, or at what period they gained their hold upon the Slavonic peoples, neither history nor tradition can say. All that the Russian peasant cares to know about them is, that they formed the favourite solace of generation after generation of his ever-toiling and often suffering ancestors, and that the songs which belong to them have been for the most part carefully handed down from parent to child from some remote period of time of which he has but a very vague idea. Nor have the researches of the learned thrown any very clear light on the subject, nothing definite being known even as to the origin of the word Khorovod—one of which the equivalent, among many of the Slavonians, is the simpler term *Kolo*, a circle.

But it is not on the history of the Khorovod that it is proposed to dwell at present, but rather on the songs associated with it, on the poetical delineations of Russian social life for which it has offered itself as at once canvas and frame, on the long series of versified domestic dramas towards the performance of which it has from immemorial times contributed successive generations of actors. To the student of the popular poetry of Russia the Khorovod is one of the most instructive, as well as interesting, of the institutions of the country. How rich in popular poetry that country is but few foreigners are thoroughly aware. And indeed there are many of its natives who have but a very slight idea of the poetic wealth amassed by the great body of their countrymen—the full appreciation, and the careful study of the songs of the common people being among the results of comparatively recent times.

A vein of natural and genuine poetry runs through the thought and speech of the Russian peasant, and so in the songs which accompany him through life there is a true poetic ring. But it is not on their poetic charm alone that their value depends. They have the additional merit of frequently offering a faithful picture of the manners of the people by or among whom they are sung; of often echoing the expressions, and embodying the sentiments, of the many millions of Russian men and women of low degree, with whose inner lives it is not easy to become acquainted. As in the Builinas, or "metrical romances," to which the people love to listen,—fragmentary epics dealing with the adventures of princes and heroes,—the dimly-seen form of the historical past of Russia is supposed by most of their commentators to reveal itself; so in the songs of the villagers, by common consent, may be recognized the principal features of the life led within the family circle by the Russian peasants. On them, remarks one of the principal collectors of his country's popular poetry[1], their songs have no slight influence. Commencing at the side of his cradle, song accompanies the Russian man during the games of his childhood and the sports of his youth, and gives expression to his earliest feelings of love. In the ears of the girls it is always ringing; and if it depicts in sombre hues the unwelcome change from maiden freedom to wedded subjection, it also paints, in glowing colours, the happiness of mutual attachment. To the husband and wife it suggests many a form of loving words, and teaches them how, with croons about the "evil Tartars" of olden days, to lull their babes to sleep, and to soothe the restlessness of their elder children. Song lightens the toil of the working hours, whether carried on out of doors, amid exposure to sun and wind, and rain and frost, or within the stifling hut, by the feeble light of a pinewood splinter; it enlivens the repose of the holiday, giving animation to the choral dance by day and the social gathering by night. The younger generation grows up, and song escorts the conscript son to the army, the wedded daughter to her new home, and mourns over the sorrow of the parents of whom their children have taken what may be a last farewell.

[1] Ruibnikof, III. p. iii.

Then comes the final scene of all, and when the tired eyes are closed for ever, and the weary hands are crossed in peace, song hovers around the silent form, and addresses to its heedless ears passionate words of loving entreaty. Nor does its ministering cease even then, for, as each returning spring brings back the memory of the past together with fresh hopes for the future, song rises again above the graves of the departed, as, after the fashion of their pagan ancestors, the villagers celebrate their yearly memorial of the dead.

Who composed these songs no one can say, and even what date ought to be assigned to them cannot well be determined. The mythical fragments have evidently come down from heathen times, bearing the unmistakable stamp of great antiquity; and many of the ritual songs, including those relating to marriage, have probably been sung for many hundreds of years. But the majority of the songs with which we have to do at present, those used by Khorovod performers, must be referred, so far at least as their present form is concerned, to a much later date. Judging by their structure, says Tereshchenko[2], these songs belong to different, but not distant periods. A few of those which will presently be quoted, such as the "Millet Sowing," the "Titmouse," and the "Poppy Growing," he attributes to the Sixteenth Century, but the rest to the Seventeenth or Eighteenth. As to their composers, he

[2] IV. 136.

continues, all that we can determine about them is that they must have belonged to the common people, for otherwise they never could have expressed with so much sympathy the simple thoughts and feelings of the villagers, or described with such accuracy, and with so complete a freedom from artificial embellishment, the commonplace occurrences of village-life. The latter part of this criticism is not likely to be disputed, but as regards the dates of the songs Tereshchenko's arguments have not been universally accepted as conclusive.

When a holiday arrives, in fine spring weather, even the saddest looking of Russian hamlets assumes a lively aspect[3]. In front of their wooden huts the old people sit "simply chatting in a rustic row," the younger men and women gather together in groups, each sex apart from the other, and talk about their fields and their flocks, their families, and their household affairs. Across the river they see their horses, free from labour for the day, browsing in the green meadows; above the copse rises the blue cupola of a neighbouring church; beyond the log-houses a streak of road stretches away into the distance, and loses itself among the woods which darken the plain and fringe the horizon. Along the village street and the slope towards the river stroll the girls in their holiday array, merrily wending towards the open space in which the Khorovods are always held, and singing as they go—

[3] Tereshchenko, IV. 136—140.

The beautiful maidens have come forth
From within the gates, to wander out of doors.
They have carried out with them a nightingale,
And have set the nightingale upon the grass,
On the grassy turf, on the blue flowers.
The nightingale will break into song,
And the beautiful maidens will begin to dance;
But the young wives will pour forth tears.
" Play on, ye beautiful maidens,
While you still are at liberty in a father's home,
While you still lead a life of ease in the home of a mother."

When the appointed spot is reached they form a circle, take hands, and begin moving this way and that, or round and round. If the village is a large one a couple of Khorovods are formed, one at each end of the street, and the two bands move towards each other singing a song which changes, when they blend together, into the Byzantium-remembering chorus—

  To Tsargorod
   Will I go, will I go.
  With my lance the wall
   Will I pierce, will I pierce.

After this they proceed with their games and songs under the guidance of the *Khorovodnitsa*, or leader of the dance. If they become tired of performing by themselves, they invite the village youths to join them, singing—

The bright falcons have met in the oak-forest:
Into the greenwood have flown the white cygnets,
Fluttering about from bush to bush,
 . . . .

Pondering, considering,
" How shall we make ourselves nests ?
How shall we build ourselves warm nests ?"
  Didi, Ladi, Didi, Ladushki !
" How shall we maidens form our Khorovod ?
How shall we fair ones begin new carols ?"

Often, however, the Khorovod remains composed of girls alone, and then she who plays the male part in any of what may be called the little operettas which they perform, sometimes adopts a man's hat or cap, in order to be in keeping with her assumed character. Of these brief metrical dramas, the number of which is considerable, the following may be taken as specimens:

In the *Murmanka Shlyapa*, the " Murman Cap[4]," a drunken *Pan*, or Lord, comes staggering in, followed by a *Pan'ya*, or Lady. Presently his cap falls off, and he orders the Lady to pick it up. The chorus sings—

> From the Prince has come a drunken Lord,
> He has dropped his Murman cap.
> To the Lady young the Lord has cried,
> "Come hither, come hither, O Lady young,
> Pick up, pick up, my Murman cap."

The Lady, in the pride of her maiden liberty, replies—

> " I, my Lord, am not thy handmaid;
> I am the handmaid of my father
> And of my mother."

---

[4] The Murmanki were large caps, richly adorned with fur, worn in old times by the Grand Dukes and Boyars. The word may possibly be corrupted from the name Norman.

The chorus recommences—

From the Prince has come a drunken Lord,
He has dropped his Murman cap.
To his Lady young the Lord has cried,
"Come hither, come hither,
My Lady young,
Pick up, pick up,
My sable Murman cap."

By this time the Lady has become his wife, so she no longer refuses to obey his commands, but replies with humility,

"My Lord, I am thy handmaid,
I will pick up thy sable Murman cap,
And I will place it on thy daring head[5]."

The idea of the despotic power of the husband is expressed still more strongly in the favourite game of "A Wife's Love." A youth and a girl, or more frequently two girls, one of whom wears a man's hat, take their place in the middle of the circle of singers, who begin—

Wife, I am going,
To walk through the bazaar[6].
Wife, my wifie,
Hard is thy heart.
Wife, I will buy thee
Muslin for a sleeve.
Wife, my wifie,
Hard is thy heart.
See, wife, here is
Muslin for a sleeve.

[5] Tereshchenko, IV. 158.

[6] The Kitai-Gorod, or China-Town of Moscow, is part of the bazaar outside the Kremlin. It takes its name from Kitaigrod in Podolia, the birthplace of Helena, the mother of Ivan the Terrible.

The husband offers his present. At first his wife will not look at it; presently she snatches it from his hand, and flings it on the ground. The chorus sings,

> Good people, only see!
> She does not love her husband at all!
> Never agrees with him, never bows down to him,
> From him turns away!

The second act is similar to the first. The husband buys his wife a golden ring, but it fares no better than his former present.

Then comes the third and final act, in which the husband cries—

> Wife, I will go
> To the bazaar—
> Wife, I will buy thee
> A silken whip.

This time when he brings his new offering, and says—

> There, wife,
> Is your dear present!

She looks upon him affectionately, he gives her a blow with the whip, and she bows low before him and kisses him, while the chorus sings—

> Good people, only see!
> How well she loves her Lord!
> Always agrees with him, always bows down to him,
> Gives him kisses.

And the satisfied husband concludes with the words,

> Wife, my wifie,
> Soft is thy heart'.

[7] Tereshchenko, IV. 238.

The subject of wife-beating plays a considerable part in Russian popular poetry. The following song may serve as a specimen of the manner in which it is treated.

Across the Don a plank lay, thin and bending ;
No foot along it passed.
But I alone, the young one, from the hill,
I went along it with my true love dear,
And to my love I said :
O darling, dear!
Beat not thy wife without a cause,
But only for good cause beat thou thy wife,
And for a great offence.
Far away is my father dear,
And farther still my mother dear ;
They cannot hear my voice,
They cannot see my burning tears[*].

The "Millet-Sowing," the "Hedge" and the "Beer-Brewing" will occur in a later chapter : the "Geese," the "Sparrow," and many others of the same kind, ought to be described among the "games" of which the Russian people possess so rich a store, rather than among their poems, and therefore we will not dwell upon them at present, but there are a few others in which historical allusions occur, and which therefore seem to deserve especial attention. Such, for instance, are the "Titmouse" and the "Oak Bench."

The subject of the first is marriage. The Bulfinch, after many unsuccessful attempts, determines to get married ; so his sister, the Titmouse, invites

[*] Shein, I. 403.

the birds to her dwelling, in order that he may choose a spouse. The person who represents the Bulfinch wanders about inside the Khorovod, seeking for his bride among its members, who sing—

> Beyond the sea the Titmouse lived; not grand,
> Not sumptuous was her state—but beer she brewed,
> Bought malt, and borrowed hops. The Blackbird brewed,
> And the distiller was the Eagle grey.
> " Grant us, O Lord, that we the beer may brew,
> May brew the beer, the brandy may distil—
> We will invite as guests the little birds."
> The widow Owl, though uninvited, came.
> The Bulfinch wandered through the passages,
> The Owl caressed the feathers of her head.
> Among themselves the birds began to say,
> " Why ever don't you marry, Bulfinch dear?"
> " Fain would I marry could I find a bride.
> I'd take the Linnet—only she's my mother.
> I'd take the Titmouse—only she's my sister.
> I'd take the Magpie—but she chatters so.
> But there, across the water, lives the Quail:
> Neither my mother nor my aunt is she:
> Her do I love, and I will marry her[9]."

This song is said to have been written during the reign of Ivan the Terrible (A.D. 1533—1584) but to have been prohibited for a time, on account of its containing allusions to the life of a certain influential Boyar.

In the "Oak Bench" a girl sits pensively in the middle of a circle of young people who, with linked hands, move around her, singing—

[9] Tereshchenko, IV. 280.

By the river side
Lies an oaken bench,
An oaken plank—
On that oaken bench
Sits a fair young Swede,
In a blue pelisse,
With a girdle of silk.

Presently some of the youths leave the circle and lay hands on her—

There have come dragoons,
Young cavaliers,
They have seized, have laid hold of the Swedish woman,
Have set her in a carriage,
Have taken her along the banks of the Moskva.

The prisoner begins to weep, on which some of the youths console her, others strike up merry music, and the rest break into a lively dance—

The Swedish woman has begun to weep piteously,
But the dragoons console her,
They strike upon their drums,
They tootle on their fifes.

At the sight of so much merriment the captive forgets her sorrows, and joins her warders in the dance, while the chorus sings—

The Swedish woman has grown more joyous,
The Swede has begun to dance,
And having danced she has bowed low.
Well done! O, ye dragoons!
Ye know how to seize a Swedish woman,
And at consoling a Swedish woman are ye expert[1].

[1] Tereshchenko, IV. 165.

This song is one of many similar relics of the war between Peter the Great and Charles the Twelfth of Sweden.

But such chants as this, although rendered interesting by their historical associations, are not remarkably poetic. It may be as well, therefore, before going farther, to give some specimens of songs which possess intrinsic as well as accidental merit, prefacing them, however, by a few words of deprecatory criticism.

There are two points in which these dramatic sketches of Russian life may seem defective to foreign eyes—they may appear to lack variety of form, and still more to be wanting in contrast of colour. Nor can it be denied that they are often monotonous and sombre. In former days, at least, the ideas of their composers not unnaturally revolved in a narrow circle. In the choice of their themes, the popular poets seldom ventured off the beaten track; in the treatment of their subjects they rarely deviated from the ordinary method. And the tone of their compositions, undoubtedly, is apt to be painfully subdued. Although one of the saddest features of Russian peasant life, the slavery which weighed so heavily on the mass of the people from the time of Boris Godunof to that of Alexander II., is seldom, if ever, alluded to in the popular songs, yet a settled gloom too often prevails in many of the pictures they offer, unbroken by a sparkle of high light, unrelieved by a touch of warm colour. In this, however, they are not out of keeping with the landscape of certain parts of Russia, suggestive as they are of grey plains dotted with sad brown huts, or of dark forests where no sound is heard but the sighing of the wind through the pines. But such drawbacks being admitted, it is only fair to recognize the merits also of these songs of the people—the untutored freshness of their thought, the nervous vigour of their language, the musical ring of their versification, their complete freedom from the sickly affectation, the wearisome sentimentality, and the tawdry ornamentation of the mock pastorals and spurious idylls of the age in which very many of them were composed. Unfortunately it is next to impossible to give in a translation, however faithful it may be, any idea of the greater part of these merits. The stuffed nightingale of the taxidermist is but a poor exchange for the living songster of the woodland.

Love is, of course, the inspirer of the great majority of these songs, but it is generally the darker side of love which they reveal; it is on its sorrows, its disappointments, its betrayals, that they lay most stress. The separation of lovers, for instance, is one of their favourite themes. Generally it is a girl who bewails her lot, lamenting over the departure of him who is so dear to her. Such is the case, for instance, in the following lyric—

> Valley of mine, sweet valley!
> O thou wide valley!
> Within that valley
> A Guelder-rose tree grew,

And on that tree
There sat a Cuckoo kookooing.
" Wherefore, O my Cuckoo,
Art thou kookooing ? "
" Wherefore, O sad maiden,
Art thou sorrowing ? "
" How can I, poor Cuckoo,
Cease from kookooing ? "
" How can I, sad maiden,
Cease from sorrowing ? "
" One green garden had I—
And that is withering ! "
" One dear friend had I—
And he is departing !
Alone does he leave me,
The young one, alone [2] ! "

Sometimes it is the youth who mourns for a lost love—stolen away from him perhaps by a richer rival.

" Why, O Dove, art thou so joyless ? "
How can I, poor Dove, be joyous ?
Late last night my mate was with me.
My mate was with me, on one wing she slept,
Slept on one wing, embraced me with the other,
With the other embraced me, calling me her dear one.
" Dear beloved one ! Dovelet blue !
Sleep, yet do not sleep, my dovelet,
Only do not, sleeping, lose me, darling."
The Dove awoke, his mate was gone !
Hither, thither, he flung himself, dash'd himself,
Hither, thither, in homes of Nobles,
Homes of Nobles, Princes, Merchants.
In a Merchant's garden did I find my Dove,
In a Merchant's garden, underneath an apple-tree ;

[2] Shcin, I. 310.

Underneath an apple-tree, wounded sore with shot!
The Merchant's son had wounded my Dove,
Wounded her with a weapon of gold[3].

But the desertion is generally on the part of the "good youth." The girl's heart remains faithful to its love.

> Misty is the sunlight, misty;
> None the sun can see.
> Mournful is the maiden, mournful:
> None her grief can tell.
> Not her father dear, nor her mother dear,
> Nor her sister dear, dovelet white.
> Mournful is the maiden, mournful.
> "Canst not thou find a solace for thy woe?
> Canst not thou thy dear friend forget?
> Neither by day nor yet by night,
> Neither at dawn nor by the evening glow?"
> Thus did the maiden in her grief reply—
> "Then only my dear love will I forget,
> When my swift feet shall under me give way,
> And to my side my hands fall helplessly;
> What time my eyes are filled with dust,
> And coffin boards my bosom white conceal[4]."

When her lover is taken from her, a girl is sometimes described as being so crushed by the blow that she can no longer endure to live. Such a despair as this is described in a song which commences with a broken-hearted youth's complaint—

> "Keep watch no more by night, dear love,
> The waxen taper burn no more,

---

[3] Shein, I. 323. The last line is translated from another copy.
[4] Sakharof, I. iii. 208.

No more await me at the midnight hour.
Ah me! our sunny days have passed away,
The stormy wind has carried off our joys,
And scattered them across the open plain!
My father has arranged,
My mother has enjoined,
That I should take another as my wife!
There blaze not in the sky two suns,
Nor shine two moons,
Nor can the youth's heart two loves know.
My father I will not disobey,
My mother's behests I will fulfil.
And I will take another as my wife—
Another will I wed—Death early wooed,
Death early wooed by violence!"
Then melted into tears the maiden fair,
And thus with tears she spake:
" Oh thou, my love, my eye's delight!
No dweller in the white light will I be
When thou art gone, my source of hope!
The swan knows not two mates,
Two mates the dove knows not,
Nor I two loves."
No longer keeps she watch by night,
But still the waxen taper burns.
Upon the table stands a coffin new,
Within the coffin lies the maiden fair[5].

A maiden whose parents wish her to marry a stranger and give up her " hope, her heart's beloved," exclaims in her grief—

> Forth will I go
> To the meadows green.
> With outcry loud
> On Harm will I call.

[5] Sakharof, I. iii. 208.

"Come hither, come hither,
Ye beasts of prey!
Here is luscious food—
Come tear me to shreds!
Only leave untouched
My beating heart,
And bear it away
To the hands of my dear one.
Ah! there let him see
How fondly I loved him[6]."

Sometimes it is death that steps in between two lovers and separates them for ever. Here is part of a song expressing the passionate grief of a youth whose "dovelet dear," whose "sweet cygnet," has passed away "at the rising of the bright sun."

O winds, warm winds,
Warm autumn winds,
Breathe not, ye are not wanted here.
But hither fly ye stormy winds
From the Northern side;
Asunder rend moist mother earth,
And furrowing the open field,
The open, sweeping plain,
Reveal to me the coffin planks,
And let me for the last of times,
To my beloved one say farewell[7].

And here is a slightly modified extract from another, in which is heard the wailing of a "fair maiden" at the death-bed of her lover. As he lies there in his last agony, at his right hand stand his father and mother, on his left his brother and his sister. At the

[6] Sakharof, I. iii. 206.   [7] Sakharof, I iii. 204.

head of his couch are his friends. "Opposite his heart" stands the "fair maiden" weeping and bitterly lamenting.

> If God would grant my love his health,
> Were it but for one idle day,
> Though it were only for one little hour—
> Then would I wander with my love,
> Would tread the mossy turf,
> Would pluck the flow'rets blue,
> Would weave a garland for my love,
> And place it on my darling's head.
> Then homewards leading him in glad content,
> Would say, "My hope, my love!
> We two will keep together, love,
> Nor part, my darling, till at death
> We say farewell for ever to the light:
> Leaving behind us some such fame as this—
> That we two loved each other tenderly,
> And loyally, my love, together died [8]."

To the tears of a wife the songs attach less importance than to those of "a dear friend," or of a mother or a sister. In one instance a brave youth lies dead beside a thicket in the plain—

> There weeps his mother—as a river runs;
> There weeps his sister—as a streamlet flows;
> There weeps his youthful wife—as falls the dew.
> The sun will rise and gather up the dew [9].

And indeed a dying husband often seems to think less about the sorrow of his wife than about that of his parents and his children—

---

[8] Sakharof, I. iii 207.   [9] Sakharof, I. iii. 209.

Not for my kinsman do I grieve,
Nor for my youthful wife—
But for my little ones I grieve.
My darling little ones are left,
Dear little tiny innocents,
To suffer pangs of hunger and of cold[1].

Not only do the songs frequently describe the indifference which is likely to attend upon marriages contracted without the intervention of love, but they find a fruitful theme in the hatred into which that indifference sometimes deepens. Many of the most striking among them are devoted to tales of crime, especially to stories of poisoning. One of them, for instance, which is said to be founded on fact, describes with repulsive realism the murder of an old husband by his young and faithless wife. But it is generally the husband who makes away with his wife, sometimes merely because he is tired of her, sometimes in order that he may fill her place with one who is nearer to his heart.

It is generally by the agency of poison that a husband rids himself of the wife who has become an encumbrance—

Thanks, thanks to the blue pitcher!
It has rid me of my cares, my longings!
Not that cares afflicted me.
My real affliction was my wife.
"Hast not thou long been ailing, wife?
Get worse and worse then, wife,
Make haste to die!
Then shall I lead a freer life."

[1] Sakharof, I. iii. 204.

I will take a sharp axe;
I will seek the green copse;
I will fell a young pine;
I will build a new room;
I will set in it a glazed stove,
And I will take to myself a young wife,
And to my children a cruel stepmother.
But the children answered him and said:
"Be thou burnt with fire, thou new room!
And do thou die, O cruel stepmother!
But rise, rise again, O our own mother dear[2]!"

In many cases the poisoner is a girl, who, driven wild by passion or hate, avenges her real or fancied wrongs by the deadly cup.

Through the meadow she went
 The wicked one;
She dug for an evil root.
"I dug for the evil root,
 Deep, deep down!
I washed the evil root,
 White, all white!
I dried the evil root
 Dry, all dry!
I pounded the evil root,
 Small, so small.
I dressed the evil root,
 Dressed it—and meant it
For my cruel love.
To the lot of my own dear brother
 That evil root fell.

---

[2] Shein, I. 358. The epithet applied to the stepmother is a purely conventional one. Just as in the songs an axe is always called sharp, a pitcher blue, a hand white, a girl beautiful, and a youth or a horse "good," so is the stepmother always styled *likhaya*, malicious.

At eventide, my brother
  Began to moan.
At midnight, my brother
  Called for the priest.
With the grey light, my brother
  Passed away.
"Bury me, my sister
  Between three roads;
The Petersburg and the Moscow
  And the road that leads to Tver.
All who pass by
  Will pray to God,
And on thee, sister,
  A curse invoke[3]."

In one song, which bears the stamp of a foreign origin, and is probably of a mythical character, a sister intentionally offers a deadly draught to her brother, with the design of consuming him with fire. He happens, however, to let a drop fall from the cup on his horse's mane, which instantly begins to burn. Thereupon he cuts off her head at once, remarking that she is a snake and no sister of his. But this piece of oriental savagery is merely a lyrical setting either of ideas connected with the old and deeply rooted belief in witchcraft, of which an account will be given in another chapter, or of some mythological fragment which has given rise to various stories of a somewhat similar kind; as, for instance, that of Arthur's narrow escape from death at the hands of Guendolen—an incident which Sir Walter Scott borrowed, in his "Bridal of Triermain," from the German

[3] Shein, I. 328.

tale of how Count Otto of Oldenburg was invited by a fairy maiden to drink from a magic horn, and how he let a portion of the proffered beverage fall on his white steed, the hair of which it immediately burnt off[4]. But whatever may be its origin, it decidedly must not be looked upon as in any way typical of the relations existing between brothers and sisters in Russia. On these relations the Russian songs do not dwell nearly so much as the Servian, but still there are to be found among them expressions of brotherly or sisterly love or regret. Of such a nature is the following lament, which is interesting, moreover, inasmuch as it contains one of the allusions to the Tartars—those terrible enemies who used to overrun the land—which are to be met with in Russian popular poetry so much less often than might have been expected.

> In his garden green
> A youth sowed flowers,
> And having sown them, wept,
> "Ah me! blue flow'rets dear,
> Who is to water you?
> To shelter you from evil frosts?
> My father and my mother are too old,
> A sister had I once,
> But she for water to the Danube went.
> Was she drowned in the Danube's waves?
> Was she lost in the forest dark?
> Did the wolves her body rend?
> Or evil Tartars carry her away?
> In the Danube had she been drowned,
> Turbid with sand the Danube's waves would roll;

---

[4] Thorpe's Northern Mythology, III. 128. *Deutsche Sagen*, 541.

If the wolves had her body rent,
Scattered across the plain her bones would lie.
If the Tartars had carried her off,
Surely some tidings would have reached my ears [5]."

In one instance a husband's mere wish proves fatal to his "evil wife." It must be remembered that death was usually represented by the Slavonians, unless under strong ecclesiastical influence, as a female being.

> Against my will was I married;
> I have taken an evil wife.
> An evil one, not to my liking,
> Neither in feeling nor thought.
> Lovingly live with her—that will I not.
> Across the stream will I go,
> Love will I make to the girls.
> As for that wife of mine
> I will go pray for her death.
> Along the bank of the stream
> Death, the beautiful, goes.
> " Ho there! My beautiful Death!
> Turn thee back again, Death!
> Make an end of my wife!"
> Scarce had I spoken—when Death
> Began her work with my wife.
> Scarce had I time to look round—
> Shrouded in linen white was her corpse!
> Struck was the stroke on the bell[6].

One more extract may be given, in which an unnatural husband longs for his wife's death. The cry of A—oo[7] which occurs in it is the Slavonic equivalent

---

[5] Sakharof, I. iii. 205.   [6] Shein, I. 356.
[7] The vowel sounds a, u, pronounced as in Italian.

of the Australian Coo-ey, and is a call with which the woods of Russia may be heard ringing in summer and autumn, when the young people wander through them gathering nuts and berries—

Out in the dreamy woods,
There goes wandering a fair maiden,
That fair maiden, darling Mashenka.
Masha was gathering berries and mushrooms,
Ere she'd gathered her berries and mushrooms,
She lost her way in the gloomy forest,
Began to A-oo to her dear friend.
"A-oo! A-oo! Thou dear friend,
Not far art thou, dear; wilt not thou answer to my call."
"I cannot answer to thy call,
For over me are watchers three—
Watchers three—three stern ones they.
The first watcher—my wife's father,
The second watcher—my wife's mother,
The third watcher—my young wife."
"We will find him, we will consume him with fire;
Consume him with fire; cast him into the swift stream."
"Oh! arise, thou terrible storm-cloud!
Strike dead my wife's father!
Pierce her mother with thy arrow,
Beat my young wife to death with the rush of rain!
But spare, spare, the fair maiden,
The fair maiden my olden love [8]."

In the next song the "olden love" dies, and the news of her death is brought to him to whom she used to be dear, but with whom fate has not allowed her to be linked—

[8] Shein, I. 341.

From under the stone, the white stone,
Fire blazes not, nor pitch seethes,
But a youth's heart is seething.
Not for his father dear, nor for his mother dear,
Nor for a young wife well-beloved,
Seethes the heart of the youth;
But for a maiden well beloved,
For her who used to be his love.
" There had reached me broken tidings
That the maiden fair was ill.
Quickly follows them a letter—
The maiden fair is dead.
I will sadly to the stable:
Lead my good—my best horse forth,
Hasten to the church of God,
Tie my horse beside the belfry,
Stamp upon the mould.
Split open, damp Mother Earth!
Fly asunder, ye coffin planks!
Unroll, O brocade of gold!
Awake, awake, O maiden fair,
O maiden fair, my olden love [9]!"

A great number of the songs are devoted to the sorrows of a young wife, condemned to live with an old and uncongenial husband. The following is one of the most characteristic of her complaints. It may be as well to take this opportunity of remarking that when poetry which deals with the various relationships of married life has to be rendered into English, the poverty of our own family nomenclature, compared with that of Russia, is very cramping to a translator. Such odious terms as father-in-law, mother-in-law, and the rest of the endearing appella-

[9] Quoted from an old MS. by Shein, I, 324.

tions of a spouse's kinsfolk so ominously terminating in law, are all but inadmissible, and it is absolutely impossible to find English equivalents for many of the numerous Slavonic names for persons mutually affected by the various degrees of consanguinity and connexion. Inherited by the Slavonians from their Aryan ancestors in Central Asia, they have been retained by them in many instances all but intact, and they remain among them to bear witness to the strength of their domestic attachments, to the vigour of their family life.

THE WIFE.

Fain would I be sleeping, dreaming:
Heavy lies my head upon the pillow.
Up and down the passage goes my husband's father,
Angrily about it keeps he pacing.

CHORUS.

Thumping, scolding, thumping, scolding,
Never lets his daughter sleep.

FATHER-IN-LAW.

Up, up, up, thou sloven there!
Up, up, up, thou sluggard there!
Slovenly, slatternly, sluggardish slut!

THE WIFE.

Fain would I be sleeping, dreaming:
Heavy lies my head upon the pillow.
Up and down the passage goes my husband's mother,
Angrily about it keeps she pacing.

CHORUS.

Thumping, scolding, thumping, scolding,
Never lets her daughter sleep.

Mother-in-Law.

Up, up, up! thou sloven there!
Up, up, up! thou sluggard there!
Slovenly, slatternly, sluggardish slut!

The Wife.

Fain would I be sleeping, dreaming:
Heavy lies my head upon the pillow.
Up and down the passage steals my well-beloved one,
All so lightly, softly, keeps he whisp'ring.

The Lover.

Sleep, sleep, sleep, my darling one!
Sleep, sleep, sleep, my precious one!
Driven out, thrown away, married too soon[1]!

If the last song was dark with discontent, the next is expressive of the utter blackness of despair. The word rendered in it by sorrow is the Russian *Gore* meaning misfortune, calamity, woe, a being who, as will be seen farther on, often figures in the popular tales—as for instance, in that in which a poverty-stricken wretch tries to keep up appearances by singing, and hears another voice in unison with his own, for which he cannot account until he discovers that it belongs to *Gore*—to misery, who is keeping him company. The fish into which sorrow is supposed in the song to turn itself, is the *Byelaya Ruibitsa*, a large Caspian fish, probably the largest with which the poet was acquainted.

---

[1] Shein, I. 306.

Whither shall I, the fair maiden, flee from Sorrow?
If I fly from Sorrow into the dark forest,
After me runs Sorrow with an axe.
"I will fell, I will fell the green oaks;
I will seek, I will find the fair maiden."
If I fly from Sorrow into the open field,
After me runs Sorrow with a scythe.
"I will mow, I will mow the open field;
I will seek, I will find the fair maiden."
Whither then shall I flee from Sorrow?
If I rush from Sorrow into the blue sea—
After me comes Sorrow as a huge fish.
"I will drink, I will swallow the blue sea:
I will seek, I will find the fair maiden."
If I seek refuge from Sorrow in marriage—
Sorrow follows me as my dowry.
If I take to my bed to escape from Sorrow—
Sorrow sits beside my pillow.
And when I shall have fled from Sorrow into the damp earth—
Sorrow will come after me with a spade.
Then will Sorrow stand over me, and cry triumphantly,
"I have driven, I have driven, the maiden into the damp earth[2]."

As these dolorous laments might leave on the mind of the reader the erroneous impression that Russian popular poetry is of a morbid character, it will be as well to give at least one specimen of a love-song, in which the pathetic does not deepen into the tragic.

The little wild birds have come flying
From beyond the sea, the blue sea.
The little birds go fluttering
About the bushes, over the open field,
All have their mates and rejoice in love.

[2] Shein, I. 322.

Only the good youth, Alexándrushka,
A homeless orphan in the wide world,
Grieves like a pining cuckoo,
And melts away in burning tears.
The poor lad has no one,
No one in the wide world to fondle him,
No one ever brings joy to the orphan,
Uttering words of kind endearment.
Should he go out into the open field—
There to trample underfoot his cares,
His misery and his bitter longing—
His longing and his misery not to be shaken off—
Or should he go out into the dark forest,
His sorrow will not fly away.
The heart of the good youth
Is eaten up with care.
He fades, he withers in his loneliness,
Like a blade of grass in the midst of a wild plain.
To the youth not even God's light is dear!
But Dunya dear has taken pity
On the poor fellow, on the orphan.
She has caressed the homeless one,
She has spoken to him terms of endearment,
The beautiful maiden has fallen in love
With the lad, Alexándrushka—
She has covered him with her silken veil,
She has called him her darling, her beloved one—
And his sorrow and sighing have passed away[3].

During the summer months, as has already been observed, it is in the Khorovods that songs are chiefly to be heard, their period varying in different localities, and being most prolonged in the neighbourhood of towns or in places where manufactories bring together large numbers of young people. In the villages, as

[3] Tereshchenko, II. 345. Sakharof, I. iii. 130.

soon as the harvest and other field-labours are over, and the evenings begin to grow dark and long, commence the social gatherings of the young people called *Posidyelki, Besyedui, Dosvitki*, etc. In the greater part of Russia the Posidyelka prevails—so called from *posidyet'*, to sit awhile. This is how it is described by Tereshchenko:—

When the appointed evening comes, the village girls take their work to a cottage selected for the purpose, and there spend some hours in spinning and combing flax, hemp, and wool. As they sit at their work they lighten it with much laughter and chattering, discussing their domestic affairs, or the character of their sweethearts, or they sing such songs as—

"Spin, my spinner!
Spin, idle not!"
"Gladly would I have spun,
But to the neighbour's I'm called
At the Besyeda to feast."

or—

The green copse
All night moaned—
But I, poor Dunya,
All night sat up,
Waiting for my love[4].

At first they all spin away steadily, but about a couple of hours after supper-time they throw aside their work, and take to playing games. By degrees the youths make their appearance, and exchange greetings with the girls. After a time the distaffs,

[4] Tereshchenko, v. 156.

spindles, combs, and hackles are put away, and the young people begin dancing to the sound of reed pipes, balalaikas, and other musical instruments, or of songs sung by the girls in chorus, such as—

> Remember, dear, remember,
> My former love,
> How we two together, my own, would wander,
> Or sit through the dark autumnal nights,
> And whisper sweet secret words.
> " Thou, my own, must never marry.
> I, the maiden, will never wed."
> Soon, very soon, my love has changed her mind :
> "Marry, dear, marry ! I am going to wed[5]."

Sometimes the songs are of a very melancholy nature, as, for instance :—

> Oak wood, dear oak wood,
> Green oak wood of mine !
> Why moaning so early ?
> Low bending thy boughs ?
> From thee, from the oak wood,
> Have all the birds flown ?
> One bird still lingers,
> The cuckoo so sad,
> Day and night singing kookoo,
> She never is still.
> Of the wandering falcon
> The cuckoo complains.
> He has torn her warm nest,
> He has scattered her young,
> Her cuckoolings dear.
>
> In her lofty chamber
> A maiden fair sits ;
> By the window she weeps

[5] Tereshchenko, v. 157.

As a rivulet flows,
As a spring wells she sobs.
Of the wandering youth
The maiden complains—
From her father and mother
He lured her away
To a strange far off home,
Strange, far off, unknown,
He has lured her—and now
Fain would fling her aside[6].

In the middle of a series of such melancholy songs as these, the girls will suddenly begin to dance. "The performers (says Tereshchenko) stand facing each other, and beat time to the music with their feet; then they turn round in opposite directions, change places, and anew stamp on the ground, and anew turn round." If they dance to the sound of song, the women and girls form a circle around them, as in the Khorovod, and sing what are called *plyasovuiya pyesni*, dance-songs—from *plyasát'*, to dance. Here is a specimen. In the original, each alternate line is composed of the exclamation, *Akh! moy Bozhin'ka!* followed by a repetition of the last words of the preceding line:—

Ah! on the hill a pine-tree stands!
   Ah! dear Lord! a pine-tree stands!
Under the pine a soldier lies!
   Ah! dear Lord! a soldier lies!
Over the soldier a black steed stands,
With its right hoof tearing up the ground,
Water it seeks for its soldier lord.

[6] Tereshchenko, v. 159.

"Water, my steed, thou wilt not find.
From the ground the soldier will never rise.
Gallop, my steed, by bank and brae,
By bank and brae, gallop on to my home.
There will come to greet thee a grey-haired dame,
That grey-haired dame is my mother dear.
There will come to greet thee a lady fair—
That lady fair is my youthful wife—
To greet thee will little lordlings come—
Those little lordlings my children are.
They will join in caressing thee, my steed—
They will join in questioning thee, my steed.
Say not, my steed, that I bleeding lie—
But tell them I serve in my troop, dark steed,
In my troop I serve, my step I gain."
His death gains the soldier beneath the pine,
His death! dear Lord! beneath the pine [7].

To the *Posidyelki* of Great-Russia correspond the Little-Russian *Dosvitki*, so called because the young people keep up their amusements *do svita*, till the dawn, and the White-Russian *Supretki*. On spring and summer evenings, also, are held social festivals which often last all night, and which in White-Russia are called *Dozhinki*, and in Little-Russia *Vechernitsui* —from *vecher*, evening. These *Vechernitsui* often led in old times to quarrels, and even to murders, among the hot-blooded Cossacks; but it is said that it was always very rare for them to be accompanied by any bad consequences so far as the girls who took part in them were concerned. Each girl is attended at these gatherings by her regular and acknowledged sweetheart, and his attentions almost

[7] Tereshchenko, v. 165.

always end in marriage. This is the case, also, at the *Posidyelki, Besyedui*, etc., of Great Russia. A singular amount of liberty is conceded to the rustic lover, but he would meet with general reprobation were he to take advantage of his position, and then attempt to evade making amends for his wrong-doing.

Of the Besyedas in the Olonets Government—one of those outlying districts in the north-east of Russia, in which the songs of old times have been best preserved—a very pleasant and picturesque account has been given by Ruibnikof, a collector to whom students of Russian folklore are deeply indebted. When October comes, he says, the young men of each village choose some clean and spacious cottage, and meet in it almost every evening during the winter months. These gatherings commence at seven o'clock, and last till a late hour. Each of the men pays the owner of the cottage from two to three kopecks a night for the right of entry, or from twenty-five to thirty [from tenpence to a shilling] for the whole season. When music is required, they make a special collection for the purpose. As a general rule the girls are admitted free, but in some districts they pay their share of the expenses.

If we follow the guidance of Ruibnikof to one of these merry gatherings, we find ourselves in a spacious *izbá*—a term applied to the whole cottage as well as to its "keeping-room". Its ceiling is made of interlacing planks. On the left of the door is a brick stove, with ample space between it and the wall, and liberal accommodation for sleepers on the *polati*, or raised flooring carried from the stove to the opposite side of the room. Along the walls stretch benches, and above them shelves. One of the walls is pierced by three windows, the middle one of which, called the red or fair window, is somewhat larger than the others, and at the end of that wall is the corner of honour where stand the *icónui*, or holy pictures, with a lamp burning before them. The scene is lighted up by a number of candles placed on the cross beams and shelves.

Before long the room becomes full. Not only the immediate neighbours, but also the lads and lasses from the surrounding villages have met together, some of them coming from places as much as eight or nine miles distant. The girls occupy the benches extending from the stove to the centre window, dressed for the most part in thin chemises with short sleeves, and in red sarafans, or stuff petticoats, fastened at the waist with a girdle of ribbon. Round their necks are thrown handkerchiefs of different colours, but not so as to hide their necklaces of glass beads. In their ears are large earrings, also of glass. On their heads they wear a network of horsehair, decorated with lace and beads, to which some add a sort of ornamented coronet of glass beads. The old people and the married couples sit near the stove and take no active part in the amusements, unless it be that here and there some old woman holds a lighted fir wood splinter for the benefit of the guests. Near the door stands the owner of the cottage and collects the entrance-money. The young men stroll about on the side opposite that occupied by the girls, most of them dressed in blue caftans, though here and there a *burlak*, a man who is in the habit of working for wages in Petersburg, wears a long surtout, "or even a Palmerston-Paletot[8]."

After a time the amusements of the evening begin, games and dances following each other in regular order, attended by songs, which are not chosen capriciously at the will of the singers, but are accepted in accordance with the dictates of established usage. Hour after hour the singing goes on until the party breaks up, the lights are put out, and, escorted by their " dear friends," the girls speed home across the snow.

It would be easy to give picture after picture of a similar kind, in which should be portrayed the bright side of social life among those Russian peasants who remain faithful to the old manners and customs of their ancestors. But to do full justice to the subject a whole volume would be required, and not a mere introductory chapter. And so we will tarry no longer in the region of the picturesque, but will proceed to clear the way for the discussion of the mythical and ritual or ceremonial songs which have to follow, by giving a rapid sketch of some divisions of the general subject which have not yet been noticed.

The songs which have been quoted in the preceding pages belong for the most part to the class of those called *Golosovuiya* (*golos* = voice) or *Protyazhnuiya*,

---

[8] Ruibnikof, III. 427—429.

long drawn out (*protyagát'* = to prolong). One of them, however—that of the wounded soldier—has already been referred to the division of the *Plyasovuiya*, or dance-songs. The song in which the wife begs not to be beaten except for good cause, is ranked in the collection from which it is taken among the *Obryádnuiya*, or Ritual and Ceremonial Songs, inasmuch as it specially belongs to the *Obryád* [feast or ceremony] of the *Toloka*, or friendly assistance rendered to a man by his neighbours at harvest time. Of the *Obryádnuiya Pyesni*, by far the most important class of Russian songs[9], a detailed account will be given farther on, those of a mythical nature being taken together, and the *Svádebnuiya Pyesni*, or Marriage Songs, [*Svad'ba* = marriage] of which one or two specimens have already been given, being discussed in a separate chapter, as also will be the *Zapláchki*, or Wailings for the Dead. Of five other divisions, to which a considerable space has been devoted by Sakharof in his collection, it will be sufficient merely to give a few specimens.

Of these five divisions, four comprise, together with some others, the " Cossack Songs," " Robber Songs," "Soldier Songs," and "Historical Songs," most of which may be arranged together as descendants or imitators of the old semi-historical poetry of Russia. There exist in the memories of the people, as has already been observed, a vast number of poems called Builínas—

[9] The word " song " is used here in the sense in which we generally employ it. The Russian term *Pyesni* is applied to poems of all kinds, epic as well as lyric.

fragmentary epics, to which neither our metrical romances nor our historical ballads exactly correspond, although they offer certain points of resemblance—and the historical songs, and most of the others of which we have just spoken, are generally written in the same style and metre as the Builínas, and often contain scraps of poetry which have been borrowed from them. As a general rule, however, there is not much poetry to be found in the "Soldier Songs," or "Historical Songs" in Sakharof's collection. As for the "popular poetry" laboriously produced now-a-days in the towns, and unblushingly fathered upon soldiers and gipsies, it is not worthy of serious notice, contrasting as it does most unfavourably with that which flowed spontaneously in olden days from the well of Russian undefiled. Here and there, however, in remote parts of the country, the old Slavonic faculty of improvisation still lives among the peasantry, and sometimes gives birth to metrical effusions which are caught up by their hearers, and so added to the common stock of current song.

"Almost every woman," says Ruibnikof, speaking of the neighbourhood of Lake Onega, "can give expression to her feelings of distress, either by constructing a new lament (*zapláchka*), or by adapting an old one to the circumstances." And he proceeds to speak of a *zapláchka* improvised by a young woman of the neighbourhood. A first cousin of hers died, and all the family bitterly lamented his loss. But his cousin's grief was expressed in a lyrical form with such force and clearness, that her *zapláchka* immediately acquired notoriety, and was adopted by other women, who now sing it whenever a similar calamity befalls them[1]. Some idea of its nature may be obtained from the following extract, which forms about a third of the whole:—

> Against my mother do I make complaint,
> Who did not let me go, unhappy me,
> To him, the dear, the loved,
> My cousin dear.
> Grieving I would have sat
> The sick, the painful bed beside.
> Sadly would I have begged
> My cousin dear to speak.
> Perchance to me he might have spoken, said
> If only just one secret word
> Which I would then have sadly told
> To my dear aunt beloved.
>
> Unhappy that I am, I would have given
> To death, swift-footed, keen,
> My raiment gay,
> My pleasant way of life,
> And all my golden store ungrudgingly . . .
> But never would have let my cousin dear depart[2].

Of the Cossack and Robber Songs given by Sakharof, and the other songs called *Udaluiya*—bold, daring, courageous, etc.—some are not a little prosaic; but there are also many of them that are as remarkable for their freshness and vigour, as for the interesting nature of the historical allusions they contain. The Cossack Songs are generally about the Don or the Volga; along the banks of those rivers ride the Cossack horse, or on their waters float the

---

[1] Ruibnikof, III. xlvii.   [2] Ruibnikof, III. 423.

Cossack boats. In one song a young Cossack, riding away on a foray, sorrowfully parts from his betrothed; in another he sends from his last field a farewell message to his home. In all of them breathe the same feelings of courage, of loyalty, of independence, the same attachment to a free life, the same contempt for death. Of the Tsar himself they speak, as a general rule, with devotion; but his messengers are not always treated with respect. One of the songs, for instance, describes how a great Boyar (probably a certain Prince Dolgoruky), starts from Moscow for "the quiet Don Ivanovich," boasting that he will hang up all the Cossacks. They, suspecting his intention, meet together and form a great circle, in the middle of which he takes his stand and begins to read aloud "the Tsar's Ukases." When he comes to the royal titles the Cossacks all doff their caps, but he keeps his on,—

> Thereupon they rose in commotion,
> Flung themselves upon the Boyar,
> Cut off his proud head,
> And threw his white body into the quiet Don;
>
> And having killed him, they said to his corpse,—
> "Respect, Boyar, the Gosudar,
> Don't go glorying or giving yourself airs before him."
>
> Then they went to the Tsar with their confession :—
> "O thou, Father orthodox Tsar!
> Judge us according to a just decision,
> Order to be done to us what pleaseth thee.
> Thou art master of our bold heads[3]."

[3] Sakharof, I. iii. 238.

A subject which is frequently treated in the songs is that of a Cossack who lies grieving in a dark prison. In one instance he entreats his parents to ransom him, but they say they cannot do so; then he turns to the "fair maiden" whom he loves, and she immediately hastens to release him. In another song a prisoner who has lain for twenty-two years in "a dark dungeon without windows or doors," within the white stone walls of "the famous city of Azof," hears "His Sultanic Majesty, the Turkish Tsar himself" go by, and calls out to him, demanding that he may be set free, adding,—

> If thou dost not order me to be let out,
> I will at once write a letter,
> Not with pen and ink,
> But with my burning tears,
> To my comrades on the quiet Don.
> The glorious, quiet Don will rise in anger;
> The whole Cossack circle will fly to arms;
> They will shatter the Turkish forces,
> And lead thee, O Tsar, away into captivity.

On hearing this "His Sultanic Majesty" immediately cries to his "field-marshals,"—

> "Set free the brave youth,
> The brave youth, the Don Cossack,
> Let him go to his Russian land,
> To his White Tsar[4]."

Of a more poetic nature is the following address to the favourite river of the Cossacks :—

---

[4] Sakharof, I. iii. 237.

Father of ours! famous, quiet Don!
Don Ivanovich, our nourisher!
Great praise of thee is spoken,
Great praise and words of honour.
That thou didst swiftly run in olden days,
Swiftly but all clearly didst thou run.
But now, our nourisher, all troubled dost thou
    flow,
Troubled unto thy depths art thou, O Don.
Then glorious, quiet Don thus made reply,—
" How otherwise than troubled can I be ?
I have sent forth my falcons bright,
My falcons bright, the Don-Kazáks.
Deprived of them my steep banks crumble down,
Deprived of them my shoals are thick with sand[5]."

And so is this description of a battle with the Tartars :—

Beyond the famous river Utva,
Among the Utvinsk hills,
In a wide valley,
A cornfield was ploughed.
Not with the plough was the field ploughed,
But with keen Tartar spears.
Not with a harrow was the field harrowed,
But with swift feet of horses.
Not with rye, nor with wheat, was the field sown,
But that cornfield was sown
With bold Cossack heads.
Not with rain was it moistened,
Not with strong autumn showers;
That field was moistened
With burning Cossack tears[6].

Most of what have been styled the " Robber

---

[5] Sakharof, I. iii. 240.   [6] Sakharof, I. iii. 243.

Songs" are reminiscences of the famous insurrection of the Don Cossacks, headed by Stenka Razín, against the Tsar Alexis Mikhailovich. For several years that insurgent chief maintained his power along the course, not only of the Don, but also of the Volga, forcing the merchant-ships which sailed down that river to pay him tribute, and at times setting the country in a blaze, from Simbirsk to the Caspian. Both on land and on the rivers, as well as on the Caspian Sea, he long set the forces of the Tsar at defiance. Once he surrendered, and promised to live peaceably, but he soon broke out into even more furious revolt than before. At last he was beaten near Simbirsk, and soon afterwards was taken prisoner and sent to Moscow, where he was put to a cruel death in the year 1672. In one of the Songs the Sun is entreated to rise " above the high hill, above the green oak wood, above the landmarks of the brave youth Stepan Timofeevich, called Stenka Razín," for the thick fogs of night lie heavy on the hearts of the insurgents :—

Rise, rise, O red Sun,
Give warmth to us, poor sufferers.
No thieves are we, nor highwaymen,
We are the workmen of Stenka Razín.
Our oars we wave—a ship we board,
Our maces⁷ we wave—a caravan we seize,
A hand we wave—a maiden we carry off⁸.

---

⁷ The *Kisten* is a metal ball to which a leather strap or a short wooden handle is attached, a kind of " slung shot."
⁸ Sakharof, I. iii. 227.

The last survivor of a band which has been crushed in fight makes his way slowly homewards through the dark forests, sadly thinking of his comrades who are either dead or in prison. Arriving at a river, he is rowed across it by the ferrymen, but no sooner does he reach the other side than he feels that death is close at hand, so he cries,—

Bury me, brothers, between three roads,
The Kief and the Moscow, and the Murom famed in story.
At my feet fasten my horse,
At my head set a life-bestowing cross,
In my right hand place my keen sabre.
Whoever passes by will stop;
Before my life-bestowing cross will he utter a prayer,
At the sight of my black steed—will he be startled,
At the sight of my keen sword—will he be terrified.
"Surely this is a brigand who is buried here!
A son of the brigand, the bold Stenka Razín[9]!"

When these freebooters are taken prisoners, they make it a point of honour to maintain a defiant demeanour in the presence of their capturers. One

---

[9] Sakharof, I. iii. 226. The same idea occurs at the end of our own ballad of "Robin Hood's Death and Burial:"—

> "Lay me a green sod under my head,
>   And another at my feet:
> And lay my bent bow by my side,
>   Which was my music sweet;
> And make my grave of gravel and green,
>   Which is most right and meet.
> Let me have length and breadth enough,
>   With a green sod under my head:
> That they may say, when I am dead,
>   Here lies bold Robin Hood."

of them is asked by the Tsar himself whether he has had many companions in his forays, and who they were with whom he robbed and stole. This is his answer:—

"I will tell thee, O source of hope, orthodox Tsar,
All the truth will I tell to thee, the whole truth.
The number of my companions was four.
My first companion—the dark night,
My second companion—a knife of steel,
My third companion—my good steed,
My fourth companion—a tough bow,
And my messengers were keen arrows."

Whereupon the Tsar compliments him upon his knowledge of how "to steal and to make bold reply," and rewards him with "a lofty dwelling in the midst of the plain, with two pillars and a cross-beam."

It is not always a freebooter whose courage in the presence of his enemies is lauded in the songs. In one of them it is a *Knyaz Boyárin*, a Boyar Prince, who is going to the scaffold amid the tears of his family, and who prefers death to the humiliation of asking for pardon—in another the bold criminal is " a great Boyar, the Strelitz Ataman," condemned to death "for treason against the Tsar's Majesty"—an allusion, no doubt, to the executions which took place under Peter the Great, after the failure of the Third Insurrection of the *Stryel'tsui*, the Russian Prætorians, in the year 1698. As the Ataman [Hetman] is being led to the block from the Kremlin—

In front of him goes the terrible headsman,
Bearing in his hand a sharp axe ;

After him follow his father and his mother,
His father and his mother and his young wife;
They weep as a river flows,
Their sobbing is like the sound of a rushing stream,
And amid their sobs they incessantly entreat him.
"O child, dear child of ours!
Humble thyself before the Tsar,
Offer him thy confession.
Perchance the Gosudar Tsar will pardon thee,
Will leave thy bold head on thy strong shoulders."
Hard as a stone grows the heart of the brave youth;
He stiffens his neck and defies the Tsar,
Not listening to his father and mother,
Not pitying his young wife,
Feeling no sorrow for his children.
He was led to the Red Field,
And there his bold head
Was struck off from his strong shoulders [1].

Many of the songs are devoted to love. Here, for instance, is the outline of a romantic story. A brave youth leaves his native Ukraine, and enters into the service of "the King of Lithuania," who shows him great favour. The King has a fair daughter, whose heart is won by the young Cossack, a fact of which her father is made aware by the youth's "own evil brothers," who repeat the idle boastings in which he had indulged when under the influence of strong drink. The King in his wrath orders his favourite to be taken out at once to the place of execution. His commands are obeyed, and the youth soon stands at the foot of the gallows:—

On the first step mounted the youth:
"Farewell, farewell, my father and my mother!"

[1] Sakharof, I. iii. 224.

On the second step mounted the youth:
" Farewell, farewell, my kith and kin !"
On the third step mounted the youth :
" Farewell, my sweet Princess !"
The Princess heard the voice afar off,
She hastened into her lofty chamber,
She seized her golden keys,
She opened a silver coffer,
She took two steel daggers,
And pierced her white bosom.
In the open field swings the brave youth,
On the daggers bends down the Princess and dies[2].

The only consolation which the bereaved father can find is that of cutting off the heads of the fatal informers.

By way of conclusion, the following romance of robber life may be given :—

It was in the city of Kief
That there lived a rich widow :
Nine sons had she,
Her tenth child was a daughter dear;
Her did her brothers carefully bring up,
Brought her up and gave her in marriage,
To a young dweller by the sea,
To a rich Boyár.
He took her to the seaside,
And there they lived a year, two years,
But in the third year they grew weary,
And set off to pay her mother a visit.
They travelled one day, they travelled two days,
The third day they made a halt,
To cook kasha, and to let their horses graze.
It was not evil crows that flew down on them,
It was evil robbers who pounced upon them.

[2] Sakharof, I. iii. 230, 231.

The husband they put to death,
His child they flung into the sea,
His wife they kept as a prisoner,
And after that they lay down to sleep.
But one of their number did not lie down to sleep,
Did not lie down, but prayed to God,
And took to questioning the captive.
" Moryanka, Moryanka, Moryanushka[3],
From what city dost thou come?
Who are thy father and thy mother?"

The captive tells her story in the words with which the song opens, to the horror of her listener.

With a loud cry exclaimed he then—
" O brothers, brothers of mine!
No mere dweller by the sea have we slain,
We have slain the dear husband of our sister!
No mere child have we flung into the sea,
But our own sister's son!
No mere seaside woman have we taken captive
We have taken captive our own sister!
Sister dear, our own sister!
Do not tell this to our mother.
We will find thee another husband,
We will endow thee more richly than before."

But with tears does the sister reply,—

" With whatsoever ye may endow me,
Ye cannot bring my dear one back to life[4]."

Of the Soldier Songs some refer to the wars with Sweden, as, for instance, one in which "General

---

[3] Moryanka means a female dweller by the seaside. Moryanushka is an affectionate diminutive of the word.
[4] Sakharof, I. iii. 228.

Boris Petrovich Sheremetef" marches out of Pskoff, and his troops "chase the Swedish general up to the very walls of Dorpat;" and another in which a girl tells her mother of a dream she has had—how in a vision of the night she saw a steep hill on which lay a white rock; and on this rock grew a cytisus bush, on which sat a dark blue eagle, holding in its claws a black crow. To which the mother replies that she will explain the dream:—

The steep hill is stone-built Moskva,
The white rock is our Kreml Gorod,
And the cytisus bush is the Kremlin palace;
The dark blue eagle is our father the Orthodox Tsar,
And the black crow is the Swedish King.
Our Gosudar will conquer the Swedish land,
And the King himself will lead into captivity[5].

Many of them refer to various military and naval exploits, one describing how a Russian Admiral terrified the Turks, another telling how the blood of the infidels was poured forth at the taking of Azof, and a third embodying the expressions used by the Orthodox Tsar himself, as he steered across the Caspian Sea one of a fleet of thirty Russian ships.

Some of the most interesting are devoted to the soldier's sorrows. In one, for instance, we see the young conscript enrolled among the "Imperial dragoons," and hear him lament as his long locks fall before the official scissors:—

"Not for my black curls do I mourn,
But I mourn for my own home.

[5] Sakharof, I. iii. 232.

> In my home are three sorrows,
> And the first sorrow is—
> I have parted from my father and mother,
> From my father and from my mother,
> From my young wife,
> From my orphaned boys,
> From my little children⁶."

In the days when long terms of military service were the rule, a conscript was generally looked upon as lost to his native village, and the occasion of his departure was one of great sorrow and mourning. Here is a song which used to be sung by the relations of a recruit when he took leave of his home, in a district of the Archangel Government. The inhabitants of the village, old and young, would collect on such an occasion, and amid sobs and tears would listen to the sad lament:—

> Warm, warm, O red Sun!
> Shine, shine, O bright Moon [Myésyats]!
> Together with the clear stars,
> Together with the bright Moon [Luná],
> So that we, the old thieves-bloodsuckers,
> May be able to see to go to the dram-shop
> To go to the dram-shop and take counsel:
> From the rich to take—and not to restore,
> From the poor to take—and so to ruin.
> Beyond the brook, beyond the river,
> In the house of an old widow
> Is her only son Ivánushko—
> Of him will we make a soldier.
> Good and pleasing is he by nature,
> Favour has he found in the eyes of the girls,
> Of service has he been to all the commune⁷.

⁶ Sakharof, I. iii. 234.   ⁷ Ruibnikof, III. 460.

In another song we witness the setting out of a mighty army:—

> The powerful army of the White Tsar,
> Going, brothers, to the Prussian land.

Sturdily the soldiers march, "all joyous, all powdered;" one only of them is sad, for after him follows a fair maiden, bitterly weeping. "Do not weep," he says, trying to comfort her,—

> Not thou alone art unhappy,
> I also, the bold youth, am sad—
> Going to a far-off land—
> To an unknown, far-off land
> Do I go in the service of the Gosudar[8].

In a third it is not for his own sorrows that the soldier weeps. His tears flow for the mighty monarch who is no more:—

> Ah! thou bright moon, bátyushka!
> Not as in old times dost thou shine,
> Not as in old, in former times,
> For from the evening to the midnight hour,
> From the midnight hour till the grey dawn,
> Dost thou hide thyself behind clouds,
> Dost thou cover thyself with black vapour.
> So was it with us, in Holy Russia.
> In Petersburg, that famous city,
> In the church of Peter and Paul,
> At the right side of the choir,
> By the tomb of the Emperor,
> By the tomb of Peter the First,
> Peter the First, the Great,
> A young sergeant prayed to God,

[8] Sakharof, I. iii. 235.

Weeping the while, as a river flows,
For the recent death of the Emperor,
The Emperor, Peter the First.
And thus amid his sobs he spake,—
" Split asunder, O damp mother Earth
On all four sides—
Open, ye coffin planks,
Unroll, O brocade of gold—
And do thou arise, awake, Gosudar,
Awake Batyushka, Orthodox Tsar.
Look upon thy army dear,
The well loved, the brave.
Without thee are we all orphans,
Having become orphans, have we lost all strength [9]."

This song may serve also as a fair specimen of the class styled "Historical." The faculty of composing Builínas, or what are usually styled the real historical poems of Russia, is supposed by some writers to have existed among the people till the time of Peter the Great, and then to have expired during the great social revolution brought about by that monarch. Of these Builínas—whether of the Vladímir cycle, or of the series referring to Iván the Terrible, Alexis Mikhaílovich, and other Tsars who lived after the Tartar period—I hope at some future period to give a detailed account. At present it is rather with lyric than with epic poetry that I propose to deal, and therefore I will not dwell any longer on the "Historical Songs," and those of a similar nature. But before parting with the subject, it may not be amiss to say a few words about the Builínas and their reciters.

[9] Sakharof, I. iii. 232.

Until the beginning of the present century very few persons even suspected that Russia could boast of possessing a national epos. It was vaguely reported that a considerable mass of more or less historical poetry was floating about in the memories of the people, but little had been done to secure and preserve it. From time to time small collections were made, one of the most interesting of which, so far as English readers are concerned, is that which is now at Oxford, having been formed by Richard James, an English clergyman, a great number of whose manuscripts are preserved in the Bodleian Library. He was in Moscow in the summer of 1619, and spent the ensuing winter in the extreme north, where he was detained on his return home by way of Archangel. His collection consists of six poems, chiefly relating to events which had recently taken place in Russia[1].

In the year 1804 there appeared at Moscow a book which extended the growing knowledge that there existed in Russia a rich mine of historical poetry. This was the work entitled "Ancient Russian Poems," containing 26 out of the 61 old "epic poems" which purported to have been collected by a certain Kirsha Danilof, towards the middle of the 18th century, at the Demídof mining works, in the Government of Perm. Fourteen years later the entire collection was edited by Kalaidovich. No farther steps of any importance were taken till about twenty

[1] Professor Buslaef has written an interesting article on these poems. *Ist. Ocherki,* I. 470—548. They have been printed by the St. Petersburg Academy of Sciences.

years ago the St. Petersburg Academy of Sciences began to publish a rich collection of national songs, and some ten years later the first parts appeared of the two great collections made, the one by P. B. Kiryeevsky, and the other by P. N. Ruibnikof. The former is still in progress, the latter was completed in the year 1867.

With respect to the contents of these two rich storehouses of national poetry—for the building up of which the greatest credit is due to the patient explorers and collectors just mentioned, and their aiders or supervisors, such scholars, for instance, as Aksákof, Bezsónof, Busláef, Dahl, Kostomárof, and many others —the theory most in repute in Russia is that they are all poetic relics of the past history of the country, and that in them may be studied its successive phases, from the far-off days of heathenism to the period of social revolution under Peter the Great, when, together with many other things appertaining to the past, the faculty of composing "epic" poetry dwindled away. But it should also be mentioned that another theory exists, but meets with only scant favour, to the effect that the poems which are regarded as records of Russia's earliest days are merely renderings of eastern romances, which have been borrowed by Russian minstrels from Mongol and Turkish sources, and altered in accordance with Russian ideas. Into the questions raised by the antagonism of these two theories I hope, at the fitting time, to enter; at present I content myself with stating their existence.

According to one of the supporters of the first

theory[2], the epos of the Builínas may be divided into certain cycles, each of which has its own poetic characteristics, and is to some extent expressive of the outer and inner life, the actions and the sentiments, of its own period. The earliest of these cycles is supposed, by the school of critics to which he belongs, to be that which deals with the mythical personages generally known as the " Elder Heroes," and considered to be " evident personifications of the Powers of Nature." Closely connected with it is the Cycle named after Vladímir the Great, and containing a number of fragmentary epic poems chiefly relating to the deeds of the " Younger Heroes "—the Russian Paladins of ancient days, whose somewhat shadowy forms are seen grouped around that of Vladímir himself, the Slavonic counterpart of Arthur or of Charlemagne, as he holds high revel within the halls of Kief.

Next in order of time to the Vladímir, or Kief Cycle, is placed that of Novgorod, prized for the pictures of life it is supposed to offer during the days of that ancient Republic's pride and prosperity. The fourth place is occupied by the Royal or Moscow Cycle, which deals with really historic characters and events, and ultimately resolves itself into the classes of Historical and Soldier Songs of which notice has already been taken.

As a specimen of the mythical Builínas, we may take the story of Svyatogor. He is one of the most

---

[2] See Maikof, " On the Builínas of the Vladímir Cycle," p. 1.

striking of the "Elder Heroes." His name is derived from his dwelling-place, which is *v svyatuikh gorakh*, "among the Holy Mountains." He is of gigantic stature, and his weight is such that the earth itself can scarcely support him. His strength is so prodigious that it is a burden even to himself. On one occasion, however, it proves insufficient. Svyatogor, we are told, has made himself ready to start on an expedition:—

He saddles his good horse,
And he goes forth into the open field.
With Svyatogor is no one equal in strength,
And the strength through his veins
Courses with right living force.
Heavily laden is he with strength as with a weighty
    burden.

See now, Svyatogor exclaims :—
"Could I but find its equal in weight[3]
I would lift the whole earth!"
Svyatogor riding over the steppe
Lights upon a little wallet[4].
He takes his whip and pushes the wallet—it does not
    move :
He tries to move it with a finger—but it does not
    yield :
He grasps it from on horseback with one hand—but
    it will not be lifted.

[3] *Tyaga* seems to mean here the equivalent of the earthly weight. In order to lift the earth Svyatogor must find a standing-place capable of supporting him when so heavily burdened. The remark is somewhat similar to that attributed to Archimedes.

[4] *Peremetnaya Sumochka*, a pair of wallets or bags, fastened together so as to be thrown across the shoulders or the saddle.

"Many a year have I ridden about the world,
But to such a wonder has my riding never brought me,
Such a marvel have I never seen before;
That a little wallet
Will not move, nor yield, not let itself be lifted!"
Down from his good steed lights Svyatogor,
With both hands he seizes the wallet,
Lifts the wallet a little higher than his knees:
But into the earth up to his knees sinks Svyatogor,
Down his white face pours a stream not of tears, but of blood[5].

Ilya Muromets, the representative of the younger race of heroes, has been told by the mystic beings who infused almost matchless strength into his formerly crippled limbs, that he might safely fight with all the heroes he might meet except three or four—the first of the exceptions being Svyatogor. Accordingly, after a time he saddles his good steed, and goes out in search of adventures. One day, as he rides afield, he sees a white tent beneath a tall oak, and in the tent is a huge bed, on which he lies down. Going to sleep, he slumbers on for three days and three nights,—

On the third day his good steed
Hears a loud roar from the northern side:
Damp mother earth staggers,
The dark forests rock,
The streams overflow their steep banks.

Then the good steed strikes the ground with its hoofs, but cannot wake Ilya until it cries aloud with

[5] Ruibnikof, I. 32.

a human voice, and tells him that Svyatogor is coming to the tent. Ilya leaps to his feet, lets his horse go free, and climbs up among the branches of the oak. Thence he sees how—

There comes a hero taller than the standing woods,
Whose head reaches to the fleeting clouds,
Bearing on his shoulders a crystal coffer.
The hero comes to the green oak,
Takes from his shoulder the crystal coffer,
Opens the coffer with a golden key:
Out comes thence a heroic woman.
Such a beauty on the whole earth
Had never been seen, never been heard of.

As soon as she leaves the coffer she proceeds to spread a sumptuous table, and Svyatogor eats and drinks, and then goes into the tent and falls asleep. His wife comes out from the tent, sees Ilya in the tree, and orders him to come down. This part of the narrative is almost identical with a portion of the story told in the first chapter of the "Arabian Nights," but the sequel is different. After Ilya has obeyed,

The beautiful one, the hero's wife,
Placed him in her husband's vast pocket,
And aroused her husband from his deep sleep.
The hero Svyatogor awoke,
Placed his wife in the crystal coffer,
Locked it with the golden key,
Sat upon his good horse,
And started for the Holy Mountains.
Then his good horse began to stumble,
And the hero struck it with his silken whip
On its stout haunches.
Then the horse said, with a human voice,—

"Formerly I carried the hero and the hero's wife,
But now I bear the hero's wife and two heroes.
No wonder that I stumble!"
And the hero Svyatogor drew out
Ilya Muromets from his pocket,
And began to question him,
As to who he was and how he came
Into his deep pocket.

Ilya tells him all that has happened, and Svyatogor, after making himself a widower, enters into a bond of fraternity with him, adopting him as his "younger brother," and instructing him in all the science with which it befits a hero to be acquainted. The two comrades afterwards travel on together "to the Northern Mountains," and on their way they come to a great coffin.

On this coffin was written this inscription,—
"Whosoever is destined to lie in this coffin,
He will lie down in it."
Ilya Muromets lay down in it;
For him was the coffin too long and too broad.
Down lay the hero Svyatogor:
Him did the coffin fit.
Thus spake the hero,—
"The coffin is made exactly for me.
Now lift the lid, Ilya,
Cover me up."
Thus answered Ilya Muromets,—
"I will not lift the lid, elder brother,
Nor will I cover thee up—
No little joke is this thou art playing,
Intending to bury thyself."
Then the hero took the lid and closed the coffin
    with it himself.
But when he wished to raise it,

In no manner could he do so.
He struggled and strove hard to lift it,
And he cried aloud to Ilya Muromets,
"Ah! younger brother!
Surely my fate has found me out;
I cannot lift the coffin-lid,
Do thou try to lift it."

Ilya Muromets tried to lift the coffin-lid [the story goes on to say in prose], but what could he do! Then thus spoke the hero Svyatogor,—
"Lift up my sword of steel, and strike across the coffin-lid."
But to lift Svyatogor's sword of steel was beyond the strength of Ilya Muromets. Then the hero Svyatogor called to him and said:
"Bend down to the coffin, to the little chink that is in it, and I will breathe upon thee with heroic breath[6]."
So Ilya bent down, and the hero Svyatogor breathed upon him with his heroic breath. Then Ilya felt that thrice as much strength as he had possessed before was added unto him, and he lifted the sword of steel, and struck across the coffin-lid. From that mighty blow wide flew the sparks, and where the sword of steel had struck, on that spot stood out a ridge of iron.
Again did the hero Svyatogor call to him—
"I stifle, younger brother, once more try to strike with the sword—this time along the coffin-lid."
Ilya Muromets struck the coffin lid lengthways, and there also there sprang up a ridge of iron.
Again the hero Svyatogor exclaimed,—
"My breath deserts me, younger brother. Bend down to the chink, and I will breathe on thee once more, and will give over to thee all my great strength."

⁸ The breath (*dukh*) was supposed to be intimately connected with the soul (*dusha*).

But Ilya Muromets replied,—
"Strength enough have I, elder brother. Were it otherwise, and had I more, the earth would not be able to support me."
Then spake the hero Svyatogor,—
"Well hast thou done, younger brother, in that thou didst not obey my last command. I should have breathed on thee with the breath of the grave, and thou wouldst have lain dead near me. And now farewell! Take to thyself my sword of steel, but fasten to my coffin my good heroic steed. No other than I can hold that steed in hand."
Then passed out of the chink his dying breath, and Ilya bade farewell to Svyatogor, made fast his good steed to his coffin, girded Svyatogor's sword of steel on his loins, and went his way into the open field[7].

As a specimen of the romances which are referred partly to the mythical cycle, and partly to that named after Vladimir, we may take the story of the hero Sukhman, as told in a Builina heard by Ruibnikof near Petrozavodsk. One day a great feast is being held at Kief, in Vladimir's palace. By the evening the guests have waxed merry and boastful over their cups.

"The fool brags of his young wife,
The idiots vaunt their wealth of gold,
But the wise man boasts of his old mother."

Only Sukhman utters no vaunt, sitting in silence at the oaken table. Noticing this, Vladimir asks what ails him; has he not received the wine-cup in his turn, or has some drunkard insulted him, or has he been allotted a lower seat than that to which his father's merits entitle him? He replies:—

[7] Ruibnikof, I. 33—42.

"The wine-cup came to me in its proper course,
And my seat is that which my father's son may claim,
And no drunkard has insulted me."

Still, he says, he will not yield like the rest to merriment and boasting; but this he will do: he will bring to Vladimir a white swan, caught by his hands without having been wounded. Having thus spoken, he rises from table, quits the festal hall, saddles his good steed, and rides away till he comes to a blue sea, into which lead creeks with quiet waters. Creek after creek does he examine, but in none of them "swim either geese, or swans, or small grey ducks." So, as he cannot think of returning empty-handed to Kief, he determines to ride on to the banks of "Mother Dnieper."

When he reaches that river, he sees that Mother Dnieper is not flowing as she used to flow, but all her waters are turbid with sand. "Why dost thou not flow as of old, Mother Dnieper?" he cries. "How can I flow as of old?" replies the river, and then goes on to complain that she is beset by forty thousand pagan Tartars, who are building bridges across her.

"By day they build bridges; by night I sweep them away;
Utterly at the end of her strength is Mother Dnieper."

Sukhman resolves to attack the infidels, so he sets his horse at the river, and clears it at a bound. Then he tears an oak out of the ground, and uses it as a club against the Tartars, when he comes up with them. Each swing of his terrible weapon "cuts a street in their ranks," each backhanded sweep "clears away a cross-street." At length all the Tartars are killed, with the exception of three who hide among the willow bushes which fringe the Dnieper's shore, and await Sukhman, with arrows fitted to their bowstrings. He follows them, and puts them to death, but not before he has been pierced by three arrows. Of these, however, he makes light, pulling them out, and "applying poppy leaves to his bleeding wounds."

On his return to Kief, when he is asked for the "live and unwounded swan" he had promised, he describes the victory he has obtained, but Vladimir will not believe him.

> He ordered his trusty servants,
> Seizing Sukhman by the white hands,
> To fling the brave youth into a dark dungeon.

And he sends his nephew Dobruinya to Mother Dnieper, to make inquiries about Sukhman's conduct. Dobruinya visits the field of battle, sees the bodies of the dead Tartars, and carries back to Kief the fragments of the great oak which Sukhman had shattered in the fight. Vladimir hears his report, and cries:—

> "What ho! my trusty servants!
> Swiftly run to the deep dungeon;
> Lead Sukhman forth,
> Bring him before my bright eyes.
> I will show favour unto the youth
> For this his great service,
> And recompense him with towns and suburbs,

Or with villages and hamlets,
Or with countless wealth of gold at will."

So they hasten to the dungeon, and tell Sukhman that he is to reap the reward of his brave deeds. And Sukhman comes out from the dungeon, and goes forth into the open field—
But then spake the brave youth these words :—
"The Sun[8] knew not how to show me favour;
The Sun knew not how to reward me;
So now his bright eyes shall not behold me!"
He tore the leaves of the poppy
From off his bleeding wounds;
And thus did Sukhman speak :—
"Flow on, O, Sukhman-River,
From out of my burning blood;
My burning blood shed uselessly[9]!"

Having given these specimens of the contents of the two great collections of national poems recently published in Russia, I will attempt to convey some idea of the manner in which those poems were collected. The best method of doing so seems to be to condense the graphic account of his exploring journeys drawn up by one of the chief compilers, P. N. Ruibnikof. How great was his industry may be measured by the fact that its results fill four large volumes. These contain 236 Builínas, the number of verses in the entire work amounting to rather more than 50,000. Kiryeevsky's collection, the whole of which has not yet been published, is on fully as great a scale.

[8] *Solnuishko*, or "Dear Sun," a name frequently given to Vladimir in these poems.
[9] Ruibnikof, I. 26—32.

In the course of the year 1859 Ruibnikof, who was then employed upon Government business in Petrozavodsk, a town situated on the western shore of Lake Onega, was informed that a number of old and curious songs were preserved among the rural population of the Olonets Government, and during the ensuing winter he betook himself to the task of collecting these "memorials of national poetry," making especial use of the opportunity afforded him by a visit which he paid to the Shungsk Fair, whither he was sent in search of certain statistics. Thither, he was informed, numbers of *Kaliki* (in modern days generally blind psalm-singers) formerly used to repair, and there they would sit by the churchyard and sing songs to crowds of listeners. But in the year 1850 " the police had begun to drive the singers away from the churchyard, and would no longer allow them to sing in the streets." At his urgent request, however, the Police-master contrived to find a couple of minstrels, and brought them to his lodgings. " When they had warmed themselves and talked a little," he says, " I began to ask them to sing any thing they knew. At first they would not, but when I had myself recited something to them from memory out of the *Kniga Golubinaya*, they began first one *Stikh* (religious poem), and then another, and sang through all the pieces they knew." From their dictation Ruibnikof wrote down a number of poems. Eventually he induced the police authorities to cease from harassing them, and so " from that time they again appeared at the Fair, took up their old quarters by the churchyard, and once more solicited alms from the public by singing religious poems."

About the same time he became acquainted with a celebrated *Voplénitsa* or professional "Wailer." The Wailer is, as we shall see farther on, a personage of no small importance in a Russian community, for it is she who sees that old customs are religiously preserved at marriages and funerals, and on other solemn occasions. She it is who teaches the bride to mourn in becoming verse for the loss of her "maiden freedom," and prompts the widow and the orphan to wail as befits them over the coffin or the grave of the departed. The particular Wailer in question enjoyed so widely spread a reputation that she was often summoned to remote spots, even to a district inhabited by Old-Ritualists, who kept up ancient customs with great strictness, and were, as a general rule, able to do their own "howling" for themselves. From her he obtained a number of good wedding songs and funeral "complaints."

But so far as Builínas were concerned, only rumours reached his ears. The Shungsk people did not care for such things. The Chinovniks (or civil officials) thought his interest in them was a proof of sheer idleness, the merchants gave up their minds to business alone, and the rest of the community seemed to him to be by no means well disposed towards such profane poetry as is represented by the Builína. In that part of the country the Russian Puritans known as Old-Ritualists abound, and they, according to Ruibnikof,—with whom, however, Hilferding has recently declared himself completely at variance on this point—feel for secular poetry what was felt in olden days by the Slavonic framers of the rules drawn up for persons leading an ascetic life, who were forbidden "to sing Satanic songs or to scandalize the profane world."

But he was told that there was a certain tailor called Butuilka (or the Bottle), who was in the habit of roaming from village to village, and of singing Builínas as he worked. Ruibnikof immediately set off in search of him, twice crossing Lake Onega on the ice, and once traversing its waters in a wretched boat, but he could not succeed in finding him. It was not till 1863 that he made the poetical tailor's acquaintance.

In the summer of 1860 Ruibnikof received a roving commission to collect statistics about the Government of Olonets. This gave him an excellent opportunity of studying the manners and customs of the peasantry in remote districts, and he profited by it to the uttermost. It is well known, he says, how difficult it is for a *Bárin*—a "gentleman"—and how especially difficult it is for a Chinovnik, or Government official, to gain the confidence of the common people, or to obtain from them any details about their way of living. Still, if they see that their visitor respects their customs, and is of a sympathetic nature, they are by no means inaccessible. On the contrary, they readily respond to his advances. It is an advantage to the inquirer to wear the national dress. "But his dress is not the main point. What he must do is to respect the independence of the religious beliefs of the people, the characteristics of their way of life, the hard labour of the agriculturist and the artisan, and at the same time to fling aside all bookish prejudices and fine airs. In that case the peasant will not refuse to recognize as a brother even a man who has received a university education, and will readily tell him all he wants to know." And so, "one fresh May morning," having donned the dress of the common people, Ruibnikof went down to the quay at Petrozavodsk, and began to look for a boat to take him to the other side of Lake Onega. The ice had scarcely had time to thaw, but boats had already begun to arrive from different parts of the lake, laden with butter, eggs, and meal, and manned by peasants who gave their services as rowers in return for a free passage. There was, however, only one boat from that part of the shore to which he wished to go. So in it, although it could offer but small accommodation, he was obliged to start. The boat left the quay at night, rowed by three men and a woman, but had not got far on its way when a strong head wind arose, and about six o'clock in the morning the weary rowers were glad to take refuge under the lee of a desolate little island about eight miles from Petrozavodsk. Ruibnikof landed and walked to a small hut intended for the benefit of weather-bound mariners, but it was full of peasants, for several other boats had been forced to take shelter from the storm, so he made himself some tea at a wood fire which was burning outside, and then lay down to sleep on the bare ground.

Before long he was awakened by strange sounds.

Some one was singing beside the fire. He had heard many songs, but never such a one as that to which he was now listening. " Lively, fantastic, joyous, it now streamed rapidly along, and now with broken flow seemed to recall to mind something antique, something forgotten by our generation." For a time Ruibnikof remained betwixt sleeping and waking, unwilling to move, " so pleasant was it to remain under the influence of an entirely new impression." Half slumbrously he could see a group of peasants sitting a little way off, listening to a song sung by a grey-haired old man, with a full white beard, keen eyes, and a kindly expression of countenance. When one song was ended another began, which turned out to be one of the Novgorod Builínas.

When the second song came to an end Ruibnikof got up and made acquaintance with the singer, a peasant named Leonty Bogdanovich. He heard many Builínas sung afterwards, he says, and that by skilled minstrels, but their performance never again produced the strong impression which was made upon him by the broken voice of the old singer to whom he listened that stormy spring morning, on the desolate island amid the wild waves of Lake Onega.

After spending some hours in friendly chat with the peasants, who formed a circle round the wood fire, Ruibnikof agreed to change boats and to accompany some of his new acquaintances to their village. One of the party was the singer, who helped to speed the hours by singing snatches of song to the men and by gossiping with the women. His age was seventy years "with a tail," but he was brisk and hearty, though "he had known but few good days in his life." About midday the boat came to the "Monk"—a long and narrow sandbank in the middle of the lake, much dreaded in stormy weather—and towards evening it was gliding between the indented shores of a secluded gulf, dotted with many islands. Here and there appeared villages and hamlets, and along the edge of the water were cottages, and little piers to which skiffs were attached. On went the voyagers, Leonty Bogdanovich singing the following song, in which the rest joined in chorus—

It is not the cuckoo that is mourning in the moist wood,
Nor the nightingale that is sadly complaining in the green garden,
Alas, it is a good youth who tearfully laments in a time of need.

. . . . .

My mother can I not recall to mind,
And who was it who gave to me, the orphan, to eat and to drink?
To me, the orphan, did the Orthodox Commune give to eat and to drink,
To me, the good youth, did mother Volga give to drink,
My yellow curls did a beauteous maiden twine.

And late in the evening they landed below the village of Seredka.

That evening as Ruibnikof was sitting in the cottage of the old singer, Leonty Bogdanovich, who had insisted on showing him hospitality, he was told by his host that the two best *skaziteli*—or reciters—of the neighbourhood lived close by, their names being Kozma Ivanof Romanof and Trofim Grigorief Ryabinin. "Take me to Ryabinin to-morrow morning," said Ruibnikof. "No," replied Leonty. "I must give him notice first. He is a proud man, and a stubborn one. If you don't persuade him beforehand, you'll get nothing out of him."

The next day Ruibnikof wandered about the village, and made acquaintance with a number of the cottagers, many of whom afterwards came to spend the evening with him. While they were talking and telling him stories, an old man of middle height, stoutly built, with flaxen hair and a small grey beard, stepped across the threshold. This was Ryabinin.

To Ruibnikof's request that he would sing "about some hero or other," he at first refused to accede. "It would be improper to recite profane songs at present," he replied, "to-day is a fast. One should sing religious songs." Ruibnikof explained that there could be no sin in reciting Builínas, which treated of "ancient Princes and Holy-Russian heroes," and at last Ryabinin allowed himself to be persuaded, and first said and then sang one of the epic poems. Such was the commencement of Ruibnikof's acquaintance with a "reciter" from whom he afterwards obtained three-and-twenty Builínas.

Ryabinin was well off for a peasant, having a good allotment of land, and making a fair livelihood by fishing. The other fishermen held him in great respect "on account of his knowledge of epic poetry," and used to take it in turns to do his share of the work when they were out fishing in common, in order that they might listen to his songs. He had acquired his stock of poetry partly by listening to an uncle who was a celebrated "reciter," and to a certain Kokotin, who kept a *traktír*, or tavern, at St. Petersburg, and who was a great lover of Builínas, of which he had a collection in manuscript. But his chief instructor had been one Ilya Elustaf'ef, the principal reciter of the whole province of Olonets, "who knew a countless number of Builínas, and could sing for whole days about different heroes." The peasants used to gather round him and say, "Now, then Ilya! sing us a Builína." And he would reply, "Give me a poltina (half a rouble); then I'll sing a Builína." And if one of the richer peasants produced the coin the old man would at once commence his recital. In this respect Ryabinin differed from him, for his pride prevented him from taking money from Ruibnikof, who says, "In spite of my urgent request, he would not consent to receive any thing from me in return for what he had taught me. When I, at my departure, gave his eldest daughter a handkerchief, he immediately presented me with an embroidered towel, and thought fit to account for his gift, and the reception of my present, as follows:—'When friends part for a long time, it is customary among us to exchange presents by way of remembrance.'"

A few days after his arrival Ruibnikof made the acquaintance of the other reciter, Románof. This was a blind, white-haired old man of ninety, who lived in a rude hut with an old woman to wait upon him. He had for his support the rent derived from his allotment of ground, and also a sum of six roubles allowed him yearly by the *Duma* or council. The rent he received each year for his piece of ground was paid in kind, and amounted to 20 poods of rye flour,—the pood being equal to about 36 lbs.—a pood of salt, a pood of groats, and three loads of hay. Moreover he kept a cow, and had money laid up for " a black day."

Románof was very willing to sing, and when he was invited to do so he poured forth Builína after Builína which he had learnt in early days. In former times, according to his account, it was customary for the old men and women to meet together and make nets, and then the " reciters " used to sing Builínas to them.

From Románof fourteen Builínas were obtained by Ruibnikof, who, after his return home to Petrozavodsk, kept up the acquaintance he had made with him and with Ryabinin. Besides these two, he became acquainted with several other "reciters," such as Shchegolenkof, for instance, a tailor who wandered about the neighbouring villages in search of work, being too weak to undertake field-labour, and whose niece also was able to sing several poems. On one occasion Ruibnikof was taken to see another woman who could sing. At first she refused to do so, but eventually complied with his request while suckling her babe. He is of opinion " that women have their own *bab'i starinui* (women's old poems), which are sung by them with special pleasure, but not so readily by the men,"—but this statement has been contradicted by Hilferding. In another village an old woman sang him a *starina*, having previously stipulated for a small piece of money in return.

Among the other singers whom Ruibnikof turned to account was Terenty Jevlef, a surly man of fifty, living in a solitary hut he had constructed for himself; Andrei Sarafanof, a middle-aged man occupied in fishing; and Peter Ivanof Kornilof, an elderly blind man living with his relations, and deriving a fair livelihood from the rent paid him for the use of his share of the communal lands. On one occasion a singer of local fame was summoned, who sent back word that he was too ill to come. Ruibnikof set off in search of him, and arriving at his cottage was told that he had gone off to the woods. Thither he went in search of him, and having found him, asked him why he had taken to flight in so unnecessary a manner. The singer explained that he had got into trouble about a fire in the woods, and that he had fancied Ruibnikof was an officer of the law who had come to inflict legal penalties upon him. As soon as Ruibnikof had told him his real mission, the peasant's fear left him, and he took his place beside the stump on which his visitor had sat down, and then and there sang him a Builína.

In one of the villages Ruibnikof found an excellent singer, Nikifor Prokhorof by name, who sang away to him during the whole of two evenings, his cottage being full of peasants all the time. " The old people listened silently, and the younger ones also sat quietly, only now and then interrupting the story by their exclamations. But at the most exciting passages they fidgetted a little on their seats, and bent forwards towards the reciter, as, for instance, when he told them how Ilya's son, not recognizing his father, bent his tough bow and shot an arrow into Ilya's white tent. From Nikifor Prokhorof, who gained his living by field-labour, Ruibnikof obtained twelve Builínas.

In the town of Pudoj, as Ruibnikof was informed, builine poetry used once to be held in great respect. Sixty years ago the merchants and other townspeople, even the civil officials being included in the number, used to meet together in the evenings on purpose to listen to Builínas; but long before his visit they had gone out of fashion. Fortunately he made the acquaintance of a young man, Andrei Sorokin, who kept an inn which his father had kept before him, and who was in the habit of telling stories and reciting ballads to his customers. "Travellers go to him in the evening and often sit up all night listening to his long stories about different heroes."

In the Kargopol district Ruibnikof found that the *Kalíki*, who looked on their singing and reciting from a thoroughly commercial point of view, asked payment for all that they contributed in the way of ballad poetry or hymns. "Up to this time," he says, "I had been accustomed to offer money of my own accord in return for singing, especially when I took away a peasant from his work. Some of the singers refused to take my money, others accepted it, either as a gift or as a recompense for their loss of time."

One of the *Kalíki* had a cottage of his own, but

scarcely ever lived in it, preferring to go about with his comrades to fairs and markets, and there to gain money by singing "spiritual songs." Along the river Onega live numbers of sectaries, who are very fond of such poetry, though they profess to object to all that is mundane. In the Archangel Government, however, where there are rich peasants in the villages, this *Kalika* sometimes recited Builínas.

Sometimes an attempt was made to deceive Ruibnikof. A peasant named Bogdanof, for instance, who had received some money from him for singing Builínas, wanted to earn more, so he "recalled to mind a number of fragments of tales, legends, and traditions, and did his best to weave them into a Builína." The result was unsatisfactory, but the minstrel was not to be discouraged; going to a *Kabak*, he fortified himself with strong liquors and returned to the attack. Failing a second time, he betook himself to a neighbour, who told him a *starina*, which he tried to repeat to Ruibnikof, breaking down, however, at the end of the first ten lines. Eventually he became so troublesome that he had to be abruptly sent about his business. Another time a village "scribe" brought Ruibnikof half-a-dozen poems which he professed to have heard, but which he had really transcribed bodily from the printed collection of Kirsha Danilof. With Butuilka (the Bottle) whose real name was Chukkoef, Ruibnikof made acquaintance in 1863. He is the possessor of a good piece of land, but his main income is derived from tailor's work, in quest of which he spends nearly the whole winter, wandering from village to village in one of the districts bordering on Lake Onega. He afterwards visited Ruibnikof at Petrozavodsk, and there sang to him all the Builínas he knew.

In some of the districts around Lake Onega, as, for instance, in those of Petrozavodsk and Pudoj, the remains of the old epic poetry are carefully preserved by the rural population. Every peasant there "is acquainted with the contents of some Builínas, and with the names of certain heroes," and every intelligent man of a certain age has a Builína or two committed to memory. Even if he thinks at first that he knows nothing about them, he will, if he reflects awhile, find at least fragments of them coming into his mind. In some places they are chiefly retained in the memories of the *Skazíteli*, or reciters, who sing them from a love for poetry, in others they are only to be heard from the *Kalíki*, who make a livelihood out of them. As a general rule the singers have learnt them from their fathers or grandfathers. Most of the *Kalíki* make a point of handing them down to their children. "But the greater part of the reciters," says Ruibnikof, "leave no heirs for their poetic stores, and in the course of twenty or thirty years, after the deaths of the best representatives of the present generation of singers, the Builínas, even in the Government of Olonetz, will be preserved in the memories of but a very few members of the rural population[1]."

[1] Ruibnikof, III. pp. vi—lii. Hilferding, however, denies that the Builínas are dying out.

CHAPTER II.

MYTHOLOGY.

SECTION I.—THE OLD GODS.

At some remote period, of which very little is known with certainty, but when, it may be supposed, what are now the various Slavonic peoples spoke the same tongue and worshipped the same gods, some kind of mythological system, in all probability, prevailed among them, of which only a few fragments have come down to the present day. Among these relics of an almost forgotten past, by no means the least important are the songs which have been preserved by the people in their different dialects, handed down as a precious heirloom from one generation to another, and watched over with a jealous care which has prevented them from entirely losing their original characteristics. In ancient times they seem to have belonged to some great mass of national poetry, some collection of Slavonic Vedas, in which the religious teaching of the day was embodied. Of it, as a whole, there can now be formed only a dim conception, but of several of its separate features it is possible to gain at least some idea by studying and piecing together the fragments of popular poetry which exist, more or less abundantly, in every land that is inhabited by a Slavonic population. Each land has its own songs now, but there is such a strong family likeness between all these memorials of old times as clearly points to a common origin, whether they come from the shores of the Baltic or of the Adriatic, whether they form the heritage of the "Orthodox" Russian or Servian, or of the "Catholic" Pole or Czekh. It is mainly with the songs which are still current in modern Russia that it is proposed to deal at present, but almost every inference that may be deduced from their testimony, with reference to the old days of heathenism, can be supported also by that of their kin among the Slavonic brethren of the Russians, as well as among their Lettic cousins.

Before entering upon the subject of these songs it will be as well to say a few prefatory words about the mythological system which they illustrate—to attempt to sketch the principal features of the religious worship of the old Slavonians, and to convey some idea of the process by which the venerable deities whom they adored have, in the course of time, become transformed into the capricious and often grotesque beings with whom the superstition of the Russian peasant peoples the spiritual world. The task is not one which can be completed in a satisfactory manner, for there is a lack of precise information on the subject, and the writers who claim to pronounce upon it with authority not seldom differ among themselves. But it is to be hoped that the remarks which are about to be made here will, at least, help to render intelligible the fragmentary songs which are to follow them.

The Slavonians—says Solovief, in the introduction to his "History of Russia"—remember nothing about their arrival in Europe, though tradition still speaks—even if history be silent—of their early sojourn along the banks of the Danube, and of their being compelled to move thence, under the pressure of some hostile force, apparently towards the north-east. So thick are the clouds which hang over this period of their history, that it is difficult to obtain any thing like a clear view of what was happening before some of their number built Novgorod on the shores of Lake Ilmen, and others founded, near the conflux of the Dyesna and the Dnieper, what was to become the chief city of South Russia, and gave it the name of Kief.

About the time of the foundation of that city, the country adjacent to the Dnieper seems to have been inhabited chiefly by two great tribes, the Drevlyáne, or Foresters [*Drevo* = a tree], and the Polyáne, or Field-people [*Pole* = a field], of whom the latter were, as might be supposed from their name, the milder and more civilized. Of the Drevlyane the old chroniclers have spoken with great harshness, but those writers may have been somewhat biassed by their theological hatred of stiff-necked idolators.

The religion of the Eastern Slavonians—among whom may fairly be included the ancestors of at least a great part of the present Russians—appears to have been founded, like that of all the other Aryan races, upon the reverence paid, on the one hand to the forces of nature, on the other to the spirits of the dead. They seem to have worshipped the sun, the moon, the stars, the elements, and the spirits whom they connected with the phenomena of the storm, personifying the powers of nature under various forms, and thus creating a certain number of deities, among whom the supremacy was, sooner or later, attributed to the Thunder-God, Perun.

These Eastern Slavonians seem to have built no regular temples, and—in striking contrast with the Lithuanians, not to speak of some of the Western Slavonians—they appear not to have acknowledged any regular class of priests. Their sacrifices were offered up under a tree—generally an oak—or beside running water, and the sacred rites were performed by the Elders, or heads of family communities. The modern Russian word for "family," *Sem'ya*—it should be observed—originally had the same meaning as *Suprugi*, man and wife. The word which supplied its place was *Rod*, which meant family in its widest sense, including the whole of a man's relatives, his Clan, as it were, or *Gens*[1]. The chief of the *Rod* exercised the functions of priest, king, and judge. Prophets seem to have existed in the persons of certain wizards—*Volkhvui*—of whom very little is known, but who probably resembled to a considerable degree the Finnish Conjurors.

[1] Solovief, *Istoriya Rossii*, I. 317.

The cultus of ancestors formed an important part of the religious system of the old Slavonians, who attributed to the souls of the dead passions and appetites like to those which sway the living, and who attached great importance to the manifestation of respect for the spirits of their forefathers, and especially for that of the original founder of the family. The worship of the Slavonic Lares and Penates, who were, as in other lands, intimately connected with the fire burning on the domestic hearth, retained a strong hold on the affections of the people, even after Christianity had driven out the great gods of old; but the spiritual beings to whom reverence was paid gradually lost their original dignity, until at last the majestic form of the household divinity became degraded into that of the Domovoy—the house-spirit in whom the Russian peasant still firmly believes, the Brownie, or Hobgoblin, who once haunted our own firesides.

Such are the most salient points of the old Slavonic mythology. We will now examine it a little more in detail, commencing with the ideas attached by the early inhabitants of Russia to those solar gods who are supposed by many eminent scholars to have originally held higher rank than the wielder of the Thunderbolt, Perun [2].

---

[2] The following extract from Mr. Talboys Wheeler's description of the religion of the "Vedic people" ("History of India," I. 8) seems to be perfectly applicable to the primitive Slavonians. "Their Gods appear to have been mere abstractions: personifications of those powers of nature on whom they relied for good

The most ancient among these deities is said to have been Svarog, apparently the Slavonic counterpart of the Vedic Varuna and the Hellenic Ouranos. His name is deduced by Russian philologists from a root corresponding with the Sanskrit *Sur*—to shine, and is compared by some of them with the Vedic *Svar*, and the later word *Svarga*, heaven.

The Sun and the Fire are spoken of as his children; the former under the name of Dazhbog, the latter under that of Ogon'. According to an old saying, Svarog is given to repose, deputing to his children the work of creation and the task of ruling the universe [3].

That Dazhbog was the Sun seems clear, and it appears to be proved that he was identical with Khors, who is sometimes spoken of as a different personage. The word *Dazh* is said to be the adjectival form of *Dag* [Gothic, *Dags*, German, *Tag*], so that Dazhbog is equivalent to Day-God. That the

---

harvests. But from the very first there appears to have been some confusion in these personifications, which led both to a multiplicity of deities, and the confounding together of different deities."

[3] Buslaef, "On the Influence of Christianity on the Slavonic Language," p. 50. Afanasief, "Poetic Views of the Slavonians about Nature," I. 64, 65. Solovief decidedly identifies Perun with Svarog. See his "History of Russia," I. 82, 322. Buslaef, in his "Historical Sketches," says "The epoch of Perun and Volos . . . was preceded by another, one common to all the Slavonians—the epoch of Svarozhich, who among us in the East received the name of Dazhbog."—*Ist. Och.* I. 364. I shall not refer in this chapter to the celebrated epic "On the Expedition of Igor," as I wish to reserve that poem for a future occasion.

word *Bog* stands for God is already well known, as also that it "reappears among us in the form of Puck, Bogy, and Bug [4]."

That Ogon', Fire, [pronounced Agón, = Agni], was considered the son of Svarog, the Heaven, is supposed to be proved by the evidence of a thirteenth century writer, who says [5] of the Slavonians, "They pray to Ogon', whom they call Svarozhich," or Svarog's son—the "Zuarasici" mentioned by Dietmar. We shall see, a little farther on, how many traces still appear to exist, in the speech and the customs of the modern Russians, of the worship once paid to Ogon', and on his account to the domestic hearth, or to the stove which eventually took its place—a worship which was closely connected with that of which the spirits of ancestors were the objects.

We now come to the deity who ultimately became the supreme god of the Slavonians—Perun, the Thunderer. In dealing with him we shall by no means be treading upon certain ground, but we shall at least have escaped from the limbo to which the lapse of time has assigned the dimly-seen form of Svarog.

Russian mythologists identify the name of Perun with that of the Vedic Parjanya. Whether the latter was an independent deity, or whether his name was merely an epithet of Indra, does not appear to be certain, nor are philologists agreed as to whether

---

[4] G. W. Cox's "Mythology of the Aryan Nations," II. 364.
[5] In the *Slovo nyekoego Khristolyubtsa*.

THE OLD GODS. 87

Parjanya means "the rain" or "the thunderer;" but "it is very probable that our ancestors adored, previously to the separation of the Aryan race, a god called Parjana, or Pargana, the personification of the thundering cloud, whom they believed to rouse the thunder-storm, to be armed with the lightning, to send the rain, to be the procreator of plants, and the upholder of justice. Afterwards the Græco-Italian nation, bent on the adoration of Dyaus, forgot him entirely; the Aryans of India and the Teutonic tribes continued to worship him as a subordinate member of the family of the gods, but the Letto-Slavonians raised him to the dignity of a supreme leader of all other deities [6]."

In the hymns addressed to Parjanya in the Rig Veda he is called "the thunderer, the showerer, the bountiful, who impregnates the plants with rain," and it is said that "Earth becomes (fit) for all creatures when Parjanya fertilizes the soil with showers [7]." Sometimes "he strikes down the trees" and destroys "the wicked (clouds)," at others he "speaks a wonderful gleam-accompanied word which brings refreshment [8]," and gives birth "to plants for man's enjoyment."

The description of Parjanya is in all respects

---

[6] Dr. G. Bühler, in an excellent article "On the Hindu God 'Parjanya,'" contained in the "Transactions of the Philological Society," 1859, pt. 2, pp. 154—168. See also his essay on the same subject in vol. i. of Benfey's *Orient und Occident*.

[7] "Rig Veda," v. 83. Prof. Wilson's translation.

[8] "Rig Veda," v. 63. Dr. Bühler's translation.

applicable to the deity worshipped by the different branches of the Slavo-Lettic family under various names, such as the Lithuanian *Perkunas*, the Lettish *Perkons*, the Old Prussian *Perkunos*, the Polish *Piorun*, the Bohemian *Peraun*, and the Russian *Perun*[9].

According to a Lithuanian legend, known also to other Indo-European nations, the Thunder-God created the universe by the action of warmth—*Perkunas wis iszperieje*. The verb *perieti* (present form *periu*) means to produce by means of warmth, to hatch, to bear, being akin to the Latin *pario*, and the Russian *parit'* [1].

In Lithuania Perkunas, as the God of Thunder, was worshipped with great reverence. His statue is said to have held in its hand " a precious stone like fire," shaped " in the image of the lightning," and before it constantly burnt an oak-wood fire. If the fire by any chance went out, it was rekindled by means of sparks struck from the stone. His name is not

---

[9] According to Dr. Bühler the word *Perkuna* is " exactly equivalent to a Sanskrit *Parjana*, to which the affix *ya* was added without change of signification." With respect to the absence of the *k* in the Slavonic forms of the name he says, " This elision may perhaps be attributed to the position of the *r*. As a group of consonants formed by *rk* or *rg* would be in disharmony with the phonetic rules established in the Slavonic languages, and the usual transposition of the liquid was not effected, an unusual remedy only could hinder the violation of the laws of the language." —Phil. Soc. Trans. 1859, p. 164. See also the *Deutsche Mythologie*, 156.

[1] Afanasief, P. V. S. I. 249.

yet forgotten by the people, who say, when the thunder rolls, *Perkúns grumena*, and who still sing *dainos*[2] in which he is mentioned. In one of these a girl who is mourning for the loss of her flowers is asked,—

> Did the north wind blow,
> Or did Perkunas thunder or send lightnings?

In another it is told how when

> The Morning Star held a wedding-feast,
> Perkunas rode through the doorway,
> Struck down the green oak.

And in a third the following myth is related about the marriage of the Moon, a male deity in the Slavo-Lettic languages:—

> The Moon wedded the Sun
> In the first spring.
> The Sun arose early
> The Moon departed from her.
> The Moon wandered alone,
> Courted the Morning Star.
> Perkunas greatly wroth
> Cleft him with a sword.
> " Wherefore dost thou depart from the Sun?
> Wandering by night alone?
> Courting the Morning Star?"
> Full of sorrow [was his] heart[3].

Among the kindred Livonians a feast used to be celebrated at the beginning of Spring, during which

---

[2] *Dainà* (plur. *Dainos*) is a Lithuanian word for a song. It is not used, however, in the case of a song of a serious or religious cast, which bears a special name.

[3] Nesselmann's *Littauische Volkslieder*, No. 2.

the following prayer is said to have been uttered by the officiating priest:—

"Perkons! father! thy children lead this faultless victim to thy altar. Bestow, O father, thy blessing on the plough and on the corn. May golden straw with great well-filled ears rise abundantly as rushes. Drive away all black haily clouds to the great moors, forests, and large deserts, where they will not frighten mankind; and give sunshine and rain, gentle falling rain, in order that the crops may thrive[4]!"

Among many of the Western Slavonians the name of this thunder-god is still preserved under various forms in the speech of the people. The White-Russian peasant to this day uses such expressions in his wrath as "Perun smite thee!" and the Slovaks have retained a curse, "May Parom show thee his teeth!" that is to say, "May the lightning strike thee[5]!"

In a most valuable collection of Lettish songs, recently published at Wilna, in Lett and Russian, there occur several allusions to Perkons, either regarded as the thunder-god or as the thunder itself. In one we are told that—

> Father Perkons
> Has nine Sons:
> Three strike, three thunder,
> Three lighten.

Another states that—
> Perkons drove across the sea,
> In order to marry beyond the sea:

[4] Quoted by Dr. Bühler from Lasicius, *De Diis Samogitarum* I have not as yet succeeded in verifying the quotation.
[5] Afanasief, P.V. S. I. 251.

Him the Sun followed with a dowry
Bestowing gifts on all the woods :
To the Oak a golden girdle,
To the Maple motley gloves.

And a third addresses the Thunderer as follows :—

Strike, O Perkons, the spring
To the very depths—
In it the Sun's daughter yesterday was drowned
While washing golden goblets [6].

According to a Polish tradition, the mother of the thunder is called Percunatele, a name which is applied in part of Russian Lithuania as an epithet of the Virgin Mary, who is called Panna [Lady] Maria Percunatele. In the Government of Vilna the second of February is devoted to the *Presvyataya Mariya Gromnitsa*, the Very Holy Mary the Thunderer, and during service on that day the faithful stand in church holding lighted tapers, the remains of which they keep by them during the rest of the year, lighting them before their holy pictures from time to time when storms impend [7].

In " Great-Russia," or Russia proper, the name of Perun has disappeared from the memory of the common people, and it has left scarcely any traces behind. Only two Russian localities, says Schöpping, bear names which seem to be derived from his, and one of them is in Kief, and the other in the Govern-

---

[6] *Pamyatniki Latuishskago Narodnago Tvorchestva, etc.*, p. 315, 316 (" Memorials of Lettish Popular Poetry," collected and edited by Ivan Sprogis), Wilna, 1868.

[7] Schöpping's R. N. p. 195.

ment of Novgorod, both places directly under Varangian influence—his theory being that the Scandinavian rulers of Russia were the chief promoters of the worship of Perun [8]. In their treaties with the Greeks they swore by Perun and Volos, and some commentators have supposed that the former was the peculiar deity of the Scandinavian rulers, and the latter that of their Slavonic subjects. At all events, Volos has retained his hold on the memory of the Russian peasants, while Perun has become forgotten, and his attributes have been transferred to the Prophet Elijah and various Christian Saints [9].

The descriptions we have of the appearance presented by the statues of Perun all come from the west and south-west. In Kief, it is said, he had

[8] Buslaef, however, a far higher authority, holds (*Ist. Och.* I. 360) "that Perun was a generally worshipped Slavonic deity long before the division of the Slavonians into their Eastern and Western branches."

[9] The following facts will serve to show how treacherous is the ground on which the antiquarian has to tread while endeavouring to discover such remains as may elucidate the early history of Slavonic Mythology. The name of the god Zuarasici, or Suarasici, mentioned by Dietmar, was misprinted in Wagner's edition Luarasici. Led astray by this mistake, Schafarik, one of the most erudite of Slavonic scholars, wrote the name Lua-Razic, and explained it as meaning Lion-King. Afterwards, however, when the spelling was corrected, he saw that the name was merely a slightly altered form of Svarozhich. More unfortunate were the mistakes mentioned by Schöpping (R. N. p. 16), which derived a god Uslyad, or "Golden Moustaches," from a couple of words describing the personal appearance of Perun, and evolved a mysterious deity called Dazhb, or Dashuba, out of a common-place contraction of Dazhboga, the genitive case of Dazhbog, the Day-God.

a statue of which the trunk was of wood, while the head was of silver, with moustaches of gold, but little more is known about it, except that it bore among its weapons a mace. White-Russian traditions, says Afanasief, describe Perun as tall and well-shaped, with black hair, and a long golden beard. He rides in a flaming car, grasping in his left hand a quiver full of arrows, and in his right a fiery bow. Sometimes he flies abroad on a great millstone, which is supported by the mountain-spirits who are in subjection to him, and who, by their flight, give rise to storms. Perun, in many respects, corresponds with Thor, and one of the points of similarity is the mace which he bears, answering to Thor's hammer, Mjölnir, the name of which may be compared with the Russian words for a hammer and for lightning, *molot* and *molniya*[1]. Ukko, also, the Finnish Thunder-God, has his hammer, and the Lithuanians used to pay special honour to a great hammer with which a certain giant—perhaps Perkunas—had freed the Sun from imprisonment.

In the Spring, according to a White-Russian tradition, Perun goes forth in his fiery car, and crushes with his blazing darts the demons, from whose wounds the blood is sometimes described as streaming forth. That is to say, the lightning pierces the clouds at that season of the year, and causes them to pour forth rain.

The myth is one which the Slavonians doubtless

---

[1] *Deutsche Mythologie*, 1171.

brought with them from some such climes as those in which "anxious multitudes watch the gradual gathering of the sky, as day by day the long array of clouds enlarges; but there is no rain until a rattling thunderstorm charges through their ranks, and the battered clouds are forced to let loose their impetuous showers. 'This,' says the Veda, 'is Indra, who comes loud shouting in his car, and hurls his thunderbolt at the demon Vritra.'"[2]

After Perun's statue at Kief had been flung into the Dnieper by St. Vladimir, and that at Novgorod had been cast into the Volkhof[3], and the people who used to worship him had accepted just so much of Christianity as left them what the chronicler called "two-faithed," then his attributes were transferred to a number of the personages whom the new religion brought into honour. In the minds of most of the people he became changed into the Prophet Ilya, or Elijah, from whose fiery chariot the lightnings

---

[2] Mrs. Manning's "Ancient India," I. 16.

[3] "The people of Novogorod formerly offered their chief worship and adoration to a certain idol named Perun. When subsequently they received baptism, they removed it from its place, and threw it into the river Volchov; and the story goes, that it swam against the stream, and that near the bridge a voice was heard, saying, 'This for you, O inhabitants of Novogorod, in memory of me;' and at the same time a certain rope was thrown upon the bridge. Even now it happens from time to time on certain days of the year, that this voice of Perun may be heard, and on these occasions the citizens run together and lash each other with ropes, and such a tumult arises therefrom, that all the efforts of the Governor can scarcely assuage it."—Herberstein, Mr. Major's translation, vol. II. p. 26.

flashed and the thunders pealed as they had done in days of yore from that of Perun. The fame of his battles with the demons survived in the legends about the Archangel Michael, the conqueror of the powers of darkness, and other traditions relating to him may be traced in stories told about the Apostle Peter, or about Yury the Brave, our own St. George [4].

Perun's bow is sometimes identified with the rainbow, an idea which is known also to the Finns. From it, according to the White-Russians, are shot burning arrows, which set on fire all things that they touch. In many parts of Russia (as well as of Germany) it is supposed that these bolts sink deep into the soil, but that at the end of three or seven years they return to the surface in the shape of longish stones of a black or dark grey colour—probably belemnites, or masses of fused sand—which are called thunderbolts, and considered as excellent preservatives against lightning and conflagrations. The Finns call them Ukonkiwi—the stone of the thunder-god Ukko, and in Courland their name is Perkuhnsteine, which explains itself [5].

In some cases the flaming dart of Perun became, in the imagination of the people, a golden key. With it he unlocked the earth, and brought to light its concealed treasures, its restrained waters, its captive founts of light. With it also he locked away in safety fugitives who wished to be put out of the

[4] Afanasief, "Poetic Views," I. 251, 771.

[5] Afanasief, "Poetic Views," I. 248. Grimm, *Deutsche Mythologie*, 164.

power of malignant conjurors, and performed various other good offices. Appeals to him to exercise these functions still exist in the spells used by the peasants, but his name has given way to that of some Christian personage. In one of them, for instance, the Archangel Michael is called upon to secure the invoker behind an iron door fastened by twenty-seven locks, the keys of which are given to the angels to be carried to heaven. In another, John the Baptist is represented as standing upon a stone in the Holy Sea [i. e. in heaven], resting upon an iron crook or staff, and is called upon to stay the flow of blood from a wound, locking the invoker's veins " with his heavenly key." In this case the myth has passed into a rite. In order to stay a violent bleeding from the nose, a locked padlock is brought, and the blood is allowed to drop through its aperture, or the sufferer grasps a key in each hand, either plan being expected to prove efficacious. As far as the key is concerned, the belief seems to be still maintained among ourselves.

According to the mythologists, Perun's golden key is the lightning with which in spring he rends the winter-bound earth and lets loose the frozen streams —offices more usually performed by the sun—or pierces the clouds, and frees the rains which are imprisoned in those airy castles. These spring rains have always been looked upon as specially health-giving, and from that idea, as some commentators suppose, arose the myth of the Water of Life which figures in the folk-lore of so many different races.

The Slavonic tales, like those with which we are more familiar, abound in accounts of how a dead hero is restored to life by means of this precious liquid, which is sometimes brought by the Whirlwind, the Thunder, and the Hail, sometimes by their types the Raven, the Hawk, the Eagle, and the Dove. But they differ from most of the similar stories in this respect. They have two species of what is called the "strong" or the "heroic" water. The one is called "the dead water" (*mertvaya voda*); the other the "living [or vivifying] water" (*zhivaya voda*). When the "dead water" is applied to the wounds of a corpse it heals them, but before the dead body can be brought to life, it is necessary to sprinkle it with the "living water." When that has been done, the corpse first shudders and then sits up, usually remarking "How long I have been asleep[6]!"

In other stories the representative of Perun recovers gems or treasures which evil spirits have hidden away within mountains or under deep waters —[that is to say, he brings out the lights of heaven from behind the dark veil of winter, or from out of the depths of the cloud-sea?] Sometimes, however, it is Perun who dies, and then remains lying veiled in a shroud [of fog?] or floating over dark

[6] In the Rámáyana, the monkey-chief, Hanuman, is sent to the Himalayas to fetch four different kinds of herbs, of which the first restore the dead to life, the second drive away pain, the third join broken parts, and the fourth cure all the wounds inflicted by Indrajit's arrows.

waters in a coffin [of cloud, until the spring recalls him to life ?].

As among other peoples, so among the Slavonians, the oak was a sacred tree, and was closely connected with the worship of the thunder-god. The name *dub*, which is now confined to the oak, originally (like the Greek *drus*) meant a tree or wood, as may be seen in such words as *dubina*, a cudgel. Afterwards it was used to designate the hardest and most long-lived among trees, and that which was consecrated to the Thunderer, the oak. Its name in Servian is *grm*, or *grmov*, a form which is evidently akin to the Russian onomatopœic word *grom*, the thunder. As has already been stated, the fire which burnt before the statue of Perkunas was fed with oak-wood, and so profoundly did the old Lithuanians respect their sacred oaks, which they carefully hedged around, that, when they accepted Christianity, they protested against those trees being hewn down, even when they consented to their idols being overthrown.

The ideas which were associated with the fern in other lands are current also in Russia. At certain periods of the year it bursts into golden or fiery blossoms, but they disappear almost instantaneously, for evil spirits swarm thickly around them, and carry them off. Whoever can gather these flowers will be able to read the secrets of the earth, and no treasures can be concealed from him. But to obtain them is a difficult task. The best way is to take a cloth on which an Easter cake has been blessed, and the knife with which the cake has been cut, and then go into the forest on Easter Eve, trace a circle with the knife around the fern, spread out the cloth, and sit down within the circle, with eyes steadily fixed upon the plant. Just at the moment when the words "Christ is arisen!" are sung in the churches, the fern will blossom. The watcher should then seize it and run home, having covered himself with the cloth, and taking care not to look behind him. When he has reached home he should cut his hand with the knife and insert the plant into the wound. Then all secret things will become visible to him [7].

The fern-gatherer must remain in the magic circle until he has secured the flowers, otherwise the demons will pull him to pieces. They do all they can to prevent his obtaining the fiery blossoms, attempting to overcome him by a magic sleep, and causing the earth to rock, lightning to flash, thunder to roar, flames to surround the intruder, so that success is rare. These magic blossoms, which appear on St. John's day at Midsummer, as well as on Easter-day, are called among the Croats, says Afanasief, by the name of *Perenovo Tsvetje*, or Perun's Flower [8].

The lightning was endowed by ancient fancy with the faculty of sight, and the flash of the summer lightning, when it gleams for a moment across the

---

[7] According to a tradition preserved in the Government of Kherson. Afanasief, P. V. S. II. 379.

[8] A number of similar traditions about the fern, gleaned from German sources, will be found, in an English dress, in Mr. W. K. Kelly's "Curiosities of Indo-European Tradition and Folk-lore," pp. 181—200.

heavens, and then hides itself behind the dark clouds, is still associated by the people in many places with the winking of an eye. Thus the Little-Russians call the summer lightning *Morgavka* [*morgat'* = to wink], and say as they look at it, "*Morgni, Morgni, Morgavko!*" "Wink, wink, Morgavko!" The stories of the Bohemians and Slovaks tell of a giant named Swifteye, whose ardent glances set on fire all that they regard, so that he is compelled to wear a bandage over his eyes; and the Russian stories describe a wondrous Ancient with huge eyebrows and enormously long eyelashes. So abnormal has been their growth, that they have darkened his vision, and when he wishes to gaze upon " God's world," he is obliged to call for a number of powerful assistants, who lift up his eyebrows and eyelashes with iron pitchforks. In Servia he appears in the form of the Vii, a mysterious being, whose glance reduces not only men, but even whole cities, to ashes. Nothing can be concealed from his eyes when they are open, but they are almost always covered by their closely-adhering lids, and by his bushy brows. When his eyelids have been lifted by the aid of pitchforks, his stare is as fatal as was that of Medusa. This wielder of baleful regards is supposed to have been one of the many forms under which the popular fancy personified the lightning—his basilisk glance, so rarely seen, being the flash which remains hidden by the clouds, till the time comes for it to make manifest its terrible strength.

There is a well-known Lithuanian story, in which

Perun occupies an intermediate place between that of a deity and of a demon. According to it a young Carpenter once went roaming about the world with Perkun and the Devil. Perkun thundered and flashed lightnings, so as to keep off beasts of prey, the Devil hunted, and the Carpenter cooked. After a time they built a hut, and lived in it, and began to till the land and to grow vegetables. All went well for a while, but at last a thief took to stealing their turnips. The Devil and Perkun successively tried to catch the thief, but only got well thrashed for their pains. Then the Carpenter undertook the task, providing himself beforehand with a fiddle. The music he drew from this instrument greatly pleased the thief, who appeared in the form of a *Laume*, or supernatural hag, and besought a music-lesson. The Carpenter, under the pretence of making her fingers more fit for fiddling, induced her to place them in a split tree-stump, from which he knocked out a wedge, and so captured her. Before he let her go he made her promise not to return, and took away her iron waggon, and the whip with which she had belaboured his comrades.

Time passed by and the three companions agreed to separate, but could not decide who should occupy the hut. At last they settled that it should belong to that one of their number who succeeded in frightening the two others. First the Devil tried his hand, and raised such a storm that he drove Perkun out of the house. But the Carpenter held out bravely, praying and singing psalms all night. Next Perkun put forth all his terrors, and frightened the Devil horribly by his thunder and lightning, but the Carpenter still held his own. Last of all the Carpenter set to work. In the middle of the night up he drove in the Laume's waggon, cracking her whip, and uttering the words he had heard her use while she was stealing turnips. Immediately away flew both the Devil and Perkun, and the Carpenter was left in possession of the house[9].

The statue of Perun, at Kief, stood upon a piece of rising ground, on which were set up also the images of several other gods—Khors, Dazhbog, Stribog, Simargla, and Mokosh. Of these Khors and Dazhbog are supposed, as has already been observed, to have been two forms of one deity, the Sun-god, and Stribog was the God of Winds. Of the others very little indeed is known. Simargla is generally taken to be a corruption of Sim and Regl, the names of two deities who are so shrouded in obscurity that one commentator—in default of all trustworthy evidence—has had recourse to a somewhat rash comparison of their names with those of the Assyrian gods mentioned in the Second Book of Kings [ch. xvii. ver. 30]: "And the men of Cuth made Nergal, and the men of Hamath made Ashima[1]." In pursuance of a similar idea Mokosh has been taken to be a female deity, and has been likened to Astarte. But these are the wildest of conjectures. The name

[9] Schleicher, *Litauische Märchen*, 141-5.
[1] See the Russian "Journal of the Ministry of National Enlightenment," 1841, II. 37—39, 41—43.

of Stribog, the God of the Winds, is derived from a word *Stri* (= the air, or a certain state of the atmosphere), and may still be recognized in various geographical designations, such as Stribog's Lake (*Stribozhe Ozero*), etc.

On the other deities known to the Western Slavonians there is no occasion to dwell at present, for they do not figure in the popular prose or poetry of Russia. Some of their names are probably synonyms, and it will be sufficient to say of such forms as Svyatovit, Radigast, and Yarovit that Professor Sreznyevsky considers them as different appellations of the Sun-god, preserved by various Slavonic races. The belief attributed to the Western Slavonians in the warring principles of good and evil, in Byelbog, the White God, the representative of light—and in Chernobog, the Black God, the representative of darkness—is supposed by some writers to have once been common to the whole Slavonic family, the Russians included, for geography has preserved the names of the antagonistic deities in divers places. In Russia, for instance, there are the Byeluie Bogi, near Moscow, the Troitsko-Byelbozhsky Monastery in the diocese of Kostroma, and Chernobozh'e, in the Porkhof district. Among the White-Russians the memory of Byelbog is still preserved in the traditions about Byelun. That mythical personage is represented as an old man with a long white beard, dressed in white, and carrying a staff in his hand, who appears only by day, and who assists travellers to find their way out of the dark forests.

He is the bestower of wealth and fertility, and at harvest time he often appears in the corn-fields, and assists the reapers. The adjective *byeloi* or *byely* [from a root *byel* or *bil*] which now means white, originally meant bright, as appears from such expressions as *byely svyet*, or *byely den*, the white (i.e. bright) light or day. In the same sense of the word the moon is often spoken of as "white," and the horses are "white" which draw the chariot of the sun[2]. The intimate connexion between Byelbog and the Light-god Bäldäg [Baldur, etc.] has been pointed out by Jacob Grimm (*Deutsche Mythologie*, p. 203).

In the Russian songs several other mythological names occur, but many of them are supposed to be merely special designations either of Perun or of Dazhbog—of the thunder or of the sun—such as Tur, Ovsen', Yarilo, etc. These may be left to be dealt with as they occur, but there are two names which are very often mentioned, and about which some discussion has arisen—those of Lado and Lada. Of these it may be as well to say a few words.

One writer has gone so far as to maintain that Lado and Lada are merely two of the meaningless refrains that occur in Russian songs[3]. But the generally received idea is that Lado was a name for the Sun-god, answering to Freyr, and that Lada was the Slavonic counterpart of Freyja, the goddess of the spring

[2] Afanasief, P. V. S. I. 92—96.
[3] Tereshchenko, v. 56. His merits as a compiler, and his demerits as a critic, have been ably pointed out by Kavelin, *Collected Works*, IV. 3—20.

and of love. In Lithuanian songs Lada is addressed as "*Lada, Lada, dido musu deve!*" "Lada, Lada, our great goddess!" And the epithet *dido*, or great, may account for the form *Did-Lado*, which frequently occurs in the Russian songs. One Lithuanian song distinctly couples the name of Lado with that of the sun. A shepherd sings, "I fear thee not, O wolf! The god with the sunny curls will not let thee approach. Lado, O Sun-Lado!" In one of the old chronicles Lado is mentioned as "The God of marriage, of mirth, of pleasure, and of general happiness," to whom those who were about to marry offered sacrifices, in order to secure a fortunate union. And nearly the same words are used about Lada, on the authority of an old tradition. In the songs of the Russian people the words *lado* and *lada* are constantly used as equivalents, in the one case for lover, bridegroom, or husband, and in the other for mistress bride, or wife. *Lad* means peace, union, harmony, as in the proverb, "When a husband and wife have *lad*, they don't require also *klad* (a treasure)." After the introduction of Christianity the reverence that was originally paid to Lada became transferred to the Virgin Mary. On that account it is that the Servians call her "Fiery Mary," and speak of her in their songs as the sister of Elijah the Thunderer, that is Perun[4].

[4] Afanasief, P. V. S. I. 227—229, and 483.

SECTION II.—DEMIGODS AND FAIRIES.

From the Gods of the Eastern Slavonians we may now turn to the inferior inhabitants of their spirit-world. In considering these we have no longer to deal almost exclusively with the past, for they still, to a considerable degree, retain their hold on the faith of the Russian peasant, and, at least in outlying districts, maintain a vigorous existence. The Church has waged war against them for centuries, and has degraded and disfigured many of them, but although their expression has in many cases become greatly altered, yet their original features may easily be recognized by a careful observer.

When Satan and all his hosts were expelled from heaven, says a popular *legenda*[5], some of the exiled spirits fell into the lowest recesses of the underground world, where they remain in the shape of *Karliki* or dwarfs. Some were received by the woods [*lyesa*], which they still haunt as *Lyeshie*, or sylvan demons, resembling fauns or satyrs; some dived into the waters [*vodui*], which they now inhabit under the name of *Vodyanuie*, or water-sprites; some remained in the air [*vozdukh*], and under the designation of *Vozdushnuie* delight in riding the whirlwind and directing the storm; and some have attached themselves to the houses [*doma*] of mankind, and have

---

[5] A popular tale is generally called a *skazka* in Russian. But if it relates to religious matters it is called a *legenda*.

thence obtained the name of *Domovuie*, or domestic spirits. The distinctions made between the various groups of demons may be referred back to a very ancient period, but their demoniacal character, and the reason given for their appearance on earth, are the results of comparatively recent ideas about the world of spirits. At least, a very great part of the opinions held by the peasants of modern Russia, with respect to these supernatural beings, are evidently founded upon the reverence paid by their forefathers to the spirits of the dead. From it, and from the ancient tendency to personify the elements, and pay divine honours to them, seem to have sprung most of the superstitions which to the present day make ghostly forms abound in woods and waters and about the domestic hearth. It is not necessary to dwell at any length in this chapter on the ideas and the customs of the Russian peasantry with respect to the dead, for they will be more fitly discussed in that devoted to " Funeral Songs," but, in order to account for the characteristics of some of the inhabitants of the Slavonic fairy-land, it will be as well to say something about the views which the old Slavonians held with reference to the unseen world. It is especially to the Domovoy or house-spirit, and the Rusalka, a species of Naiad or Undine, that they apply.

In common with the other Aryan races, the Slavonians believed that after death the soul had to begin a long journey. According to one idea it was obliged to sail across a wide sea, and therefore coins intended for the spirit's passage-money were placed in every grave. This practice is still kept up among the Russian peasants, who throw small copper or silver coins into the grave at a funeral, though in many cases they have lost sight of the original meaning of the custom. To the idea of this voyage, also, some of the archæologists are inclined to turn for an explanation of the old Slavonic custom of burning or burying the dead in boats, or boat-shaped coffins.

According to another idea the journey had to be made on foot, and so a corpse was sometimes provided with a pair of boots, intended to be worn during the pilgrimage and discarded at its termination, a custom said to linger still among the Bohemian peasants. Kotlyarevsky thinks that there is reason to suppose that a conductor of the dead was known to the old Slavonians, and as their Psychopomp he is inclined to recognize the deity whom Dlugosz mentions under the name of Nija, and compares with Pluto, but whom another old writer calls "The Leader[6]." And Afanasief thinks that some connexion may be traced between the dark dogs of Yama, which guarded the road to the dwelling-place of the Fathers, and the black dog which in Ruthenia, when a dying man's agony is greatly prolonged, is passed through a hole made in the roof over his head, in the hope of thereby expediting the liberation of the soul from the body[7]. But these are mere conjectures. What is certain is that the Slavonians believed in a road leading from this to the other

[6] Kotlyarevsky, p. 204. [7] Afanasief, P. V. S. III. 282.

world, sometimes recognizing it in the rainbow, but more often in the Milky Way. To the latter various names, associated with this old belief, are still given by the Russian peasants. In the Nijegorod Government it is called the "Mouse Path," the mouse being a well-known figure for the soul. In that of Tula it is the *Stanovishche*, the "Traveller's Halting-Place." About Perm it is known as the "Road to Jerusalem;" the Tambof peasantry call it "Baty's Road," and say that it runs from the "Iron Hills," within which are confined the Tartar invaders whom Baty used to lead—the original idea having been, in all probability, that the path led from the cloud-hills in which the spirits of the storm were imprisoned, for in the middle ages the Tartars were commonly substituted in legends for the evil spirits of an earlier age. In the Government of Yaroslaf the Raskolniks say that there is a sacred city hidden beneath deep waters, in which the "Holy Elders" live, and that Baty's Road led thither. The Holy Elders are the dead, whom the Russian peasant still addresses as *Roditeli*, a term exactly answering to the Vedic *Pitris*, or Fathers. At the head of the Milky Way, according to a Tula tradition, there stand four mowers, who guard the sacred road, and cut to pieces all who attempt to traverse it—a myth closely akin to that of Heimdall, the Scandinavian watcher of the Rainbow-bridge between heaven and earth.

A third view of the soul's wanderings was that it had to climb a steep hill-side, sometimes supposed to be made of iron, sometimes of glass, on the summit of which was situated the heavenly Paradise. And, therefore, if the nails of a corpse were pared, the parings were placed along with it in the grave, a custom still kept up among the Russian peasantry. The Raskolniks, indeed—the Russian Nonconformists, among whom old ideas are religiously kept alive—are in the habit of carrying about with them, in rings or amulets, parings of an owl's claws and of their own nails. Such relics are supposed by the peasantry in many parts of Russia to be of the greatest use to a man after his death, for by their means his soul will be able to clamber up the steep sides of the hill leading to heaven [8]. The Lithuanians, it is well known, held similar ideas, and used to burn the claws of wild beasts on their funeral pyres.

Before ascending the high hill or crossing the wide sea, the soul had to rise from the grave, and therefore certain aids to climbing were buried with the corpse. Among these were plaited thongs of leather and small ladders. One of the most interesting specimens of Survival to be found among the customs of the Russian peasantry is connected with this idea. Even at the present day, when many of them have forgotten the origin of the custom, they still, in some districts, make little ladders of dough, and have them baked for the benefit of the dead. In the Government of Voroneje a ladder of this sort, about three feet high, is set up at the time when a coffin is being carried to the grave; in some other places similar pieces

[8] Afanasief, P. V. S. I. 120.

of dough are baked in behalf of departed relatives on the fortieth day after their death, or long pies marked crossways with bars are taken to church on Ascension Day and divided between the priest and the poor. In some villages these pies, which are known as *Lyesenki*, or "Ladderlings," have seven bars or rungs, in reference to the "Seven Heavens." The peasants fling them down from the belfry, and accept their condition after their fall as an omen of their own probable fate after death. A Mazovian legend tells how a certain pilgrim, on his way to worship at the Holy Sepulchre, became lost in a rocky place from which he could not for a long time extricate himself. At last he saw hanging in the air a ladder made of birds' feathers. Up this he clambered for three months, at the end of which he reached the Garden of Paradise, and entered among groves of gold and silver and gem-bearing trees, all of which were familiar with the past, the present, and the future[9].

The abode of the dead was known to the old Slavonians under three names, *Rai*, *Nava*, and *Peklo*. They originally, it is supposed, had the same meaning, but in the course of time the first and the last became associated with two different sets of ideas, and in modern Russian *Rai* stands for Heaven and *Peklo* for Hell. The word *Rai*, in Lithuanian *rojus*, is derived by Kotlyarevsky from the Sanskrit root *raj*, and one of its forms, *Vuirei*, is compared by Afanasief with the Elysian *vireta* of Virgil. Accord-

[9] Afanasief, P. V. S. 124-5.

ing to many Slavonic traditions, this *Rai*, *Iry*, or *Vuirei* is the home of the sun, lying eastward beyond the ocean, or in an island surrounded by the sea. Thither repairs the sun when his day's toil is finished; thither also fly the souls of little children [provided that they have not died unchristened], and there they play among the trees and gather their golden fruits. There, according to a tradition current among the Lithuanians, as well as among some of the Slavonic peoples, dwell the spirits which at some future time are to be sent to live upon earth in mortal bodies, and thither, when disembodied, will they return. No cold winds ever blow there, winter never enters those blissful realms, in which are preserved the seeds and types of all things that live upon the earth, and whither birds and insects repair at the end of the autumn, to re-appear among men with the return of spring[1]. There seems to have prevailed in almost all parts of the world a belief in the existence of Happy Islands lying towards the west, the home of the setting sun, but among the Slavonians there appears to have been widely spread some idea,—due probably to the apocryphal books about Alexander of Macedon,—of eastern climes to which they attached the idea of perennial warmth and light. Thus, in Galicia, there still lingers a tradition that somewhere far away, beyond the dark seas, and in the land from which the sun goes forth to run his daily course, there dwells the happy

---

[1] For other details about this happy land, see *infra*, p. 375.

nation of the Rakhmane. They lead a holy life, for they abstain from eating flesh all the year round, with the exception of one day, "the Rakhmanian Easter Sunday." And that festival is celebrated by them on the day on which the shell of a consecrated Easter egg floats to them across the wide sea which divides them from the lands inhabited by ordinary mortals. The name of these Easterns, who seem akin to Homer's "blameless Ethiopians" explains itself. The people who were Brahmans have become Rakhmane, and their name has gradually passed, in the minds of the people, into an expression for persons who are (1) joyous, hospitable, etc., (2) soft, mild, etc., (3) dreary, weak-minded, etc [2].

The derivation of the second term for the home of the dead, *Nava*, is uncertain. The word *nav*, *nav'e*, means a mortal, and *unaviti* is to kill. Comparisons have been made by the philologists between *nava* and the Sanskrit and Greek *naus*, or the Latin *navis*, as well as with *nekus*, but all that can be deduced from such comparisons is that in *nava* there may possibly be some reference to the sea traversed by the dead, the atmospheric ocean across which the winds breathe. The primary meaning of the third designation, *Peklo*, seems to be that of a place of warmth, being derived from the same root as *Pech'*, [as a verb] to parch, [as a substantive] a stove, etc. After a time it probably acquired the signification of the

---

[2] Afanasief, P. V. S. III. 195—318. Buslaef, *Ist. Ocherki*, 492.

abode of bad souls only, and under the influence of Christian teaching it became Hell, the subterranean place of punishment in which evil spirits torment the souls of the wicked [3].

Side by side with the traditions which point to a distant habitation of the dead, there exist others in which the grave itself is spoken of as the home of the departed spirit. "Dark and joyless is our prison-house," is the reply constantly made by ghosts when questioned as to their habitation. "Stone and earth lie heavy on our hearts, our eyes are fast closed, our hands and feet are frozen by the cold." Especially during the winters do the dead suffer; when the spring returns the peasants say, "Our fathers enjoy repose," and in Little-Russia they add, "God grant that the earth may lie light on you, and that your eyes may see Christ[4]!" It is this idea of residence in the material grave that lies at the root of the custom of periodically visiting and pouring libations on the tombs of departed relatives, with which we shall meet in the section devoted to funeral songs.

The old heathen Slavonians seem to have had no idea of a future state in which present wrongs should be redressed, or griefs assuaged. They appear to have looked on the life beyond the grave as a mere prolongation of that led on earth—the rich man retained at least some of his possessions; the slave remained a slave. Thus wedded people were supposed to live together in a future state, an opinion

[3] Kotlyarevsky, 199—202.   [4] Tereshchenko, v. 28.

on which some of the funeral ceremonies of the present day are founded, and which, in heathen times, frequently induced wives to kill themselves when their husbands died. The Bulgarians hold the same doctrine even at the present day, and therefore among them widows seldom marry. Nor does a widower often find any one but a widow who will accept him, for in the world to come, it is supposed, his first wife will claim him and take him away from her successor.

After death the soul at first remains in the neighbourhood of the body, and then follows it to the tomb. The Bulgarians hold that it assumes the form of a bird or a butterfly, and sits on the nearest tree waiting till the funeral is over. Afterwards it sets out on its long journey, accompanied by an attendant angel. The Mazovians say that the soul remains with the coffin, sitting upon the upper part of it until the burial is over, when it flies away. Such traditions as these vary in different localities, but every where, among all the Slavonic people, there seems always to have prevailed an idea that death does not finally sever the ties between the living and the dead. This idea has taken various forms, and settled into several widely differing superstitions, lurking, for instance, in the secrecy of the cottage, and there keeping alive the cultus of the domestic spirit, or showing itself openly in the village church, where on a certain day it calls for a service in remembrance of the dead. The spirits of those who are thus remembered, say the peasants, attend the service, taking their place behind the altar. But those who are left unremembered weep bitterly all through the day[5].

In the mythic songs and stories current among the old Slavonians the soul of man was represented under various forms, by numerous images. Ancient traditions affirmed that it was a spark of heavenly fire, kindled in the human body by the thunder-god. And in accordance with this idea the superstition of the Russian peasant of to-day often sees ghostly flames gleaming above graves, not to be banished till the necessary prayers have been said—still believes that of a wedded couple that one will die the first whose taper was first extinguished at the time of the marriage ceremony. In the Government of Perm the peasants hold that there are just as many stars in the sky as there are human beings on earth, a new star appearing whenever a babe is born, and disappearing when its corresponding mortal dies. In Ruthenia a shooting star is looked upon as the track of an angel flying to receive a departed spirit, or of a righteous soul going up to heaven. In the latter case, it is believed that if a wish is uttered at the moment when the star shoots by, it will go straight up with the rejoicing spirit to the throne of God. So, when a star falls, the Servians say "Some one's light has gone out," meaning some one is dead.

Besides being likened to fire and a star, the soul is often represented by Russian tradition as a smoke, or

[5] Kotlyarevsky, 199.

vapour, or a current of air. In the *Stikhi*, or popular religious poems, the Angel of Death receives the disembodied spirit from " the sweet lips " of the righteous dead, an idea which prevails also among the people of South Siberia, who hold that a man's soul has its residence in his windpipe. A shadow, also, is as common a metaphor for the soul in Russia as elsewhere, whence it arises that, even at the present day, there are persons there who object to having their silhouettes taken, fearing that if they do so they will die before the year is out. In the same way, a man's reflected image is supposed to be in communion with his inner self, and therefore children are often forbidden to look at themselves in a glass, lest their sleep should be disturbed at night. In the opinion of the Raskolniks a mirror is an accursed thing, invented by the devil.

The butterfly seems to have been universally accepted by the Slavonians as an emblem of the soul. In the Government of Yaroslav, one of its names is *dushichka*, a caressing diminutive of *dusha*, the soul. In that of Kherson it is believed that if the usual alms are not distributed at a funeral, the dead man's soul will reveal itself to his relatives in the form of a moth flying about the flame of a candle. The day after receiving such a warning visit, they call together the poor, and distribute food among them. In Bohemia tradition says that if the first butterfly a man sees in the spring is a white one, he is destined to die within the year. The Servians believe that the soul of a witch often leaves her body while she is asleep, and flies abroad in the shape of a butterfly. If during its absence her body be turned round, so that her feet are placed where her head was before, the soul-butterfly will not be able to find her mouth, and so will be shut out from her body. Thereupon the witch will die. Gnats and flies are often looked upon as equally spiritual creatures. In Little-Russia the old women of a family will often, after returning from a funeral, sit up all night watching a dish in which water with honey in it has been placed, in the belief that the spirit of their dead relative will come in the form of a fly, and sip the proffered liquid.

A common belief among the Russian peasantry is that the spirits of the departed haunt their old homes for the space of six weeks, during which they eat and drink, and watch the sorrowing of the mourners. After that time they fly away to the other world. In certain districts bread-crumbs are placed on a piece of white linen at a window during those six weeks, and the soul is believed to come and feed upon them in the shape of a bird. It is generally into pigeons or crows that the dead are transformed. Thus when the Deacon Theodore and his three schismatic brethren were burnt in 1681, the souls of the martyrs, as the " Old-Believers " affirm, appeared in the air as pigeons. In Volhynia dead children are supposed to come back in the spring to their native village under the semblance of swallows and other small birds, and to seek by soft twittering or song to console their sorrowing parents. The cuckoo, also, according to Slavonic superstitions, is intimately connected with the dead. In Little-Russia she flies to weep over corpses. The Servians and Lithuanians look on her as a sister whom nothing can console for the loss of a brother; and in a Russian marriage-song the orphan bride implores the cuckoo to fetch her dead parents from the other world, that they may bless her before she enters on her new life.

It is evident, from what has been said, that the views of the Old Slavonians about a future state were not defined with any great precision, and it is not easy to decide what were the exact opinions they held as to the relations between the inhabitants of this world and of the other. But there can be no doubt about their belief that the souls of fathers watched over their children and their children's children, and that therefore departed spirits, and especially those of ancestors, ought always to be regarded with pious veneration, and sometimes solaced or conciliated by prayer and sacrifice. It is clear, moreover, that the cultus of the dead was among them, as among so many other peoples, closely connected with that of the fire burning on the domestic hearth, a fact which accounts for the stove of modern Russia having come to be considered the special haunt of the Domovoy, or house-spirit, whose position in the esteem of the people is looked upon as a trace of the ancestor worship of olden days. He is, of course, merely the Slavonic counterpart of the house-spirit of other lands, but his memory has been so well preserved in Russia, and so many legends are current about him, that he seems well worthy of a detailed notice.

Since the introduction of Christianity into Russia, something of a demoniacal nature has attached itself to the character and the appearance of the Domovoy, which may account for the fact that he is supposed to be a hirsute creature, the whole of his body, even to the palms of his hands and the soles of his feet, being covered with thick hair. Only the space around his eyes and nose is bare. The tracks of his shaggy feet may be seen in winter time in the snow; his hairy hands are felt by night gliding over the faces of sleepers. When his hand feels soft and warm it is a sign of good luck: when it is cold and bristly, misfortune is to be looked for.

He is supposed to live behind the stove now, but in early times he, or the spirits of the dead ancestors, of whom he is now the chief representative, were held to be in even more direct relations with the fire on the hearth. In the Nijegorod Government it is still forbidden to break up the smouldering remains of the faggots[6] in a stove with a poker; to do so might be to cause one's "ancestors" to fall through into Hell. The term "ancestors[7]" is universally applied to the defunct, even when dead children are being spoken of. When a Russian family moves from one house to another, the fire is raked out of the old stove into a jar and solemnly conveyed to the new

[6] *Goloveshki* (*golova* = head), the harder parts of logs; those burning more slowly than the others.
[7] *Roditeli* (*rodit'*, *razhdat'* = to beget).

one, the words "Welcome, grandfather, to the new home!" being uttered when it arrives. This and the following custom have been supposed to point to a time when the spirit and the flame were identified, and when some now forgotten form of fire-worship was practised:—On the 28th of January the peasants, after supper, leave out a pot of stewed grain for the Domovoy. This pot is placed on the hearth in front of the stove, and surrounded with hot embers. In olden days, says Afanasief, the offering of corn was doubtless placed directly on the fire [8].

In some districts tradition expressly refers to the spirits of the dead the functions which are generally attributed to the Domovoy, and they are supposed to keep careful watch over the house of a descendant who honours them and provides them with due offerings. Similarly among the (non-Slavonic) Mordvins in the Penza and Saratof Governments, a dead man's relations offer the corpse eggs, butter, and money, saying: "Here is something for you: Marfa has brought you this. Watch over her corn and cattle, and when I gather the harvest, do thou feed the chickens and look after the house."

In Galicia the people believe that their hearths are haunted by the souls of the dead, who make themselves useful to the family, and there are many Czekhs who still hold that their departed ancestors look after their fields and herds, and assist in hunting and fishing. Directly after a man's burial, according

---

[8] Afanasief, P. V. S. II. 67.

to them, his spirit takes to wandering by nights about the old home, and watching that no evil befalls his heirs.

In Lithuania the name given to the domestic spirits is *Kaukas*, a term which has never been thoroughly explained. They are little creatures, like the German kobolds, being not more than a foot high. The peasants sometimes make tiny cloaks, and bury them in the ground within the cottage; the *Kaukas* put them on, and thenceforward devote their energies to serving the friendly proprietor of the house. But if they are badly used or neglected, they set his homestead on fire. Similar little beings, called *Krosnyata*, or dwarfs, are supposed to exist among the Kashoubes, the Slavonic inhabitants of a part of the coast of the Baltic. The Ruthenians reverence in the person of the Domovoy the original constructor of the family hearth. He has a wife and daughters, who are beautiful as were the Hellenic Nymphs, but their favours are deadly to mortal men. In one district of the Viatka Government the Domovoy is described as a little old man, the size of a five-year-old boy. He wears a red shirt with a blue girdle; his face is wrinkled, his hair is of a yellowish grey, his beard is white, his eyes glow like fire. In other places his appearance is much the same, only sometimes he wears a blue caftan with a rose-coloured girdle. Every where he is given to grumbling and quarrelling, and always expresses himself in strong, idiomatic phrases. In Lusatia he takes the form of a beautiful boy, who goes about the house dressed in white, and warns its inhabitants, by his sad groaning, of impending woe. When hot water is going to be poured away, it is customary there to give warning to the Domovoy, that he may not be scalded.

The Russian Domovoy hides behind the stove all day, but at night, when all the house is asleep, he comes forth from his retreat, and devours what is left out for him. In some families a portion of the supper is always set aside for him, for if he is neglected he waxes wroth, and knocks the tables and benches about at night. Wherever fires are lighted, there the Domovoy is to be found, in baths [9], in places for drying corn, and in distilleries. When he haunts a bath (*banya*) he is known as a *Bannik;* the peasants avoid visiting a bath at late hours, for the *Bannik* does not like people who bathe at night, and often suffocates them, especially if they have not prefaced their ablutions by a prayer. It is considered dangerous, also, to pass the night in a corn-kiln, for the Domovoy may strangle the intruder in his sleep. In the Smolensk Government it is usual for peasants who quit a bath to leave a bucket of water and a whisk for the use of the Domovoy who takes their place. In Poland it is believed that the Domovoy is so loath to quit a building in which he has once taken up his quarters, that even if it is burnt down he still haunts it, continuing to dwell in the remains of the stove. And so they say there, " In an old stove the

[9] The Russian bath is something like the Turkish, only the heat is moist.

devil warms," for the devil and the Domovoy are often synonymous terms in the mouths of the people, who regard Satan with more sorrow than anger. In Galicia the following story is told " About the Devil in the Stove :"—

There was a hut in which no one would live, for the children of every one who had inhabited it had died, and so it remained empty. But at last there came a man who was very poor, and he entered the hut, and said, " Good day to whomsoever is in this house ! " " What dost thou want ? " cried out the Old One[1]. " I am poor ; I have neither roof nor courtyard," sadly said the new comer. " Live here," said the Old One, " only tell thy wife to grease the stove every week, and look after thy children that they mayn't lie down upon it." So the poor man settled in that hut, and lived in it peacefully with all his family. And one evening, when he had been complaining about his poverty, the Old One took a whole potful of money out of the stove and gave it him.

In Galicia and Poland a belief is current in the existence of an invisible servant who lives in the stove, is called *Iskrzycki* [*Iskra* is Polish for a spark], and most zealously performs all sorts of domestic duties for the master of the house. In White-Russia the Domovoy is called *Tsmok*, a snake, one of the forms under which the lightning was most commonly personified. This House Snake brings all

---

[1] *Dyed'ko*, grandfather.

sorts of good to the master who treats it well and gives it omelettes, which should be placed on the roof of the house or on the threshing-floor. But if this be not done the snake will burn down the house. It rarely shows itself to mortal eyes, and when it does so, it is generally to warn the heads of the family to which it is attached of some coming woe.

"Once upon a time a servant maid awoke one morning, lighted the fire, and went for her buckets to fetch water. Not a bucket was to be seen! Of course she thought 'a neighbour has taken them.' Out she ran to the river, and there she saw the Domovoy—a little old man in a red shirt—who was drawing water in her buckets, to give the bay mare to drink, and he glared ever so at the girl—his eyes burned just like live coals! She was terribly frightened, and ran back again. But at home there was woe! All the house was in a blaze!"

It is said that the Domovoy does not like to pass the night in the dark, so he often strikes a light with a flint and steel, and goes about, candle in hand, inspecting the stables and outhouses. Hence he derives a number of his names. Sometimes he appears as *Vazila* [from *vozit'*, to drive], the protector of horses, a being in shape like a man, but having equine ears and hoofs; at other times as *Bagan*, he is guardian of the herds, taking up his quarters in a little crib filled for his benefit with hay. On Easter Sunday and the preceding Thursday he becomes visible, and may be seen crouching in a corner of his stall. He is very fond of horses, and often rides them all night, so that they are found in the morning foaming and exhausted. Sometimes, also, he goes riding on a goat. When a newly purchased animal is brought home for the first time, it is customary in several places to go through the following ceremony. The animal is led to its stall, and then its possessor bows low, turning to each of the four corners of the building in succession, and says, "Here is a shaggy beast for thee, Master! Love him, give him to eat and to drink!" And then the cord by which the animal was led is attached to the kitchen-stove.

With the idea that each house ought to have its familiar spirit, and that it is the soul of the founder of the homestead which appears in that capacity, may be connected the various superstitious ideas which attach themselves in Slavonic countries to the building of a new house. The Russian peasant believes that such an act is apt to be followed by the death of the head of the family for which the new dwelling is constructed, or that the member of the family who is the first to enter it will soon die. In accordance with a custom of great antiquity, the oldest member of a migrating household enters the new house first, and in many places, as for instance, in the Government of Archangel, some animal is killed and buried on the spot on which the first log or stone is laid. In other places the carpenters who are going to build the house call out, at the first few strokes of the axe, the name of some bird or beast, believing that the creature thus named will rapidly consume away and perish. On such occasions the peasants take care to be very civil to the carpenters, being assured that their own names might be pronounced by those workmen if they were neglected or provoked. The Bulgarians, it is said, under similar circumstances, take a thread and measure the shadow of some casual passer-by. The measure is then buried under the foundation-stone, and it is expected that the man whose shadow has been thus treated will soon become but a shade himself. If they cannot succeed in getting at a human shadow, they make use of the shadow of the first animal that comes their way. Sometimes a victim is put to death on the occasion, the foundations of the house being sprinkled with the blood of a fowl, or a lamb, or some other species of scapegoat, a custom which is evidently derived from that older one of offering sacrifices in honour of the Earth Goddess, when a new house was being founded. In Servia a similar idea used to apply to the fortifications of towns. No city was thought to be secure unless a human being, or at least the shadow of one, was built into its walls. When a shadow was thus immured, its owner was sure to die quickly. There is a well-known Servian ballad—one of those translated by Sir John Bowring—in which is described the building of Skadra [the Bulgarian Scutari] by a king and his two brothers. At first they cannot succeed in their task, for the Vilas pull down at night what has been built in the day, so they determine to build into the wall whichever of the three princesses, their wives, comes out the first to bring them refreshment. The two elder brothers warn their wives, who pretend to be ill, but the youngest of the ladies hears nothing about the agreement, so she comes out, and is at once seized upon by her brothers-in-law, and immured alive.

A similar story is told about the second founding of Slavensk. The city was built by a colony of Slaves from the Danube. A plague devastated it, so they determined to give it a new name. Acting on the advice of their wisest men, they sent out messengers before sunrise one morning in all directions, with orders to seize upon the first living creature they should meet. The victim proved to be a child (*Dyetina*, archaic form of *Ditya*), who was buried alive under the foundation-stone of the new citadel. The city was on that account called Dyetinets[2], a name since applied to any citadel. The city was afterwards laid waste a second time, on which its inhabitants removed to a short distance, and founded a new city, the present Novgorod.

The Domovoy often appears in the likeness of the proprietor of the house, and sometimes wears his

---

[2] This story was told some time ago by Popof in his *Dosugi*. He called it "a Slavonian fable," but subsequent writers are inclined to look upon it as at least founded upon fact. A number of similar legends, current in various lands, are mentioned by Jacob Grimm in the *Deutsche Mythologie*, p. 1095; also by Mr. E. B. Tylor, in his "Primitive Culture" (I. 94—97), who holds that it is plain "that hideous rites, of which Europe has scarcely kept up more than the dim memory, have held fast their ancient practice and meaning in Africa, Polynesia, and Asia, among races who represent in grade, if not in chronology, earlier stages of civilization."

clothes. For he is, indeed, the representative of the housekeeping ideal as it presents itself to the Slavonian mind. He is industrious and frugal, he watches over the homestead and all that belongs to it. When a goose is sacrificed to the water-spirit, its head is cut off and hung up in the poultry-yard, in order that the Domovoy may not know, when he counts the heads, that one of the flock has gone. For he is jealous of other spirits. He will not allow the forest-spirit to play pranks in the garden, nor witches to injure the cows. He sympathizes with the joys and sorrows of the house to which he is attached. When any member of the family dies, he may be heard (like the Banshee) wailing at night; when the head of the family is about to die, the Domovoy forebodes the sad event by sighing, weeping, or sitting at his work with his cap pulled over his eyes. Before an outbreak of war, fire, or pestilence, the Domovoys go out from a village and may be heard lamenting in the meadows. When any misfortune is impending over a family, the Domovoy gives warning of it by knocking, by riding at night on the horses till they are completely exhausted, and by making the watch-dogs dig holes in the courtyard and go howling through the village. And he often rouses the head of the family from his sleep at night when the house is threatened with fire or robbery.

The Russian peasant draws a clear line between his own Domovoy and his neighbour's. The former is a benignant spirit, who will do him good, even at the expense of others; the latter is a malevolent being, who will very likely steal his hay, drive away his poultry, and so forth, for his neighbour's benefit. Therefore incantations are provided against him, in some of which the assistance of "the bright gods" is invoked against "the terrible devil and the stranger Domovoy." The domestic spirits of different households often engage in contests with one another, as might be expected, seeing that they are addicted to stealing from each other's possessions. Sometimes one will vanquish another, drive him out of the house he haunts, and take possession of it himself. When a peasant moves into a new house, in certain districts, he takes his own Domovoy with him, having first, as a measure of precaution, taken care to hang up a bear's head in the stable. This prevents any evil Domovoy, whom malicious neighbours may have introduced, from fighting with, and perhaps overcoming, the good Lar Familiaris.

Each Domovoy has his own favourite colour, and it is important for the family to try and get all their cattle, poultry, dogs and cats of this hue. In order to find out what it is, the Orel peasants take a piece of cake on Easter Sunday, wrap it in a rag, and hang it up in the stable. At the end of six weeks they look at it to see of what colour the maggots are which are in it. That is the colour which the Domovoy likes. In the Governments of Yaroslaf and Nijegorod the Domovoy takes a fancy to those horses and cows only which are of the colour of his own hide. There was a peasant once, the story runs, who lost all his horses because they were of the wrong colour. At last the poor man, who was almost ruined, bought a miserable hack, which was of the right hue. "What a horse! there's something like a horse! Quite different from the other ones!" exclaimed the delighted Domovoy, and from that moment all went well with the peasant. It is a terrible thing for a family when a strange Domovoy gets into a house and turns out its friendly spiritual occupant. The new comer plays all the pranks attributed to

"That shrewd and knavish sprite,
Call'd Robin Goodfellow,"

pinches sleepers as the fairies in Windsor Park pinched Falstaff, but without equally good reason, and renders life a burden to the haunted household. Fortunately there is a means of expelling him, which is to take brooms, and with them to strike the walls and fences, exclaiming, "Stranger Domovoy, go away home!" and on the evening of the same day to dress in holiday array, and go out into the yard, and call out to the original tenant of the hearth, "Grandfather Domovoy! Come home to us—to make habitable the house and tend the cattle!" Another means is to ride on horseback about the yard, waving a fire-shovel in the air, and uttering an incantation. Sometimes the shovel is dipped in tar. When the Domovoy rubs his head against it he is disgusted, and quits the house.

Sometimes a man's own Domovoy takes to behaving

unpleasantly to him, for the domestic spirits have a dual nature, answering to that which the old Slavonians attributed to the spirits of the storm. The same forces of nature which fattened the earth and made it bring forth harvests, often manifested themselves as destructive agents; so the Domovoy, although generally good to his friends, sometimes does them harm, just as fire is at one time friendly to man, at another hostile[3]. Every now and then, the peasants believe, a house becomes haunted by teazing, if not absolutely malicious beings, who make terrible noises at night, throw about sticks and stones, and in various ways annoy the sleeping members of the family. When the regular Domovoy does this, all he needs in general is a mild scolding. Various stories prove the truth of this assertion. Here is one of them. In a certain house the Domovoy took to playing pranks. "One day, when he had caught up the cat, and flung her on the ground, the housewife expostulated with him as follows: 'Why did you do that? Is that the way to manage a house? We can't get on without our cat. A pretty manager, forsooth!' And from that time the Domovoy gave up troubling the cats."

One of the many points in which the Domovoy resembles the Elves with whom we are so well acquainted, is his fondness for plaiting the manes of horses. Another is his tendency to interfere with the breathing of people who are asleep. Besides

[3] See Grimm's *Deutsche Mythologie*, 569.

plaiting manes, he sometimes operates in a similar manner upon men's beards and the back hair of women, his handiwork being generally considered a proof of his goodwill. But when he plays the part of our own nightmare, he can scarcely be looked upon as benignant. The Russian word for such an incubus is *Kikimora* or *Shishimora* (the French *Cauche-mare*). The first half of the word, says Afanasief[4], is probably the same as the provincial expression *shish* = Domovoy, demon, etc. The second half means the same as the German *mar* or our *mare* in nightmare. In Servia, Montenegro, Bohemia, and Poland the word answering to *mora*, means the demoniacal spirit which passes from a witch's lips in the form of a butterfly, and oppresses the breathing of sleepers at night. The Russians believe in certain little old female beings called Marui or Marukhi, who sit on stoves and spin by night. No woman in the Olonets Government thinks of laying aside her spindle without uttering a prayer. If she forgot to do so the Mara would come at night and spoil all her work for her. The Kikimori are generally understood to be the souls of girls who have died unchristened, or who have been cursed by their parents, and so have passed under the power of evil spirits. According to a Servian tradition the Mora sometimes turns herself into a horse, or into a *dlaka*, or tuft of hair. Once a Mora so tormented a

---

[4] For the derivation of the word, see also Grimm's *Deutsche Mythologie*, pp. 433 and 1104.

man that he left his home, took his white horse and rode away on it. But wherever he wandered the Mora followed after him. At last he stopped to pass the night in a certain house, the master of which heard him groaning terribly in his sleep, so he went to look at him. Then he saw that his guest was being suffocated by a long tuft of white hair which lay over his mouth. So he cut it in two with a pair of scissors. Next morning the white horse was found dead. The horse, the tuft of hair, and the nightmare, were all one.

The Domovoy generally turns malicious on the 30th of March, and remains so from early dawn till midnight. At that time he makes no distinction between friends and strangers, so it is as well to keep the cattle and poultry at home that day, and not to go to the window more than is necessary. It is uncertain whether his short-lived fury at that season of the year arises from the fact that he is then changing his coat. Some authorities hold that a kind of mania comes over him then, others that he feels a sudden craving to get married to a witch. Anyhow it is considered wise to propitiate him by offerings. These gifts can take almost any edible shape. In the Tomsk Government, on the Eve of the Epiphany, the peasants place in a certain part of the stove little cakes made expressly for the Domovoy. In other places a pot of stewed grain is set out for him on the evening of the 28th of January. Exactly at midnight he comes out from under the stove, and sups off it. If he is neglected he

waxes wroth, but he may be appeased as follows :—A
wizard is called in, who kills a cock and lets its blood
run on to one of the whisks used in baths ; with this
in hand he sprinkles the corners of the cottage inside
and out, uttering incantations the while. It may be
as well to remark, that while unclean spirits fear
the crowing of cocks, it never in any way affects the
Domovoy.

Another way of pacifying the irritated domestic
spirit is for the head of the family to go out at midnight into the courtyard, to turn his face to the
moon, and to say, "Master! stand before me as
the leaf before the grass [an ordinary formula], neither black nor green, but just like me! I have
brought thee a red egg." Thereupon the Domovoy
will assume a human form, and, when he has received
the red egg, will become quiet. But the peasant
must not talk about this midnight meeting. If he
does, the Domovoy will set his cottage on fire, or will
induce him to commit suicide.

We have already mentioned the custom of literally
or figuratively sacrificing a victim on the spot which
a projected house is to cover. Generally speaking
that victim is a cock, the head of which is cut off
and buried, in all privacy, exactly where the " upper
corner" of the building is to stand. This corner,
opposite to which stands the stove, is looked upon
with great reverence by the peasants, who call it
also the " Great" and the " Beautiful." There
the table stands on which is spread the daily meal
in which the ancestors of the family were always

supposed to participate. In all probability, says one Russian commentator, their images used to stand close by, and were transferred to the table at meal-time, but since the introduction of Christianity they have been replaced by holy icons, or sacred pictures. In that same corner every thing that is most revered is placed, as Paschal eggs and Whitsuntide verdure. Towards it every one who enters the cottage makes low obeisance. The peasants still believe that the souls of the dead, as soon as the bodies they used to inhabit are buried, take up their quarters in the cottage behind the sacred pictures, and therefore they place hot cakes upon the ledge which supports those pictures, intending them as an offering to the hungry ghosts. The sound of the death-watch is believed to be as ominous in Russia as in England. In Bohemia it is supposed to be caused by such ghosts as have just been mentioned, who are knocking in order to summon one of their descendants to join them.

The threshold of a cottage is not so important as its " front corner," but many curious superstitions are attached to it. On it a cross is drawn to keep off Maras (hags). Under it the peasants bury stillborn children. In Lithuania, when a new house is being built, a wooden cross, or some article which has been handed down from past generations, is placed under the threshold. There, also, when a newly-baptized child is being brought back from church, it is customary for its father to hold it for a while over the threshold, " so as to place the new member of the family under the protection of the domestic divinities." On the other side of the threshold that power which produces peace and goodwill in a family loses its influence, so kinsfolk ought to carry on their mutual relations as much as possible within doors. A man should always cross himself when he steps over a threshold, and he ought not, it is believed in some places, to sit down on one. Sick children, who are supposed to have been afflicted by an evil eye, are washed on the threshold of their cottage, in order that, with the help of the Penates who reside there, the malady may be driven out of doors.

Allusion has already been made to the customs observed when a Russian peasant family is about to migrate into a new house. So strange are they, that they are well deserving of a fuller notice. After every thing movable has been taken away from the old house, the mother-in-law, or the oldest woman in the family, lights a fire for the last time in the stove. When the wood is well alight she rakes it together into the *pechurka* (a niche in the stove), and waits till midday. A clean jar and a white napkin have been previously provided, and in this jar, precisely at midday, she deposits the burning embers, covering them over with the napkin. She then throws open the house-door, and, turning to the "back corner," namely to the stove, says, " Welcome, dyedushka (grandfather) to our new home!" Then she carries the fire-containing jar to the courtyard of the new dwelling, at the opened gates of which she finds the master and mistress of the house, who have come to offer bread and salt to the Domovoy. The old woman strikes the door-posts, asking, "Are the visitors welcome?" on which the heads of the family reply, with a profound obeisance, " Welcome, dyedushka, to the new spot!" After that invitation she enters the cottage, its master preceding her with the bread and salt, places the jar on the stove, takes off the napkin and shakes it towards each of the four corners, and empties the burning embers into the *pechurka*. The jar is then broken, and its fragments are buried at night under the " front corner." When distance renders it impossible to transfer fire from the old to the new habitation, as, for instance, when the Smolensk peasants migrate to other Governments, a fire-shovel and other implements appertaining to the domestic hearth are taken instead. In the Government of Perm such "flittings" take place by night. The house-mistress covers a table with a cloth and places bread and salt on it. A candle is then lighted before the holy icons, all pray to God, and afterwards the master of the house takes down the icons, and covers them over with the front of his dress. Then he opens the door which leads into what may be called the cellar, bows down, and says, " Neighbourling, brotherling! let us go to the new home. As we have lived in the old home well and happily, so let us live also in the new one. Be kind to my cattle and family!" After this they all set off for the new house, led by the father, who carries a cock and a hen. When they arrive at the cottage they turn the fowls loose in it, and wait till the cock crows. Then the master enters, places the icons on their stand, opens the cellar-flaps, and says, "Enter, neighbourling, brotherling!" Family prayer follows, and then the mistress lays the cloth, lights the fire, and looks after her cooking arrangements. If the cock refuses to crow it is a sign of impending misfortune. These customs are all of great antiquity. The part allotted in them to the icons dates, of course, from the time in which Christianity became the religion of the country, but a similar part may formerly have been played by images of domestic gods or deified ancestors. The whole ceremony is one of the most striking relics of that heathendom which once prevailed over the entire face of the land, and which still crops up in many of its remoter districts, sometimes half concealed by a Christian garb, sometimes exposing itself in downright pagan nakedness[5].

Next in importance to the Domovoy, but far superior to him in poetic interest, is the Rusálka. The Rusalkas are female water-spirits, who occupy a position which corresponds in many respects with that filled by the elves and fairies of Western Europe. The origin of their name seems to be doubtful, but it appears to be connected with *rus*, an old Slavonic word for a stream, or with *ruslo*, the bed of a river, and with several other kindred words, such as *rosá*, dew, which have reference to water. They are

[5] See Afanasief, P. V. S. II. 83—86, 109, 110, 115—119.

generally represented under the form of beauteous maidens with full and snow-white bosoms, and with long and slender limbs. Their feet are small, their eyes are wild, their faces are fair to see, but their complexion is pale, their expression anxious. Their hair is long and thick and wavy, and green as is the grass. Their dress is either a covering of green leaves, or a long white shift, worn without a girdle. At times they emerge from the waters of the lake or river in which they dwell, and sit upon its banks, combing and plaiting their flowing locks, or they cling to a mill-wheel, and turn round with it amid the splash of the stream. If any one happens to approach, they fling themselves into the waters, and there divert themselves, and try to allure him to join them. Whomsoever they get hold of they tickle to death [6]. Witches alone can bathe with them unhurt.

In certain districts bordering on the sea the people believe, or used to believe, in marine Rusalkas, who are supposed, in some places, as, for instance, about Astrakhan, to raise storms and vex shipping. But as a general rule the Rusalkas are looked upon in Russia as haunting lakes and streams, at the bottom of which they usually dwell in crystal halls, radiant with gold and silver and precious stones. Sometimes, however, they are not so sumptuously housed,

---

[6] The verb *Shchekotat'* originally meant to utter loud, piercing sounds, to laugh shrilly, and afterwards acquired the sense of to do what produces shrill laughter, to tickle. See Afanasief, P. V. S. II. 339.

but have to make for themselves nests out of straw and feathers collected during the " Green Week," the seventh after Easter. If a Rusalka's hair becomes dry she dies, and therefore she is generally afraid of going far from the water, unless, indeed, she has a comb with her. So long as she has a comb she can always produce a flood by passing it through her waving locks.

In some places they are fond of spinning, in others they are given to washing linen. During the week before Whitsuntide, as many songs testify, they sit upon trees, and ask for linen garments. Up to the present day, in Little-Russia, it is customary to hang on the boughs of oaks and other trees, at that time of year, shifts and rags and skeins of thread, all intended as a present to the Rusalkas. In White-Russia the peasants affirm that during that week the forests are traversed by naked women and children, and whoever meets them, if he wishes to escape a premature death, must fling them a handkerchief, or some scrap torn from his dress.

On the approach of winter the Rusalkas disappear, and do not show themselves again until it is over. In Little-Russia they are supposed to appear on the Thursday in Holy Week, a day which in olden times was dear to them, as well as to many other spiritual beings. In the Ukraine the Thursday before Whitsuntide is called the Great Day, or Easter Sunday, of the Rusalkas. During the days called the "Green Svyatki," at Whitsuntide, when every home is adorned with boughs and green leaves, no one dares to work for fear of offending the Rusalkas. Especially must women abstain from sewing or washing linen; and men from weaving fences and the like, such occupations too closely resembling those of the supernatural weavers and washers. It is chiefly at that time that the spirits leave their watery abodes, and go strolling about the fields and forests, continuing to do so until the end of June. All that time their voices may be heard in the rustling or sighing of the breeze, and the splash of running water betrays their dancing feet. At that time the peasant-girls go into the woods, and throw garlands to the Rusalkas, asking for rich husbands in return, or float them down a stream, seeing in their movements omens of future happiness or sorrow.

After St. Peter's day, June 29, the Rusalkas dance by night beneath the moon, and in Little-Russia and Galicia, where Rusalkas (or *Mavki* as they are there called) have danced, circles of darker, and of richer grass are found in the fields. Sometimes they induce a shepherd to play to them. All night long they dance to his music: in the morning a hollow marks the spot where his foot has beaten time. Sometimes a man encounters Rusalkas who begin to writhe and contort themselves after a strange fashion. Involuntarily he imitates their gestures, and for the rest of his life he is deformed, or is a victim to St. Vitus' dance. Any one who treads upon the linen which the Rusalkas have laid out to dry loses all his strength, or becomes a cripple; those who desecrate the *Rusalnaya* (or Rusalkas') week by working are punished by the loss of their cattle and poultry. At times the Rusalkas entice into their haunts both youths and maidens, and tickle them to death, or strangle or drown them.

The Rusalkas have much to do with the harvest, sometimes making it plenteous, and at other times ruining it by rain and wind. The peasants in White-Russia say that the Rusalkas dwell amid the standing corn; and in Little-Russia it is believed that on Whit-Sunday Eve they go out to the corn-fields, and there, with joyous singing and clapping of hands, they scamper through the rye or hang on to its stalks, and swing to and fro, so that the corn undulates as if beneath a strong wind.

In some parts of Russia there is performed, immediately after the end of the Whitsuntide festival, the ceremony of expelling the Rusalkas. On the first Monday of the "Peter's Fast" a figure made of straw is draped in woman's clothes, so as to represent a Rusalka. Afterwards a Khorovod is formed, and the assembled company go out to the fields with dance and song, she who holds the straw Rusalka in her hand bounding about in the middle of the choral circle. On arriving at the fields the singers form two bodies, one of which attacks the figure, while the other defends it. Eventually it is torn to pieces, and the straw of which it was made is thrown to the winds, after which the performers return home, saying they have expelled the Rusalka. In the Government of Tula the women and girls go out to the fields during the "Green Week," and chase the

Rusalka, who is supposed to be stealing the grain. Having made a straw figure, they take it to the banks of a stream and fling it into the water. In some districts the young people run about the fields on Whit-Sunday Eve, waving brooms, and crying, "Pursue! pursue!" There are people who affirm that they have seen the hunted Rusalkas running out of the corn-fields into the woods, and have heard their sobs and cries.

Besides the full-grown Rusalkas there are little ones, having the appearance of seven-year-old girls. These are supposed, by the Russian peasants, to be the ghosts of still-born children, or such as have died before there was time to baptize them. Such children the Rusalkas are in the habit of stealing after death, taking them from their graves, or even from the cottages in which they lie, and carrying them off to their subaqueous dwellings. Every Whitsuntide, for seven successive years, the souls of these children fly about, asking to be christened. If any person who hears one of them lamenting will exclaim, "I baptize thee in the name of the Father, and of the Son, and of the Holy Ghost," the soul of that child will be saved, and will go straight to heaven. A religious service, annually performed on the first Monday of the "Peter's Fast," in behalf of an unbaptized child will be equally efficacious. But if the stray soul, during seven years, neither hears the baptismal formula pronounced, nor feels the effect of the divine service, it becomes enrolled for ever in the ranks of the Rusalkas. The same fate befalls those babes whom their mothers have cursed before they were born, or in the interval between their birth and their baptism. Such small Rusalkas, who abound among the Little-Russian *Mavki*, are evidently akin to our own fairies. Like them they make the grass grow richly where they dance, they float on the water in egg-shells, and some of them are sadly troubled by doubts about a future state. At least it is believed in the Government of Astrakhan that the sea Rusalkas come to the surface and ask mariners, " Is the end of the world near at hand ?" Besides the children of whom mention has been made, women who kill themselves, and all those who are drowned, choked, or strangled, and who do not obtain Christian burial, are liable to become Rusalkas. During the Rusalka week the relatives of drowned or strangled persons go out to their graves, taking with them pancakes, and spirits, and red eggs. The eggs are broken, and the spirits poured over the graves, after which the remnants are left for the Rusalkas, these lines being sung :—

> Queen Rusalka,
> Maiden fair,
> Do not destroy the soul,
> Do not cause it to be choked,
> And we will make obeisance to thee.

On the people who forget to do this the Rusalkas will wreak their vengeance[1]. In the Saratof Government the Rusalkas are held in bad repute. There

---

[1] Afanasief, P. V. S. III. 244.

they are described as hideous, humpbacked, hairy creatures, with sharp claws, and an iron hook with which they try to seize on passers-by. If any one ventures to bathe in a river on Whit-Sunday, without having uttered a preliminary prayer, they instantly drag him down to the bottom. Or if he goes into a wood without taking a handful of wormwood (*Poluin*), he runs a serious risk, for the Rusalkas may ask him, " What have you got in your hands ? is it *Poluin* or *Petrushka* (Parsley)." If he replies *Poluin*, they cry, " Hide under the *tuin* (hedge)," and he is safe. But if he says, *Petrushka*, they exclaim affectionately, " Ah ! my *dushka*," and begin tickling him till he foams at the mouth. In either case they seem to be greatly under the influence of rhyme.

In the vicinity of the Dnieper the peasants believe that the wild-fires which are sometimes seen at night flickering above graves, or around the tumuli called Kurgáns, or in woods and swampy places, are lighted by the Rusalkas, who wish thereby to allure incautious travellers to their ruin ; but in many places these wandering " Wills o' the Wisp " are regarded as being the souls of unbaptized children, and so small Rusalkas themselves. In many parts of Russia the Rusalkas are represented in the songs of the people as propounding riddles to girls, and tickling and teasing those who cannot answer them. Sometimes the Rusalkas are asked similar questions, which they answer at once, being very sharp-witted.

The Servian Vilas are evidently akin to the Rusalkas, whom they equal in beauty, and generally outdo in malice. No higher compliment can be paid to a Servian maiden than to say that she is " lovely as a Vila." But once upon a time, says a story, a proud husband boasted that his wife was " more beautiful than the white Vila." His vaunt was overheard by the spirit, who exclaimed,—

" Show me thy love who is fairer than I, fairer than the white Vila from the hill."

So he took his wife by the hand and led her forth, and what he had said was true. She was three times as beautiful as the Vila, and when the Vila saw that it was so, she cried out,—

" No great vaunt is it of thine, O youth, that thy love is fairer than I, the Vila from the hill. Her a mother bare, wrapped her in silken swaddling-clothes, and nourished her with a mother's milk. But me, the Vila from the hill—me the hill itself bare, swaddled me in green leaves. The morning dew fell—nourished me the Vila; the breeze blew from the hill—rocked me the Vila[8]."

Another spiritual being of the same class is the *Poludnitsa*. Among the Lusatians, under the name of *Prezpolnica* or *Pripolnica*, she appears in the fields exactly at mid-day (in Russian, *Polden* or *Poluden*— " half-day"), holding a sickle in her hand. There she addresses any woman whom she finds tarrying afield instead of returning home for mid-day repose, and questions her on the cultivation and the spinning of flax, cutting off the head or dividing the neck of an

* Quoted from Vuk Karadjich by Buslaef, *Ist. Och.* I. 231.

unsatisfactory answerer. She seems to be akin to the *dæmon Meridianus*, "the sickness that destroyeth in the noonday[9]." It is worthy of remark that the Russian peasants make use of a verb, *Poludnovat'*, to express the action of drawing one's last breath— "His soul in his body scarcely *poludnoet*," they say. In the Government of Archangel tradition tells of "Twelve Midnight Sisters (*Polunochnitsas*), who attack children, and force them to cry out with pain[1]."

The traditions of the Russian peasants people the waters with other spiritual inhabitants besides the Rusalkas. Their songs and stories often speak of the Tsar Morskoi, the Marine or Water King, who dwells in the depths of the sea, or the lake, or the pool, and who rules over the subaqueous world. To this Slavonic Neptune a family of daughters is frequently attributed, maidens of exceeding beauty, who, when they don their feather dresses, become the Swan Maidens who figure in the popular literature of so many nations. These graceful creatures, however, as well as their royal parent, belong to the realm of the peasant's imagination rather than to that of his belief. But this is not the case with the spirits who are called *Vodyanuie*, the male counterparts of the Rusalkas. In them he still believes, and of them he often stands in considerable awe.

The Vodyany, or Water-sprite, like his kin spirit the Domovoy, is affectionately called *Dyedushka*, or Grandfather, by the peasants. He generally inhabits

---

[9] Grimm, D. M. 1114.
[1] Afanasief, P. V. S. III. 77. Buslaef, I. O. 233.

the depths of rivers, lakes, or pools; but sometimes he dwells in swamps, and he is specially fond of taking up his quarters in a mill-stream, close to the wheel. Every mill is supposed to have a Vodyany attached to it, or several if it has more wheels than one. Consequently millers are generally obliged to be well-versed in the black art, for if they do not understand how to treat the water-spirits all will go ill with them.

The Vodyany is represented by the people as a naked old man, with a great paunch and a bloated face. He is much given to drinking, and delights in carouses and card-playing. He is a patron of bee-keeping, and it is customary to enclose the first swarm of the year in a bag, and to throw it, weighted with a stone, into the nearest river, as an offering to him. He who does this will flourish as a bee-master, especially if he takes a honeycomb from a hive on St. Zosima's day, and flings it at midnight into a mill-stream.

The water-sprites have their subaqueous dwellings well-stocked with all sorts of cattle, which they drive out into the fields to graze by night. They have wives and children too, under the waves, the former sometimes being women who have been drowned, or whom a parent's curse has placed within the power of the Evil One. Many a girl who has drowned herself has been turned into a Rusalka or some such being, and then has married a Vodyany. On the occasion of such a marriage, or indeed of any subaqueous wedding, the Vodyanies indulge in such revels and mad pranks that the waters are wildly agitated, and often carry away bridges or mill-dams; at least, that is how the peasants explain such accidents as arise when the snows melt and the streams wax violent. When a water-sprite's wife is about to bear a child he assumes the appearance of an ordinary mortal, and fetches a midwife from some neighbouring village to attend her. Once a water-baby was caught by some fishermen in their nets. It splashed about joyously as long as it was in the water, but wailed sorely when it was taken into a cottage. Its capturers returned it to its father on his promising to drive plenty of fish into their nets in future—a promise which he conscientiously fulfilled. Here is one of the stories about a mixed marriage beneath the waves. Except at the end, it is very like that which forms the groundwork of Mr. Matthew Arnold's exquisite romaunt of "The Forsaken Merman." " Once upon a time a girl was drowned, and she lived for many years after that with a water-sprite. But one fine day she swam to the shore, and saw the red sun, and the green woods and fields, and heard the humming of insects and the distant sound of church-bells. Then a longing after her old life on earth came over her, and she could not resist the temptation. So she came out from the water, and went to her native village. But there neither her relatives nor her friends recognized her. Sadly did she return in the evening to the water-side, and passed once more into the power of the water-sprite. Two days later her mutilated corpse floated on to the sands, while the river roared and was wildly agitated. The remorseful water-sprite was lamenting his irrevocable loss[2]."

When a Vodyany appears in a village it is easy to recognize him, for water is always dripping from his left skirt, and the spot on which he sits instantly becomes wet. In his own realm he not only rules over all the fishes that swim, but he greatly influences the lot of fishers and mariners. Sometimes he brings them good luck; sometimes he lures them to destruction. Sometimes he gets caught in nets, but he immediately tears them asunder, and all the fish that had been enclosed in them swim out after him. A fisherman once found a dead body floating about in the water, so he took it into his boat. But to his horror the corpse suddenly came to life, uttered a wild laugh, and jumped overboard. That was one of the Vodyany's pranks. A sportsman once waded into a river after a wounded duck. The Vodyany got hold of him by the neck, and would have pulled him under if he had not cut himself loose with his axe. When he got home his neck was all over blue marks left by the Vodyany's fingers. Sometimes the Vodyany will jump on a horse and ride it to death; so, to keep him away while horses are fording a river, the peasants sign a cross on the water with a knife or a scythe. One should not bathe, say the peasants, without a cross round one's neck, or after sunset. Especially dangerous is it to bathe during

---

[2] Afanasief, P. V. S. II. 239.

the week in which falls the feast of the Prophet Ilya (Elijah, formerly Perun, the Thunderer), for then the Vodyany is on the look out for victims. During the day he generally lies at the bottom of the deep pools, but at night he sits on the shore combing his hair, or he sports in the water, diving with a splash and coming up far away; sometimes, also, he fights with the wood-sprites, the noise of their combats being heard afar off. In Bohemia fishermen are afraid of assisting a drowning man, thinking the Vodyany will be offended and will drive away the fish from their nets; and they say he often sits on the shore with a club in his hand, from which hang ribbons of various hues: with these he allures children, and those whom he gets hold of he drowns. The souls of his victims the Vodyany keeps, making them his servants, but their bodies he allows to float to shore.

Sometimes he changes himself into a fish, generally a pike. Sometimes, also, he is represented, like the western Merman, with a fish's tail. In the Ukraine there is a tradition that, when the sea is rough, such half-fishy "marine people" appear on the surface of the water and sing songs. The *Chumaki* (local carriers) go down at such times to the sea-side, and there hear those wonderful songs which they afterwards sing in the towns and villages. In other places these "sea people" are called "Pharaohs," being supposed, like the seals in Iceland, to be the remains of that host of Pharaoh which perished in the Red Sea.

DEMIGODS AND FAIRIES. 153

During the winter the Vodyany sleeps, but with the early spring he awakes, wrathful and hungry, and manifests his anger by various spiteful actions. In order to propitiate him the peasants in some places buy a horse, which they feed well for three days; then they tie its legs together, smear its head with honey, adorn its mane with red ribbons, attach two millstones to its neck, and at midnight fling it into an ice-hole, or, if the frost has broken up, into the middle of a river. Three days long has the Vodyany awaited his present, manifesting his impatience by groanings and upheavings of water. After he has received his due he becomes quiet. Fishermen propitiate him at the same season of the year by pouring oil on the water, begging him, as they do so, to be good to them; and millers once a year sacrifice a black pig to him. A goose, also, is generally presented to him in the middle of September, as a return for his having watched over the farmer's ducks and geese during the summer months.

As the Vodyany haunts the waters, so does the Lyeshy make the forest [*Lyes*] his home. He is supposed by some critics to be one of the spirits who belong to the realm of cloudland and storm, and they hold that their hypothesis is confirmed by the fact that he can assume different shapes, and alter his stature at will, at one time making himself taller than the trees of the forest, and at another shorter than the grass of the field. He often appears as a peasant dressed in a sheepskin, but ungirdled,—as is always the case with evil spirits,—and with the left skirt crossed over the right. One of his peculiarities is, that he never has any eyebrows or eyelashes. Sometimes, like a Cyclops, he has but one eye. When he appears in his own shape, and without clothes, he greatly resembles the mediæval pictures of the devil. From his forehead spring horns, his feet are like those of a goat, his head and body are covered with shaggy hair, which is sometimes as green as that of the Rusalkas, his fingers are tipped with long claws. In the Governments of Kief and Chernigof the peasants divide the Lyeshies into two classes, belonging respectively to the woods and to the cornfields. The one consists of giants of an ashy hue; the other of beings who, before the harvest, are of the same height as the growing corn, and, after it, dwindle away till they are no higher than the stubble.

The Lyeshy is malicious, and to those who do not conciliate him he often does much mischief. One of his tricks is to suck their milk from the cows. In the Olonetsk Government it is believed that a herdsman ought to give a cow every summer to the Lyeshy: if he fail to do so, the revengeful spirit will destroy the whole herd. In the Government of Archangel it is held that if the herdsmen succeed in pleasing the Lyeshy, he will see to the pasturing of the village cattle. In Little-Russia, on the other hand, he is supposed to be the protector of the wolves.

These wood-demons frequently quarrel among themselves, using as their weapons huge trees and masess of rock. The devastations, usually attributed to hurricanes, are in reality, the peasants say, due to these mighty combatants of the forest world. In the Archangel Government a story is told of a Lyeshy who quarrelled with two others of his race about some forest rights. A battle ensued, in which they overcame him, tied his hands so tightly together that he could not move, and then left him to his fate. A travelling merchant chanced to come that way, and released the captive demon, who was so grateful that he sent his benefactor home in a whirlwind, and did much for him afterwards. When the Lyeshy goes round to inspect his domains, the forest roars around him and the trees shake. By night he sleeps in some hut in the depths of the woods, and if by chance he finds that a belated traveller or sportsman has taken up his quarters in the refuge he had intended for himself, he strives hard to turn out the intruder, sweeping over the hut in the form of a whirlwind which makes the door rattle and the roof heave, while all around the trees bend and writhe, and a terrible howling goes through the forest. If, in spite of all these hints, the uninvited guest will not retire, he runs the risk of being lost next day in the woods, or swallowed up in a swamp.

All the birds and beasts which inhabit the forest are under the protection of the Lyeshy. His favourite is the bear, his only servant, who watches over him when he has taken too much of the strong drink he loves so well, and guards him from the assaults of the water-sprites. When the squirrels, field-mice, and some other animals go forth in troops upon their periodical migrations, the peasants explain the fact by saying that the Lyeshies are driving their flocks from one forest to another. In 1843 a great number of migrating squirrels appeared in certain districts of Russia, and the neighbouring peasants said that it was because a Lyeshy in the Vyatka Government had gambled away all his squirrels to a brother demon in that of Vologda, and the lost property was on its way to its new master. Similar gambling transactions are frequent among the water-sprites. Fishermen know at once why it is that certain fish suddenly desert particular spots. They have been staked and lost by the local Vodyany. But neither the Lyeshy nor the Vodyany will use a pack of cards in which any clubs occur. Any thing like the sign of the cross [or Perun's hammer-mace] is distasteful to demons.

A sportsman's success in the woods depends, to a great extent, on his treatment of the Lyeshy. In order to please that wayward spirit, he makes an offering of a piece of bread, or a pancake, sprinkled with salt, and lays it on the stump of a tree. The Perm peasants offer up prayers once a year to the Lyeshy, presenting him with a packet of leaf-tobacco, of which he is very fond. In some districts the hunters make an offering to the Lyeshy of whatever animal they first bag, leaving it for him in an oak forest. One of the incantations intended to be used by a hunter calls upon the "Devils and Lyeshies" to drive the hares into his power, and its magic force is supposed to be so great that the wood-demons must obey.

The Lyeshy is very fond of diverting himself in the woods, springing from bough to bough, and rocking himself among the branches as if in a cradle, whence in some places he is called *Zuibochnik*, [*Zuibka* = a cradle]. At such times he makes all manner of noises, clapping his hands, shrieking with laughter, imitating the neighing of horses, the lowing of cows, the barking of dogs. So loud is his laughter, say the peasants, that it may be heard for versts around. In their opinion, when the winds make the woods resound, the voice of the Lyeshy may be heard in what ignorant people might think was the creaking of branches or the crashing of stems; the sounds, also, which are erroneously attributed to an echo are in reality the calls of demons, who wish to allure an unwary sportsman or woodcutter on to dangerous ground, with the intention of tickling him to death if they can get hold of him. For in this respect the Lyeshies resemble their sisters the Rusalkas.

In olden days, when forests were larger and denser than they are now, the Lyeshy used to be constantly deluding travellers, and making them lose their way. Sometimes he would alter the landmarks, or would assume the likeness of some tree by which the neighbours were accustomed to steer. Sometimes he would himself take the form of a traveller, and engage a passer-by in conversation. His victim would chat away unconcernedly, till, all of a sudden, he found himself in a swamp or ravine. Then a loud laugh would be heard, and, looking round, he would see the Lyeshy at a little distance grinning at him. Sometimes by night a forest-keeper would hear the wailing of a child, or groans apparently proceeding from some one in the agonies of death. His only safe course under such circumstances was to go straight onwards, without paying any attention to those noises. If he followed them he would probably fall into a foaming stream, which rushed along where no stream had ever been seen before.

Wherever the Lyeshy goes, he always tries to leave no track behind, covering the traces of his footsteps with sand, or leaves, or snow. If by any chance a passer-by strikes upon the Lyeshy's recent trail, he becomes bewildered, and does not easily find his way again. His best plan is to take off his shoes and reverse their linings, and it may be as well also to turn his shirt or pelisse inside out. Besides making travellers lose their way, the Lyeshy amuses himself in many ways at their expense, blowing dust into their eyes and their caps off their heads, freezing their sledges tight to the ground, and so forth, so that a popular saying conveys this advice, " Don't go into the forest; the Lyeshy plays tricks there!" Worse than that, he often brings illness upon them, so that when any one falls ill after returning from the woods, his friends say, " He has crossed the Lyeshy's track." In order to get cured he takes bread and salt, wraps them in a clean rag, and carries them to the forest. On his arrival there he utters a prayer over his offering, leaves it as a sacrifice to the Lyeshy, and returns home with the firm conviction that he has left his illness behind him.

Sometimes the Lyeshy is described as leading a solitary life. Sometimes he has a wife and children. The *Lisunki*, or forest girls and women, are merely female Lyeshies, hairy and hideous. A Little-Russian story, closely resembling one told in Germany of a *Holzweibchen*, tells how a woman one day found a baby Lyeshy lying naked on the ground and crying bitterly. So she covered it up warm with her cloak, and after a time came her mother, a *Lisunka*, and rewarded the woman with a potful of burning coals, which afterwards turned into bright golden ducats.

If any one wishes to invoke a Lyeshy he should cut down a number of young birch-trees, and place them in a circle with their tops in the middle. Then he must take off his cross, and, standing within the circle, call out loudly, "Dyedushka!" "Grandfather!" and the Lyeshy will appear immediately. Or he should go into the forest on St. John's Eve, and fell an aspen, taking care that it falls towards the East. Then he must stand upon the stump, with his face turned eastward, bend downwards, and say, looking between his feet, " Uncle Lyeshy! appear not as a grey wolf, nor as a black raven, nor as a fir for burning: appear just like me!" Then the leaves of the aspen will begin to whisper as if a light breeze were blowing over them, and the Lyeshy will appear in the form of a man. On such occasions he is ready to make a bargain with his invoker, giving all kinds of assistance in return for the other's soul.

Sometimes the Lyeshies carry off mortal maidens, and make them their wives. But whether they intermarry or no, their weddings are always attended by noisy revels and by violent storms. If the wedding procession traverses a village, many of the cottages will be injured: if a forest, a number of its trees will fall. A peasant will rarely dare to lie down to sleep in a forest path, for he would be afraid of a wood-demon's bridal procession coming that way and crushing him in his slumbers. In the Government of Archangel a whirlwind is set down to the wild dancing of a Lyeshy with his bride. On the second day after his marriage the Lyeshy, according to the custom prevalent in Russia, goes to the bath with his young wife, and if any mortal passes by at the time, the newly-married couple splash water over him, and drench him from head to foot.

SECTION III.—STORYLAND BEINGS.

BESIDES the spiritual beings in whom the Russian peasant actually believes as haunting his house, or making themselves a habitation in the neighbouring woods and waters, there are a few fantastic creatures who belong for the most part only to his story-world, with whom he is rendered familiar by tradition, but on whose present existence he does not place implicit reliance.

Of these apparently mythic personages, who play important parts in the *Skazki*, or popular tales, the most prominent is the Yagá Bába, or, to use the more popular form of her name, Bába Yagá[3]. She is a supernatural being, who is generally represented under the form of a hideous old woman, very tall in stature, very bony of limb, with an excessively long nose, and with dishevelled hair. Her nose is sometimes described as being of iron, as also are her long pendant breasts and her strong sharp teeth. As she lies in her hut she often " stretches across from one corner to the other, and her nose goes right through the ceiling." Her usual habitation is a cottage [*izba*, dim. *izbushka*] which stands "on fowls' legs," that is, on slender supports. The door looks towards the forest, but when the hut is adjured in the right words it turns round, so that its back is towards the forest and its front towards the person addressing it. Sometimes, however, the Baba Yaga lives in a larger building, round which stands a fence made of the bones of the people she has eaten, and tipped with their skulls. The uprights of the gates are human legs, the bolts are human arms, and "instead of a lock there is a mouth with sharp teeth."

When the Baba Yaga goes abroad, she rides in an iron mortar. This she propels with the pestle, a sort

---

[3] *Baba* stands for "woman;" the meaning of the word *Yaga* (the accent falls on the second syllable) is uncertain.

of club, and as she goes she sweeps away the traces of her passage with a broom. According to some stories the Sun, the Day, and the Night are her servants, trunkless hands wait upon her, the elements fulfil her behests. She possesses a magic cudgel, a single wave of which suffices to turn any living creature into stone, and she can always avail herself of "fire-breathing horses," of "courier, [i. e., seven-leagued] boots," of "self-playing *gusli*," of a "self-cutting sword," and a "self-flying carpet." With all these means and appliances she is able to secure many victims, whom she cooks and eats, often stealing children for her table, often supplying it also with belated travellers.

The White-Russians declare that the Baba Yaga flies through the sky in a fiery mortar, which she urges on with a burning broom, and that, during the time of her flight, the winds howl, the earth groans, and the trees writhe and crack. At such times she greatly resembles the Fiery Snake, which plays a leading part in the Slavonic stories, and, indeed, the Baba-yaga and the Snake often appear to be identical personages, different versions of the same narrative employing sometimes the one name and sometimes the other for the same mythical being.

In the Ukraine the flying witch is usually called a snake; in a Slovak tale the sons of a Baba Yaga are described as "baneful snakes." One of the tastes which characterize the snake of fable is sometimes attributed to the Baba Yaga also. She is supposed "to love to suck the white breasts of beautiful women." Like the Snake, also, she keeps guard over and knows the use of the founts of "Living Water"—that water which cures wounds and restores the dead to life.

Sometimes three Baba Yagas are mentioned in a story. In that case they are usually three sisters who, in spite of their name, are not of an unkindly nature, and who assist the "fairy prince" or other hero of the tale, giving him good advice, and bestowing upon him magic presents. These seem to be connected with the "Prophetesses," or "Wise Women," who were looked upon with so much honour in the old days of heathenism, and who became degraded into vulgar witches under the influence of Christianity. But, as a general rule, the Baba Yaga is described as a being utterly malevolent, and always hungering after human flesh. According to some traditions she even feeds on the souls of the dead. The White-Russians, for instance, affirm that " Death gives the dead to the Baba Yaga, with whom she often goes prowling about. And that the Baba Yaga and her subordinate witches feed on the souls of people, and by that means become as light as spirits [1]."

In some places, when the wind bows down the ears of corn the peasants say that the Baba Yaga is running after children, with the intention of blinding

---

[1] Afanasief, *Skazki*, I. 120. It has already been observed that the Slavonians always represented Death as a female being, the word representing death in each of the Slavonic languages—in Russian *Smert'*—being of the feminine gender.

them or pounding them in an iron churn. Cornfields are specially haunted by the Baba Yaga, in remembrance of whom, perhaps, the last sheaf in harvest-time is dressed up in woman's clothes, and called the *Jitnaya Baba* — "the Corn-woman," — answering to the German *Kornpuppe*, the *Grosse Mutter* or *Die Alte* of the harvest-home. Russian critics are inclined to identify the Baba Yaga with Holda or Bertha—or, at least, with the unfavourable representations of those once kindly deities. The "wild," "iron" and "long-nosed" Bertha [*Frau Precht mit der langen Nase*] seems, indeed, to have many points in common with the Baba Yaga, especially as the latter is frequently represented as spinning. The Servian Baba Yaga, known as the "Iron Tooth," carries about live coals in a pitcher, and burns the distaffs of lazy spinners. To the mythologists the Baba Yaga appears to be an impersonification of the spirit of the storm. When she tears her way through the forest, making the trees writhe and howl as she passes, and sweeping away the traces of her progress with a broom, she is looked upon as the whirlwind. When as "a black cloud" she chases fugitive heroes, she seems to be the thunder-cloud which threatens to blot out the light of day.

Another strange being who figures in many of the stories is "Koshchei the Immortal," who is considered to be a mythical representation of Winter. His name is derived from the word *Kost'*, a bone, whence comes *Okostenyet'*, to ossify, to make hard as a bone or a stone, a figurative expression for "to freeze." As the earth is locked up by the Winter—say the Russian commentators—as the bright and blooming Spring cannot become visible till the wintry season is past, so are beautiful princesses kept in imprisonment by Koshchei, unable to show themselves to admiring beholders till his spell is broken and his power is overthrown.

Sometimes it is a hero's mother whom Koshchei suddenly carries off; sometimes it is his wife. In either case she is kept a prisoner until the hero finds out in what manner the immortal one can be rendered mortal—in what place his "death" can be discovered and brought home to him. The secret is always hard to detect, but sooner or later Koshchei is generally induced to make some such revelation as this,—"My death is in such and such a place. There stands an oak, and under the oak is a casket, and in the casket is a hare, and in the hare is a duck, and in the duck is an egg, and in the egg is my death." And when, after many adventures, the egg has been found and broken, Koshchei dies; he being "the Giant who had no heart in his body" of the Norse Tale[5], the Deccan Punchkin[6], the Witch of the German story[7]. Like the Baba Yaga, Koshchei is, in the opinion of the mythologists, one of the many forms in which is personified the Evil Spirit who wars against sunlight and fair weather, and who

[5] Dasent's "Tales from the Norse," p. 76.
[6] Miss Frere's "Old Deccan Days," p. 13.
[7] Haltrich's *Deutsche Volksmärchen aus dem Sachsenlande in Siebenbürgen*, p. 188.

is usually personified in the Russian stories under the form of a snake. In a Polish version of the "Sleeping Beauty," it is Koshchei who carries off the Princess, and throws her, as well as all the inhabitants of her father's kingdom, into a magic slumber. At last the destined rescuer comes, who conquers Koshchei and seizes his magic *gusli*. No sooner is their music heard than the sleepers all awake and return to busy life. Just as, say the mythologists, at the first sounds of the spring thunders, the sleeping, as it were petrified, realm of nature awakes from its winter slumbers. In a Russian story, Prince Ivan lives happily with his wife the Queen Marya Morevna (Mary, daughter of *More*, the sea), until one day, during her absence, he enters a forbidden chamber, and there finds Koshchei hung up and bound with twelve chains. Koshchei begs for water, saying he has hung there without drinking for ten years; and when he has obtained it, and has drunk his fill, he recovers his lost strength, bursts his chains, and flies away, carrying off the Queen as he goes. Fortunately the Prince obtains a magic steed, which eventually fells Koshchei by a kick on the forehead: so all goes well. The mythological explanation of this story is, that Marya Morevna, the fair Daughter of the Sea, is the Springtide Sun. Koshchei is the storm which is bound by the iron or icy chains of winter, and so has lost its strength. But when he has drunk his fill, he regains his vigour, bursts forth in a whirlwind, and carries off the fair Queen, i. e., after the first spring rains the thunderstorms begin to resume their strength, the winds arise, the dark clouds gather, and the sunlight suffers for a time eclipse. Then the Prince kills Koshchei and carries off the sea's fair daughter. The thunder-god Perun overcomes the storm-cloud, and the sun shines out again.

In another Russian story, the description of the manner in which Koshchei's secret as to his death is obtained from him still more closely resembles that given in the Norse tale. He first declares that his death resides in a besom, and then that it lies in the fence which surrounds the house. His fair captive has first the besom tipped with gold and then the fence. At last he divulges the secret, and the Prince gets hold of the fatal egg, and shifts it from one hand to the other till it breaks, when Koshchei, who has been "rushing from one corner to the other," gives way and dies. In another variant a snake is substituted for Koshchei, and its death lies in a little stone within the yolk of the mystic egg. In different versions of the story different animals are represented as forming the chain which secures the life of Koshchei, and of which the last link is either an egg, or a stone inside an egg; but Afanasief points out that such animals are always chosen as are frequently employed as types of the clouds—the boar, the bull, the hare, the duck. In one variant, the mythological nature of the story is even more clearly apparent, for it is expressly stated that the hero was assisted in his search for the fatal egg by the Thunder, the Wind, and the Hail.

Closely connected with Koshchei, and often identical with the Baba Yaga is the *Vyed'ma*, or Witch. Her name, as well as that of the *Vyedun*, or Wizard, springs from the root *vyed*, whence *vyedat'*, "to know." In the old heathen times the *Vyed'ma* was the *Vyeshchaya zhena*, the wise or knowing woman, and was held in high reverence. As prophetess, poetess, medicine-woman, she exercised solemn functions; she was supposed to control the elements, to be able to compel the clouds to withhold or to pour forth rain, to prevent the sun from shining, or to gladden the earth with its rays. In times of drought and famine, it is true, the whole race of warlocks, conjurors, soothsayers, and the like, whether male or female, seems to have suffered cruelly at the hands of the furious populace; but the divining profession did not fall into utter disrepute until some time after the introduction of Christianity.

In the Skazkas, however, the *Vyed'ma* is not the old Slavonian Wise Woman, but a witch of the worst possible character, a female fiend always longing to feed upon human flesh, as rapacious, but not so formidable, as the mother of Grendel, whom Beowulf slew. In one story a witch who longs to get hold of a boy called Ivashko [dim. of Ivan], gets a blacksmith to forge her "just such a thin little voice as Ivashko's mother has," and by its aid she entices him into her power. The end of the story is nearly the same as that of the Norse tale of Buttercup [Dasent, p. 146], for Ivashko contrives to escape, after getting the witch's daughter baked instead of himself.

One of the strangest of the stories of these devouring harpies is that of a witch who consumes every thing on which she can lay her hands, so that at last "only the walls remain" of the palace in which she lives. Her brother, a young prince who had left his father's home before she was born, is the only member of her family whom she has not devoured. He had been warned that his as yet unborn sister would eat him if she could, and he had managed to make his way to the abode of the "Sun's Sister," where he remained. On his way there he had made the acquaintance of certain weird sewing women, and of a "Leveller of Mountains" and an "Uprooter of Trees," but finding that they must all die some day, he had not stopped long with them. At last he pays a visit to his old home, where he sees no living thing except his sister, who receives him with cordiality, and prepares to eat him. But while she is "sharpening her teeth" he is warned of his impending fate by a mouse, so he takes to flight, and succeeds in escaping to the castle of his friend and protector, the Sun's Sister. The witch arrives soon afterwards, and, after some parley, proposes that he and she shall be weighed against each other, outside the castle, with the stipulation that the heavier of the two shall be at liberty to eat the lighter. This is agreed upon, and the Prince steps first into one of the scales. His sister prepares to get into the other, but, says the story, "no sooner did she put her foot into it than up shot Prince Ivan, and that with such force that he flew right up to the sky, and into the room of the Sun's Sister. But the Witch-Snake remained there on earth [8]".

How little is known precisely about such witches is plainly shown by the variety of explanations which this story has called forth. Investigators who treat it as a solar myth recognize the Dawn as the Sun's Sister, looking upon the devouring witch as the Night, who perpetually chases her brother the Day, and is only driven away by the interposition of the Dawn. One of the Russian songs, Afanasief remarks, begins with the words,

O Dawn, my dear little Dawn!
O Dawn, Sister of the Sun!

In the Servian songs it is the Day Star who is the Sun's Sister.

Those who consider the story to be a moral allegory, it has been suggested, may look on the Prince as the type of the soul of man, pursued by the Death-Witch, who tries to seize it and carry it off to the depths of her gloomy realm. Then comes a form of judgment. The soul is weighed in the balance, and if it is heavy with crime it goes down into the world of darkness, but if it be light it flies aloft into the realm of bliss, there to shine in heaven as a star. This seems to be going rather too far, but there appears to be good reason for supposing that the Witch is Death, and the object of her chase is the soul. In what seems to be a variant of the same story, current in Little-Russia, a man sets out to seek "the

[8] Afanasief, *Skazki*, VI. 57, p. 283.

island where there is no death." A wolf invites him to stop, but, when he hears that the wolf is to die as soon as she has uprooted an oak with her tail, he goes on. In the same way he refuses the hospitable offers of some women whom he finds sewing in a hut, and who are to die when they have used up their needles, which fill several huge boxes. At last he visits the Moon, who says, "This is how I am. When the moon in heaven is old, I am old; and when it is young, I am young also." So the man stops with the Moon a hundred years and more. At last Death, after consulting the Wolf and the Sewers, comes to the Moon, and asks for "her soul." "It isn't yours," says the Moon; but Death perseveres in her claim. At last the Moon takes the man by the head, while Death seizes him by the feet, on which he shoots up into the air, and becomes "a star which may be seen in the sky near the Moon[9]."

Somewhat of the same kind also is the Bulgarian story in which the Sun falls in love with the fair maiden Grozdanka. So on St. George's day he lets down from heaven a golden swing, which remains suspended close by her house. Small and great swing away in it, till at last Grozdanka steps into it. But no sooner has she done so than the golden swing flies up to heaven, and bears the maiden [as the eagle bore Ganymede] to her radiant lover[1].

In the story of "Truth's Triumph," in Miss Frere's "Old Deccan Days" [p. 50], much evil is wrought

[9] Afanasief, P. V. S. III. 274.   [1] Afanasief, *Skazki*, VIII. 380.

by an evil spirit, a *Rakshasa*, who has taken the form of " an ugly old woman," closely resembling the *Vyed'ma* or the Baba Yaga. She has long claws instead of hands, " her hair hangs around her in a thick black tangle," and she possesses a magic wand with which she can work wonders. The hero of the tale steals it, and when she chases him he waves it, and causes, first, a great river to flow, then a high mountain to rise, between him and her—obstacles which are frequently produced in similar emergencies by the heroes of Russian tales, who generally have recourse for the purpose to the agency of a magic comb, brush, or towel.

The three embodiments of the Spirit of Evil, generally known as the Baba Yaga, Koshchei, and the Witch, seem to be mere varieties of the general form it assumes in the stories—that of the Snake. Their names appear to be interchangeable at will with that of the great antagonist of the heroes of the Skazkas, the terrible Fiery Serpent. In one variant of a story, it is a Baba Yaga who pursues a band of fugitives; in another, it is the wife of a slain snake. Here Koshchei is seen hanging in chains in the room which the Prince is forbidden to enter, there a fettered serpent meets the eye. The mythical being who chases her brother up to the home of the Sun's Sister is spoken of as a human witch until the end of the story, but then she is called the "Witch-Snake[2]."

[2] "In process of time" (says Mr. Talboys Wheeler, speaking of the "Scythic Nágas," in his History of India, I. 147) "these

The Serpent [*Zmyei*] is described in the stories as "winged," "fiery," "many-headed." Sometimes he assumes a human form, becoming a youth of marvellous beauty in the presence of his beloved, or, when going to meet a foe, a warrior mounted on a noble charger, with a raven perched on his shoulder and a hound following at his heels. Sometimes he bears the patronymic of Goruinuich, i. e. Son of the Mountain [*Gora* = a mountain], in which case he may be the lightning, looked upon as the offspring of the aerial mountain, the cloud. In others he seems to be intended for the cloud itself, as in a story which mentions his blotting out the light of day. It seems to be in the latter capacity that he is spoken of as guarding treasures of bright metals and gleaming gems, and as carrying off and imprisoning fair maidens. In one story a snake is said to have stolen the luminaries of the night. A hero cuts off its head, and out from the slain monster issue "the Bright Moon and the Morning Stars;" and in another the Bear and the "Ocean Monster" carry off the Beautiful Princesses Luna and Zvyezda [Star][3]. But it is generally a mortal maiden with whom he elopes, and whom he retains much against her will. From such unions spring heroes of magic powers, such as Tugarin Zmyeevich, and Volkh Vseslav'evich, of whom more will be said hereafter, and also

Nágas became identified with serpents, and the result has been a strange confusion in the ancient myths between serpents and human beings."

[3] Afanasief, P. V. S. II. 535.

fiendish shapes like the Kikimori, or Incubi, which harass sleepers.

In the stories and songs the fair prisoner is generally rescued by a hero who penetrates into the castle of the Snake, and there fights and conquers him, getting possession at the same time of the "living water" [the rain?] on which depends the snake's [or the cloud's] power. This hero is supposed to be the Thunder-god, who disperses the Cloud and frees the life-bestowing Rain and the fair Sunlight. In some of the stories he bears a surname which points to his connexion with the Deity of the Hearth, being called Zapechny, or Zatrubnik, or Popyalof—from *pech* [the stove], or *truba* [the stovepipe or chimney], or *pepel* [ashes]. Sometimes the demon eats the maidens whom he carries off, the stories frequently speaking of a beautiful princess who is exposed like Andromeda, and whom a Slavonic Perseus saves from a "seven-headed snake" which is hastening to devour her.

In a few of the stories the Thunder-god himself appears under the form of a snake. The princely bridegroom has been changed by the magic spells of a foe into "a terrible serpent." But the loving bride breaks the spell by a kiss, and the serpent turns into a handsome prince, who marries his rescuer; that is, says Afanasief, the hot breath of the Goddess of Spring recalls Perun to life, and brings about a union fraught with happy consequences to the earth[4].

---

[4] See Grimm *Deutsche Sagen*, I. 13.

Sometimes a captive princess, enchanted by Koshchei or some other mythic being, is turned into a snake. In one story, the hero who rescues her has first to remain for seven years shut up in a castle of metal on a steep hill. At the end of that time the princess recovers her former shape and beauty, i. e. at the end of the seven winter months, passed in darkness and seclusion, the Goddess of the Spring regains her power, or her former charms are restored to the Earth. The idea of a serpent as a terrible enemy is now preserved in Russia only in the popular literature. By the common people of the present day snakes are there looked upon with much respect and even affection. " Our peasants," says Afanasief, " consider it a happy omen if a snake takes up its quarters in a cottage, and they gladly set out milk for it. To kill such a snake would be a very great sin." And he goes on to say that healing powers are still attributed to the heads and skins of snakes. These ideas may have been handed down from a time when serpent-worship prevailed among the Slavonians in general. The Old Prussians are said to have worshipped a fiery serpent over which priests kept careful watch. In Poland and Lithuania, according to Kromer, snakes were domesticated in the houses of the people, who honoured them as Penates, and made offerings to them of milk, eggs, cheese, and fowls. The Lusatian Wends believe that snakes sometimes do men good service, aiding them in growing rapidly rich, and requiring nothing in return but simple offerings.

Among the most striking of the Russian Snake-stories—stories which seem to be clearly nature-myths—may be mentioned the tale of Ivan Popyalof, in which it is expressly stated that "in that kingdom in which Ivan lived there was no day, but always night: that was a snake's doing." So when the snake, a twelve-headed one, had been killed by Ivan and his brothers, they cut off and destroyed its heads, "and immediately there was bright light throughout the whole kingdom." As a general rule, however, it is not openly stated that the Snake-Cloud has blotted out the light of day, or that Winter has imprisoned the Spring, but the idea is conveyed in a mythical form, common to all Indo-European folk-lore, the story relating that a fair Princess has been carried off by the Snake. She is of course always rescued by the hero of the tale, who finds out where she is confined—sometimes after having traversed the kingdoms of copper, of silver, and of gold—and kills her serpent-gaoler.

In one of the stories a Seven-headed Snake carries off a girl as she is taking food to her two brothers in the forest. The elder of the two goes in search of her, and arrives at the Snake's dwelling. He is at first cordially received, but as he can neither eat iron bread and iron beans, nor accomplish the tasks which are set him—to cut up a huge log without a hatchet, and to burn it without fire—he is killed by the irritated Snake, who takes out his eyes and puts them into a pot, and then hangs his dead body to a beam. After a time the younger brother undergoes the same fate.

As their mother is weeping one day, and complaining to God, she sees a pea come rolling along. Saying to herself, "This is a gift from God," she eats it, and the result is that she bears a son, who receives the name of Pokatigoroshek [from *katit'*, to roll, and *gorokh*, peas], and who eventually goes to look for his two brothers. Arriving at the Snake's dwelling, he devours the iron food which is offered to him; with a finger's touch he turns the huge log into dust and ashes, and then he tries his strength against the Snake. When he and the Snake grasp each other's hands, his hand "only turns blue," but the snake's is broken off. A mortal combat ensues, in which he kills the Snake, and afterwards he obtains the water of life, and resuscitates his dead brothers[1].

In a Croatian variant of this story the Snake is replaced by the Devil, *Vrag*,—a word compared by Grimm with the Old High-German *warg*, a wolf—and Pokatigoroshek becomes the being known in Russian as Malchik-s-Palchik, our Tom Thumb [*Malchik*, a boy, *palchik* dim. of *palets*; a finger].

The part assigned in most of the stories to the Snake, is, in some of them, given to a monster called Chudo-Yudo [*Yudo* = Judas: *Chudo* now means a marvel or prodigy; in olden times it was synonymous with *Velikan*, a Giant], and it often corresponds in some points with that filled by the Slavonic Neptune, the Tsar Morskoi, or Sea King, who has already been alluded to, but who is worthy of a more detailed

[1] Afanasief, *Skazki*, III. 2, pp. 6—15.

notice, as also are his daughters, the Swan Maidens, whose fair sisters are known in all lands.

In one of the Builinas, or metrical romances, the following story is told of a Novgorod trader, named Sadko :—Once in a fit of dreariness, due to his being so poor that he had no possessions beyond the *gusli* on which he performed at festivals, he went down to the shore of Lake Ilmen, and there began to play. Presently " the waters of the lake were troubled, and the Tsar Morskoi appeared," who thanked him for his music, and promised him a rich reward. Thereupon Sadko flung a net into the lake, and drew a great treasure to land. Another of the poems tells how the same Sadko, after he had become a wealthy merchant, was sailing over the blue sea. Presently his ship stopped, and nothing would make it move on. Lots were cast to find out whose guilt was the cause of this delay, and they fixed the blame upon Sadko. Then he confessed that he had now been sailing to and fro for twelve years, but had not remembered to pay fitting tribute to the King of the Waters, " to offer bread and salt to the blue Caspian." Thereupon the sailors flung him overboard, and immediately the ship once more proceeded on its way.

Sadko sank to the bottom of the sea, and there found a dwelling entirely made of wood. Inside lay the Tsar Morskoi, who said he had been expecting Sadko for twelve years, and told him to begin playing. Sadko obeyed, and charmed the Tsar, who began to dance. " Then the blue sea was troubled, and the swift rivers overflowed, and many ships with their freights were submerged." The Ocean King was so pleased with the music, that he offered the hand of any one of his thirty daughters to the musician. So Sadko married the nymph Volkhof, that being the name of the river which runs past Novgorod:

> And at midnight, during his slumber,
> He touched his young wife with his left foot—
> From his sleep arose Sadko.
> He found himself under [the walls of] Novgorod,
> And his left foot was in the river Volkhof[6].

In one of the prose stories a king, whom the chase has rendered athirst, lies down flat on the ground and drinks of the cool waters of a lake. "He drinks and suspects no danger, but the Tsar Morskoi seizes him by the beard," and holds him fast until he promises to give in ransom his infant son. When the young Prince has grown up he is taken by his father to the edge of the fatal lake, and there deserted. Acting upon the advice of a friendly sorceress, he hides among the bushes on the shore, and waits till twelve pigeons arrive, which strike the ground, and "turn into beautiful maidens, every one of them of indescribable loveliness." They fling off their clothes, run into the water, and there "play, laugh, splash about, and sing songs." After a time arrives a thirteenth pigeon, which also becomes a maiden, fairer than all the rest. Her dress [*sorochka*, a shift] Prince Ivan steals. So when her sisters have re-

---

[6] Kirsha Danilof, 343.

sumed their feathered garb, and flown away, she has to remain behind, vainly searching for her missing garment, until at last she cries,—

"Whoever you are who have my shift, come here. If you are old, you shall be my father. If middle-aged, you shall be my brother. If of my own age, you shall be my loved one."

Ivan appears, and she gives him a golden ring, tells him she is Vassilissa the Wise, the daughter of the Tsar Morskoi, and shows him the way to her subaqueous abode. Then she assumes her pigeon-shape, and flies away. Ivan enters the world beneath the waters. "There the light is just the same as with us. There the dear sun shines warmly, and there stretch ploughed lands, and meadows, and verdant groves." The Water-King receives him angrily, and sets him various difficult tasks, one of which is "to build a church of pure wax;" but he performs them all, thanks to the aid of Vassilissa and the ants, the bees, and others of her "trusty servants," and eventually he becomes her husband'.

The Water-King's daughters, who in this story take the shape of pigeons, often appear under the forms of ducks, geese, or swans. The pigeon was in ancient times consecrated to the thunder-god, and, as has already been observed, in some places Slavonic

---

' Afanasief, *Skazki*, vi. 48, pp. 205—213. The story is a Slavonic counterpart of the tales *De beiden Künigeskinner*, Kinder- und Hausmärchen, 113) and "The Mastermaid," (Dasent's Norse Tales, p. 81), but the Tsar Morskoi has more individuality than the German king or the Norse giant.

children still sing to the rain, when they want it to stop, "Do not come, O rain! Three pigeons will come flying, will take thee on their wings, and will carry thee into foreign parts." After the Russians had become Christians, they retained their reverence for the bird, but considered it ·sacred to the Third Person of the Trinity, instead of to Perun; and so to this day they look upon the slaying of a pigeon as a great sin, one which will bring a murrain upon the herds of its perpetrator. Pigeons are supposed to bring good luck with them, and to assure the house they haunt against fire. If a building does catch fire, a white pigeon will extinguish the flames if it is thrown among them; on the other hand the flying of a pigeon into a house through the window forebodes a conflagration.

In some parts of Russia the swan, also, is looked upon as a bird which ought not to be shot at, and tradition affirms that "if a swan which has been killed is shown to children, they will all die." In one of the metrical romances a hero sees a wondrous swan—its plumage all golden, its head formed of "red gold," set with pearls—and is going to let fly an arrow at it, when it cries aloud, "Do not shoot at me!" comes flying up to him, and turns into a fair maiden, who afterwards becomes his wife. In a Bulgarian song a youth meets with one of the weird beings called Vilas—the South-Slavonian Rusalkas, who, in return for a draught of water from the fountains they guard, demand "the dark eyes" of those who drink. But he does not allow the Vila "to drink out his dark eyes." He seizes her by her ruddy locks, throws her across his swift steed, and takes her to his home. There he tears off her right wing, shuts it up in a coffer, and makes her his wife. Three years pass by, and she bears a son. At the christening she is entreated to dance, but she replies that she cannot do so properly unless she is given back her missing wing. So it is restored to her, whereupon she flies away and does not return. Her husband's mother calls to her to come back, asking who is to feed her child and rock its cradle. To which she replies that if it cries for food she will "suckle it with copious dew;" if it wishes to be lulled to sleep, she will "rock its cradle with a gentle breeze[8]."

Somewhat akin to the story of how the Tsar Morskoi demanded from the king his son, is that which tells how another king had to give up both his son and his daughter to Tsar Medvyed, or King Bear. In vain does their father hide them away in an underground retreat. The Bear finds them out and carries them off. During his absence a hawk takes them on its wings, and tries to fly away with them. But the Bear returns, catches sight of them, strikes his head against the ground, and sends forth a flame, which burns the hawk's wings, and compels it to drop the fugitives. An eagle next attempts to rescue them, but meets with the same fate as the hawk. At last,

---

[8] For a detailed account of "Swan-Maidens," see Baring-Gould's "Curious Myths," etc., Second Series, p. 296.

STORYLAND BEINGS. 183

however, a bull-calf succeeds in carrying them off safely. Acting on its directions the royal children consume it with fire, and from its ashes spring a horse, a dog, and an apple-tree, all of which play important parts in the second half of the story [9].

The bear [Medvyed] is a well-known symbol of the thunder, said to be chosen partly on account of its fondness for honey [Med, which, in mythological language means rain]. The hawk, the eagle, and the bull, are all equally familiar symbols of the cloud.

In another version of the story there issues from the ashes of the bull one of those supernatural dwarfs who play so leading a part in the traditions of all nations. The Slavonic Tom Thumb, Däumling, or Petit Poucet, is generally known as the Malchik-s-Palchik, the boy [Mal'chik, from maly, small] who is only as long as a finger [palets, dim. pal'chik], or as Mizinchik [dim. of Mizinets, the little finger], just as the Old-Prussian name for a dwarf was Parstuck, from the Lithuanian pirsztas, a finger[1]. Sometimes, however, as in the story alluded to, he is called Mujichok-s-Kulachok, the little Mujik as big as a fist [our Pygmy, Kulak = πυγμή], or Mujichok-s-Nogotok, Boroda-s-Lokotok, the little Mujik as big as a finger-nail, with a beard as long as a fore-arm. In any case he is taken to be an impersonification of the lightning, his long beard being the storm-cloud.

For the Tsar Morskoi, also, as well as for his

[9] As in that of " Katie Wooden-cloak," in Dasent's Norse Tales, p. 420.

[1] *Deutsche Mythologie*, 419.

daughters, the Swan Maidens, as plausible mythological explanations have been offered as have been supplied in the cases of the Baba Yaga, Koshchei, the Witch, and the Fiery Snake. But on some of them it seems not a little hazardous to rely with any great confidence. That many of the stories of the Russian peasantry may not unwarrantably be resolved into nature-myths will, I think, become apparent to any one who carefully examines them. To such an examination I hope, in another volume, to devote fitting space. At present I must be contented with merely mentioning, without unhesitatingly adopting, the theories propounded on the subject by the Russian mythologists. This is not the place for a discussion of the sources from which are derived the stories and metrical romances current in Russia, nor for an investigation of their age; but it may be stated here that while some critics look on them as decidely ancient, and regard them as the medium through which the west of Europe has obtained much of its popular fiction, there are others who hold that those divisions of Russian folk-lore are comparatively modern. What is certain is that they have been more or less subjected to manifold influences, Scandinavian, Byzantine, Arabian, Persian, Turkish, and the like. And therefore the task of tracing a Russian story through its wanderings from its far off eastern home is by no means an easy one. But before investigating its mythical meaning, it is as well at least to attempt such a tracing, with a view to reducing it as far as possible to its original form by relieving it of the foreign matter which has adhered to it on its travels. When it has undergone that operation it is fit to be subjected to the scrutiny of the comparative mythologist.

The case of the songs of the Russian people, however, is different in this respect from that of the stories and romances. Some of them—especially such fragments as have been preserved by the peasantry of the ancient ritual and mythical hymns of their ancestors—are evidently of very great antiquity, and have probably been, comparatively speaking, but little exposed to any foreign influence. From these songs, therefore, it is allowable to expect some evidence as to old times, and, in particular, as to the religious ideas and the mythical teaching of those Slavonians who, at some early period to which we can assign no definite date, spread themselves over the great plains in the north-east of Europe. Of the songs which seem to be most closely connected with those subjects I will now endeavour to give some brief account. Unfortunately, the number of such undoubted relics of Russian heathenism is by no means great, rich as is the store of "folk-songs" possessed by the Russian people.

CHAPTER III.

MYTHIC AND RITUAL SONGS.

EACH season of the year has its own songs set apart for it in Russia, hallowed by old traditions, and linked with customs of which the original meaning has, in most cases, long been forgotten, but which still retain much of that firm hold upon the popular mind which they possessed in heathen times. In none of them are the traces of the old religion more perceptible than in the songs which are sung at Christmas-tide, chiefly in White-Russia and Little-Russia, and which bear the name of *Kolyádki*. The name of *Kolyáda*, or *Koleda*, which is given to the festival celebrated at that time has been explained in various ways, being derived by one philologist from *Kolo*, a wheel, and connected by another with *Kolóda*, a kind of yule log; but others are decidedly of opinion that it is merely an adaptation of the Roman *Kalendæ*, the word having been introduced into the Slavonic languages by way of Byzantium [1].

---

[1] The Croatian verb, *Kolyadovati*, means "to offer a sacrifice," but the word *Koleda*, as used by the Tver peasants, stands for "the daily dole of alms to the poor." In Croatia the word has retained its old heathen associations: in the Russian provinces it has yielded to the influence of Christianity. See Schöpping, *R. N.* p. 13.

However that may be, the festival which is called that of *Kolyáda*, and which the influence of the Church has to some extent converted into a celebration of the birth of Christ, seems to have referred in ancient times to the renewed life universally attributed to the Sun after the winter solstice, when the gloom of the long nights begins to give way to the light of the lengthening day. At that time, according to popular tradition, the Sun—a female being—arrays herself in her holiday robe and head-dress, takes her seat in her *teléga*, and urges her horses upon the summer track. And to this solar goddess the people have given the name of Kolyada, and a custom used once to prevail in many places, and in some may still be kept up, of representing her by a girl dressed in white, who was seated on a sledge and driven about from house to house, while *Kolyadki* were sung by the young people who attended her, and who had various presents made to them in return; such gifts being supposed to have represented the contributions to a sacrifice which used to be made in the days of old. Here is one of the songs still sung at the Christmas festivals :—

Kolyada! Kolyada!
Kolyada has arrived
On the Eve of the Nativity.
We went about, we sought
Holy Kolyada,
Through all the courts, in all the alleys.
We found Kolyada
In Peter's Court.
Round Peter's Court there is an iron fence,

> In the midst of the Court there are three rooms:
> In the first room is the bright Moon;
> In the second room, the red Sun;
> And in the third room, the many Stars.

The song then proceeds to explain that the Moon is the master of the house, the Sun is the mistress, and the Stars are their children, and concludes by wishing them good health,

> "For many years, for many years[2]."

In all probability the celestial beings were originally introduced as objects of worship; but as time went by, and new religious ideas came into play, they were employed merely for the purpose of laudatory comparison. At present they occur in many songs under different forms, and are explained in various ways. In a Ruthenian version, for instance, they are likened to God, to the Son of God, and to the Children of God, the last being, in all probability, the Angels. Instead of the Stars sometimes appear "the Bright Dawns," or they are replaced by the Rain. In one song they are "three kind guests," and in another they are "three brothers who have brought blessings with them from distant lands." In another of the Ruthenian *Kolyadki*, the Sun has a son, the young Ivan, who speaks of the "Bright Dawn" as his sister. In some of the songs, especially those sung in Bohemia, Moravia, and Bulgaria, a Christian form is given to

---

[2] Tereshchenko, VII. 56.

the idea. The Virgin Mary appears, either bathing or washing vestments in the Jordan, and directly afterwards she bears a son, and the angels come and carry him away to heaven. Or she bathes her child, and places him in the manger, and the doors of a temple are opened, and lights are lit, and Christ Himself serves at the altar. These legends are not supposed to be of Christian origin, but are looked upon as old heathen myths to which a Christian character has been given, being akin to the Lithuanian idea of Perun's mother daily bathing the weary and travel-stained Sun, and sending it forth again bright and rejoicing.

The Maiden who appears in these songs as the Virgin Mary is found in others guarding wine. Heavenly birds, in a Little-Russian *Kolyadka*, fly to her, and would fain drink the wine. She awakes and drives them away, saying that she has need of the wine for her own wedding, and for that of her brother and sister.

> The steep hill gave forth, gave forth a sound.
> On it as yet grew no silken grass,
> Grew only green wine.
> A lady fair guarded the wine,
> Guarded the wine—fell into a heavy slumber.
> There came flying heavenly birds,
> They plucked the green wine,
> And wakened the fair lady.
> Quickly did she hear that;
> She waved at them her sleeve.
> " Away with you afield, heavenly birds !
> To me myself is the wine needful,

To give in marriage my brother and my sister,
And I myself am a young betrothed one[3]."

In her the mythologists see the Dawn, to whom the part of a manager of weddings is openly ascribed in one Little-Russian song, in which it is said that—

The Moon went wandering about the heaven,
And the Moon met the bright Dawn.
"O Dawn, Dawn! wherever hast thou been?
Wherever hast thou been? Where dost thou intend
    to live?"
"Where do I intend to live? why at Pan Ivan's,
At Pan Ivan's in his Court,
In his Court, and in his dwelling,
And in his dwelling are two pleasures:
The first pleasure—to get his son married;
And the second pleasure—to give his daughter in
    marriage[4]."

Pan[5] Ivan is supposed to be some celestial being, marriages between the heavenly bodies being often mentioned in Slavonic songs—especially in those of Servia, in one of which the Day-star, so closely connected with the Dawn, arranges a marriage with the Moon, and in another the "Sun's Sister" appears as a bride, whose hand is gained by a youth in whom some see the Morning-star. A similar youth is found in a number of Little-Russian *Kolyadki*, in which he is represented as besieging a town and gaining from it a bride. He is tall and radiant, he sits within a tent made of white silk, or rides on a

---

[3] Sakharof, I. iii. 22.   [4] Sakharof, I. iii 22.
[5] The Little-Russian or Polish equivalent for the Great-Russian *Gospodin*, the German *Herr*, the French *Monsieur*, etc.

horse with a mane of gold; his sabre flashes like the
Sun, and so do the swords of his trusty comrades, who
enable him to drive away his foes and gain his bright
bride. In him Orest Miller sees the lightning which
pierces the dark clouds and rescues the fair sunlight
from eclipse, just as he recognizes some thunder-
bearer in the "proud youth" of one of the Ruthenian
Kolyadki. In it we see a dark mountain, from behind
which come a flock of sheep, and after them follows a "proud youth" with three pipes, the sound
of whose piping exercises a magic influence over all
the realm of Nature.

> The dark mountain has grown black,
> From behind it has come forth a black cloud,
> A black cloud—a flock of sheep;
> After them has come forth a proud youth,
> A proud youth to the foreground:
> He has girded himself with a straw girdle,
> From that girdle hang two or three pipes;
> The one pipe is of horn,
> The second pipe is of copper,
> The third pipe is of aurochs horn.
> Oh! when he began to sound the pipe of horn,
> A voice went through the forest;
> Oh! when he began to sound the pipe of copper,
> A voice went among the mountain tops;
> Oh! when he began to play on the aurochs pipe,
> There went up voices to the heavens[6].

Some of the Russian *Kolyadki*, also, seem to refer
to the thunder-god, for they speak of the sacrifice of
a goat, one of the animals most frequently used as
symbols of the thunder. Here is one of them :—

---

[6] Afanasief, P. V. S. III. 757.

Beyond the river, the swift river,
Oi Kolyadka!
There stand dense forests:
In those forests fires are burning,
    Great fires are burning.
Around the fires stand benches,
    Stand oaken benches.
On those benches the good youths,
The good youths, the fair maidens,
    Sing Kolyada songs,
        Kolyadka, Kolyadka!
In their midst sits an old man;
He sharpens his steel knife.
A cauldron boils hotly.
Near the cauldron stands a goat.
They are going to kill the goat.
"Brother Ivanushko,
Come forth, spring out!"
"Gladly would I have sprung out,
But the bright stone [7]
Drags me down to the cauldron:
The yellow sands
Have sucked dry my heart."
    Oi Kolyadka! Oi Kolyadka [8].

Long after heathenish rites had been generally discarded in Russia, they were kept up by the Lithuanians, among whom it was customary for the shepherds and shepherdesses to assemble and light a great fire, round which they would sing religious songs. Afterwards a goat would be brought to the fire and sacrificed by a priest, the priestly class existing among the Lithuanians. In all probability

---

[7] Literally "the fiery or inflammable stone," the epithet being in general purely conventional.

[8] Snegiref, R. P. P. II. 68.

the sacrifice described in the song was actually performed in old days in Russia as well as in Lithuania, though its memory is now preserved in popular poetry alone. Some writers, it should be mentioned, are of opinion that this song belongs to the Midsummer, rather than to the Christmas festival, the pig, and not the goat, being the animal generally sacrificed in the winter[9]. The last few lines of the song are very like, if not identical with, those which occur in the story "of the Kid Prince," a Russian counterpart of that of *Brüderchen und Schwesterchen* in the *Kinder- und Hausmärchen*.

In some of the *Kolyadki* may be found traces of cosmogonic myths, as well as fragments of others referring to the relations between the gods and mankind. To some of these deities Christian names have been given, but the old heathen forms are plainly apparent under the ill-fitting garb which a later time has carelessly flung over them; for instance, in this Carpathian *Kolyadka*:—

Afield, afield, out in the open field!
There a golden plough goes ploughing,
And behind that plough is the Lord Himself.
The holy Peter helps Him to drive,
And the Mother of God carries the seed corn,
Carries the seed corn, prays to the Lord God,
" Make, O Lord, the strong wheat to grow,
The strong wheat and the vigorous corn !
The stalks there shall be like reeds !

[9] See Schöpping, *R. N.* p. 40. He says that the names *Kolyada* and *Kupalo* were not unfrequently confused, and that the latter feast to this day bears the name of the former in Dalmatia.

> The ears shall be [plentiful] as blades of grass!
> The sheaves shall be [in number] like the stars!
> The stacks shall be like hills,
> The loads shall be gathered together like black clouds[1]."

Here the Mother of God is evidently some such benignant divinity as the Teutonic Holda. There is a tradition among the Lusatian Wends that the Virgin Mary and the infant Christ once passed by a field in which a peasant was sowing barley, and she said to him "God be with thee, good man! As soon as thou hast sown, take thy sickle and begin to reap." In a little time came a crowd of Jews in pursuit of her, and asked the peasant if he had seen a mother and child go by. "She passed not long ago," he replied, "just when I was sowing this barley." "Idiot! why that must be twelve weeks ago!" exclaimed the Jews, seeing that the barley was now ripe, and the peasant was reaping it, and they turned back. The same story is told in a Little-Russian *Kolyadka*, only the Virgin carries on her hand a hawk —one of the symbols of the Sun-god—instead of leading the infant Christ.

Perhaps the most curious of the cosmogonic *Kolyadki* is a Carpathian song, in which we find the following description of the creation of the world:—

> Once there was neither heaven nor earth,
> Heaven nor earth, but only blue sea,
> And in the midst of the sea two oaks.

---

[1] Afanasief, P. V. S. III. 758.

There sat there two pigeons,
Two pigeons on the two oaks,
And began to take counsel among themselves,
To take counsel and to say,
" How can we create the world ?
Let us go to the bottom of the sea,
Let us bring thence fine sand,
Fine sand and blue stone.
We will sow the fine sand,
We will breathe on the blue stone.
From the fine sand—the black earth,
The cool waters, the green grass.
From the blue stone—the blue heavens,
The blue heavens, the bright sun,
The bright sun, the clear moon,
The clear moon and all the stars[2]".

It is chiefly on Christmas Eve that the *Kolyadki* are sung, but the Christmas festival itself lasts until the Epiphany. The evenings during this festal period, and indeed the whole space of time included, bear the name of *Svyatki*, and to them belong a number of special games and songs. Their sacred character dates back to the period of heathenism, and on them it was customary, as it is now, for social gatherings to take place at which games were played, and songs were sung, and guesses were made about the future. These guesses or divinings—*Gadaniya* —are now for the most part kept up only among girls who wish to know something beforehand about their destined husbands. Sometimes a horse is led across a piece of wood, and, according to whether it stumbles or not, a conclusion is drawn as to the

[2] Afanasief, P. V. S. II. 466.

character of the coming man. German writers of the eleventh and twelfth centuries bear witness to the fact that a similar divining process formerly prevailed among the Baltic Slavonians, only in those days it was a lance across which the horse was driven, and the subject about which an omen was sought was the issue of an impending war. Sometimes a girl goes out into the street, and asks the first man whom she meets what his (Christian) name is; her husband will bear the same name. Sometimes she listens at the window of some neighbour's house; the mirthful or melancholy tone of the conversation she overhears serves to give her an idea of what will be the nature of her married life. Sometimes "a despairing maiden" takes a table into an empty room, lays a cloth on it, and prepares it as for a meal—only neither a knife nor a fork must appear upon it. Then she shuts herself up in the room alone, and calls to her destined husband to come and sup with her. According to tradition he may perhaps appear, heralded by the sound of the night-wind beneath the window, or by a tapping on the window pane or the door, or even "by an evil odour." When he comes the girl must keep her seat, and hold her peace until he sits down at the table. Then she asks his name, which he gives, taking something out of his pocket the while. She is then to utter certain words, on hearing which he will vanish, leaving behind him whatever it was he had brought in his pocket. Unmarried ladies of a mature age will sometimes go down to a frozen river by night, and sit there beside a hole in the ice, straining their eyes and ears for prophetic sights and sounds. She who is going to be married within the year will see her destined husband in the water; she who hears a single thump beneath the surface will remain unwedded. Such are the uses to which these "guesses" are now turned, but in olden times they seem to have referred to other subjects, and especially to the weather which the coming year was likely to bring with it. At the season when the birth, or the renewed life, of the Sun was being celebrated, thoughts of the harvest which the next summer was to ripen would necessarily arise, and to them may have been originally due the song sung on those Christmas evenings, beginning—

Glory to God in heaven, Glory!

This song is one of the most prominent among the *Kolyadki*, for with it always commences the singing of what are called the *Podblyudnuiya* Songs [3]. At the Christmas festival a table is covered with a cloth, and on it is set a dish or bowl (*blyudo*) containing water. The young people drop rings or other trinkets into the dish, which is afterwards covered with a cloth, and then the *Podblyudnuiya* Songs commence. At the end of each song one of the trinkets is drawn at random, and its owner deduces an omen from the nature of the words which have just been sung. The *Sláva*, or "Glory" Song, is as follows:—

[3] Snegiref, R. P. P. III. 8. Tereshchenko (VII. 150) says that the songs derived their name from the fact of their being sung at table during a meal.

Glory to God in Heaven, *Glory!*
To our Lord on this Earth, *Glory!*
May our Lord never grow old, *Glory!*
May his bright robes never be spoiled, *Glory!*
May his good steeds never be worn out, *Glory!*
May his trusty servants never falter, *Glory!*
May the Right throughout Russia, *Glory!*
Be fairer than the bright Sun, *Glory!*
May the Tsar's golden treasury, *Glory!*
Be for ever full to the brim, *Glory!*
May the great rivers, *Glory!*
Bear their renown to the sea, *Glory!*
The little streams to the mill, *Glory!*
But this song we sing to the Corn, *Glory!*
To the Corn we sing, the Corn we honour, *Glory!*
For the old folks to enjoy, *Glory!*
For the good folks to hear, *Glory*[4] *!*

The word translated "Lord" in the second line is *Gosudar'*, the term generally applied to the Emperor, but it seems to be used here in the sense of head of the family, lord of the household. Of the other songs of the same class there are many which are very hard to understand. The most intelligible are generally those which refer to marriage, such as the following, in which the divine blacksmith (*Kuznets*) is introduced—the Slavonic Vulcan, who became transformed in Christian times into the double saint Kuz'ma-Dem'yan [Cosmas and Demian].

There comes a Smith from the forge, *Glory!*
The Smith carries three hammers, *Glory!*
Smith, Smith, forge me a crown, *Glory!*
Forge me a crown both golden and new, *Glory!*

[4] Sakharof, I. iii. 11.

Forge from the remnants a golden ring, *Glory!*
And from the chips a pin, *Glory!*
In that crown will I be wedded, *Glory!*
With that ring will I be betrothed, *Glory!*
With that pin will I fasten the nuptial kerchief,
 Glory[5]*!*

One of the legends about Kuz'ma-Dem'yan is, that once, when he had just made a plough, a great snake tried to attack him. But no sooner had it licked a hole through the iron door of the smithy than the Saint seized it by the tongue with his pincers—as firmly as St. Dunstan seized the devil—harnessed it to the plough, and forced it to plough up the land "from sea to sea." The snake vainly prayed for a draught of water from the Dnieper; the Saint drove it till it came to the Black Sea. That sea it drank half dry, and then it burst[6].

Some of the songs sung at this time have evidently come from the regions inhabited by the South Slavonians, as, for instance, those of which the refrain is,—

O vineyard, green and red!

or the following, in which the name of the man is as foreign as that of the river,—

By the Danube, by the river,
On the steep bank,
There lies an untuned lute, *Kolyada!*
Who shall tune the lute? *Kolyada!*
Zenzevei Andryeyanovich
Shall tune the lute, *Kolyada!*
Zenzevei is away from home;

[5] Sakharof, I. iii. 12.   [6] Afanasief, P. V. S. I. 561.

He has gone to T'sargrad
To settle questions, to arrange agreements,
Kolyada⁷ !

Among the games in vogue at this season by far the most interesting is that called "The Burial of the Gold." A number of girls form a circle, and pass from hand to hand a gold ring, which a girl who stands inside the circle tries to detect. Meanwhile they sing in chorus the following verses :—

> See here, gold I bury, I bury;
> Silver pure I bury, I bury;
> In the rooms, the rooms of my father,
> Rooms so high, so high of my mother.
> Guess, O maiden, find out pretty one,
> Whose hand is holding
> The wings of the serpent—

The girl in the middle replies,—

> Gladly would I have guessed,
> Had I but known, or had seen,—
> Crossing over the plain,
> Plaiting the ruddy brown hair,
> Weaving with silk in and out
> Interlacing with gold.
> O my friends,—O dear companions
> Tell the truth, do not conceal it,
> Give, oh give me back my gold!
> My mother will beat me
> For three days, for four:
> With three rods of gold,
> With a fourth rod of pearl [8].

---

[7] Sakharof, I. iii. 17.

[8] Sakharof, I. iii. 21. There are many variants of the song, but they do not differ materially.

The chorus breaks in, singing,—
The ring has fallen, has fallen,
Among the guelders and raspberries,
Among the black currants.
. . . .
Disappeared has our gold,
Hidden amid the mere dust,
Grown all over with moss.

All this is somewhat hard to comprehend, but the explanation given by the mythologists is, that the golden ring represents the sun, hidden away and, as it were, buried by wintry storms and clouds, and that this game—the counterpart of "hunt the slipper," and many other recreations of the same kind—is in reality an ancient rite. It is evidently connected with the custom prevalent among so many nations, our own included, of hiding a ring (or a coin, or a bean) in a loaf or cake, about the time of the New Year.

According to rustic tradition, all sorts of hidden treasures are revealed at this period of the year. During the "holy evenings" between the Nativity and the Epiphany the new-born Divinity comes down from heaven and wanders about on earth, wherefore every sort of labour during that period is held to be a sin. At midnight, on the eve of each of those festivals, the heavenly doors are thrown open; the radiant realms of Paradise in which the Sun dwells, disclose their treasures; the waters of springs and rivers become animated, turn into wine, and receive a healing efficacy; the trees put forth blossoms, and golden fruits ripen upon their boughs [9].

[9] Afanasief, P. V. S. III. 741.

Ideas of this kind were common to the Teutons and to the Slaves, and a certain mysterious being, about whom very little is known, but in whose honour songs are still sung in Russia at Christmastide, seems to have had several points in common with one of the divinities known to German mythology. In the *Kolyadki* mention is made of a goddess called *Kolyada*, although no such being appears in the recognized list of old Slavonic deities, and her existence seems to have been accepted only by the popular belief, not by any properly constituted religious authorities. Similar mention is made in another set of songs, called *Ovsénevuiya*—of another divine being, also seeming to represent the Sun, to whom is given the name of Ovsén[1]. He is represented as a "good youth," who appears together with the New Year, making the way clear for it, and bringing from Paradise rich gifts of fruitfulness, which he distributes among mortals according to divine decrees. On New Year's Eve boys go about from house to house, scattering grain of different kinds, but chiefly oats, and singing *Ovsénevuiya Pyesni*, such as the following:—

> In the forest, in the pine-forest,
> There stood a pine-tree,
> Green and shaggy.
>   Oh, Ovsén! Oh, Ovsén!

---

[1] This name (pronounced *avsén*) is derived by some writers from *Oves* (pronounced *av-yós*), oats, and connected by others with *Vesná*, Spring. The Feast of Ovsén was originally on the first of March.

>   The Boyars came,
>   Cut down the pine,
>   Sawed it into planks,
>   Built a bridge,
>   Covered it with cloth,
>   Fastened it with nails.
>   Oh, Ovsén! Oh, Ovsén!
>   Who, who will go
>   Along that bridge?
>   Ovsén will go there,
>   And the New Year,
>   Oh, Ovsén! oh, Ovsén[2]!

Another songs asks,—

>   "On what will he come?"
>   "On a dusky swine."
>   "What will he chase?"
>   "A brisk little pig."

This peculiarity seems to link Ovsén with Fro or Freyr, the Teutonic sun-god, who possessed a boar, Gullinborsti, whose golden fell made the night as clear as the day, whose speed was that of a horse, and who drew the car of the god[3]. In reference, probably, to this idea, pigs' trotters, and the like, used to be offered as a sacrifice to the gods at the beginning of a New Year, and the custom still prevails in Russia of preferring such dishes at that time, and giving them away as presents.

The New Year, it may be as well to remark, began in olden times with the month of March, and this method of computation remained in force till A.D. 1348.

---

[2] Snegiref, R. P. P. II. 111.   [3] Grimm, D. M. 194.

The commencement of the New Year was then shifted to the 1st of September, an arrangement which held good till the year 1700, when it was made to begin with the 1st of January [4].

In some of the songs the name *Ovsén*, or *Govsén*, as it is sometimes written, occurs as a refrain under the form of *Tausen*. Here is one, of a later date than those which have already been quoted, in which the names of Kolyada and Ovsén are coupled.

> Peter is getting ready to go to the Horde,
> Koleda Tausen!
> Alexander fawns at his feet,
> Koleda Tausen!
> Do not go to the Horde, do not serve the king.
> Serve thou the White Tsar.
> Without thee surely can I not
> Eat bread and salt,
> Nor sleep upon a bed.
> Now must I sleep in sorrow
> On the bare boards,
> On the warm stove,
> On the ninth brick.
> Koleda Tausen [5]!

Among the many strange customs preserved among the people is a very singular one, kept up by the peasants of White-Russia, by which they express in a symbolical form the idea that the New Year brings with it to each man his allotted share of weal and woe. On New Year's Eve they lead about from

---

[4] Tereshchenko, VII. 90.
[5] Tereshchenko, VII. 123. The refrain occurs in the original at the end of almost every line.

house to house two youths. One of them, called the Rich Kolyada, is dressed in new and holiday attire, and wears on his head a wreath made of ears of rye; the other, whom they call the Poor Kolyada, wears a ragged suit and a wreath made of threshed-out straw. When they come to a cottage they wrap up each of the two youths in long coverings, and tell the owner of the house to choose one of them. If his choice falls upon the Rich Kolyada, a song is sung by his visitors, which states that a good harvest awaits him, and plenty of money; but if he chooses the Poor Kolyada, then the singers warn him that he must expect poverty and death.

In Little-Russia, on the festival of the New Year, a number of corn sheaves are piled upon a table, and in the midst of them is set a large pie. The father of the family takes his seat behind them, and asks his children if they can see him. "We cannot see you," they reply. On which he proceeds to express what seems to be a hope that the corn will grow so high in his fields that he may be invisible to his children when he walks there in harvest-time. A similar custom is said by German writers of about the twelfth century to have prevailed in their times among the Baltic Slavonians, only in that case it was a priest who hid himself behind a pile of sheaves[6].

Another custom, most religiously preserved, is the preparing of *Kásha*—a favourite Russian dish made of stewed grain—for the New Year. Kásha in this

[6] Orest Miller, *Opuit*, etc. I. 52.

case is used as a general expression for corn, or for the coming harvest, and is spoken of as a living person, as some great lady who is met on the threshold by boyars and princes, and who comes attended by two other personages of importance, " Honourable Oats," and " Golden Barley." Here is one of the formulas recited during the cooking of the New Year's Kásha. " They sowed Buckwheat, they let it shoot up all the summer long. Both fair and rosy did our Buckwheat grow up. They called, they invited our Buckwheat to visit Tsargrad, to feast at the princely banquet. Off set Buckwheat to visit Tsargrad, with Princes, with Boyars, with Honourable Oats, with Golden Barley. They awaited Buckwheat, they tarried till its coming at the Stone Gates. Princes and Boyars met Buckwheat, they set Buckwheat at the oaken table to feast. As a guest has our Buckwheat come unto us [7].

The singers of the songs about Ovsén receive presents, standing in lieu of the old contributions towards a sacrifice to the Gods, for which they ask in some such terms as

" Give us a pig for Vasíly's Eve."

The first day of the New Year being consecrated to the memory of St. Basil the Great, the previous evening bears the name of Basil's or Vasíly's Eve. In one of the Little-Russian songs it is said that " Ilya comes on Vasíly's Day," i.e. on Basil's or New Year's Day comes the Sun-god or the Thunder-

[7] O. Miller, *Chrest.* I. 5.

bearer, originally Perun, who, under Christian influences, became Elijah, or Ilya.

> Ilya comes
> On Vasíly's Day.
> He holds a whip
> Of iron wire
> And another of tin.
> Hither he waves,
> Thither he waves—
> Corn grows [8].

An idea which is intended to be conveyed by the custom of scattering seeds which is still kept up by the singers of songs to Ovsén.

The *Svyatki*—the Christmas or New Year festivities — come to an end with the Feast of the Epiphany, on the eve of which a curious custom is observed. After dark, on the 4th of January, the girls go out into the open air, and address this prayer to the stars :—

> O Stars, Stars,
> Dear little Stars!
> All ye, O Stars,
> Are the fair children
> Ruddy and white,
> Of one mother.
> Send forth through the christened world
> Proposers of marriages [9].

On the feast of the Epiphany, in some places, a number of sheaves of various kinds of corn are heaped

---

[8] Tereshchenko, VII. 109.

[9] The *Svat* (or *Svakha*) is the man (or woman) who proposes or arranges a marriage in Russia.

up in the courtyards after the morning service is over, the cattle are driven up to them, and the corn and the animals are sprinkled with holy water. This appears to be a relic of a festival observed in old times, when the cattle were first driven out afield after the winter was past, and seems to speak of a warmer clime as its birthplace, for sprinkling with water is a somewhat unseasonable custom at a time when every spring or stream is frozen. Not less inopportune is the custom which prevails in some parts of bathing on the occasion of "Meeting the Spring," the bath often having to be taken in one of the holes in the ice kept open for the purpose of procuring water during the frosty season. Either the custom has been imported from a southern land, or the date of the festival has been altered.

Such an alteration has been brought about in some cases by the Church, for the introducers of Christianity into Russia found that certain festivals, which the people had observed from time immemorial, occurred during the season of Lent. As the Clergy objected to this, but were not powerful enough utterly to abolish the feasts, they transferred them to the week preceding Lent—the *Máslyanitsa*, or "Butter-week," [*Máslo* = oil or butter] answering to the Carnival of Western Europe.

The songs appropriate to this season have almost entirely disappeared, but some idea of their nature may be obtained by a study of the customs appertaining to it, the songs and customs having always been closely connected with each other. In some parts of Russia a large sledge, drawn by twelve horses, is driven about at this time, followed by other sledges containing singers and musicians. On the principal sledge is placed a pillar with a wheel on the top, and on the wheel sits a man dressed in a peculiar style, with bells and cymbals attached to his clothes, and holding in his hands bread and a bottle of spirits. He probably represents the Sun, of which a wheel was so well known an emblem, and he seems to be a male counterpart of the girl who, as the representative of Kolyada, used to be driven about in a similar manner on the days immediately following the winter solstice.

In other places a sort of huge "Christmas Tree" is carried round, an emblem of summer fruitfulness. In Archangel an ox, resembling the French *bœuf gras*, occupies the place of honour on the sledge; and in Siberia a ship, with sails spread, conveying a figure representing "Lady Maslyanitsa," and a bear[1]. As in mythical speech a ship generally means a cloud, fraught with showers destined to enrich the earth, and the bear is one of the familiar emblems of the thunder-god, the Siberian equipage is looked upon by the mythologists as a type of the storm-compelling deity, who was supposed to make his power specially felt about the time of the vernal equinox, or an emblem of the productive powers of nature, manifesting themselves at springtide amid wind and thunder and rain.

---

[1] Snegiref, R. P. P. II. 132.

In some parts of Russia the end or death of winter is celebrated on the last day of the "Butter-week," by the burning of "the Straw Mujik"—a heap of straw, to which each of the participators in the ceremony contributes his portion. The same custom prevails in Bulgaria, accompanied by dancing round the bonfire, the firing of guns and pistols, and the singing of songs in honour of Lado or Lada, the peculiar deity of Spring. There, also, during the whole week, the children amuse themselves by shooting with bows and arrows, a custom which has descended to them from their remote ancestors, and which is supposed, by some imaginative writers, to have referred in olden times to the victory obtained by the sun-beams—the arrows of the far-darting Apollo—over the forces of cold and darkness.

In every Slavonic country, indeed, there are to be found, at this period of the year, traces of olden rites intended to typify the death of Winter and the birth of Spring or Summer. Some of them have been preserved in customs almost identical with those still kept up by various Latin or Teutonic peoples; as, for instance, the destruction of a figure representing Winter or Death. In Poland a puppet, made of hemp and straw, is flung into a pond or swamp, with the words "The Devil take thee!" Then the participators in the deed scamper home, and if one of them stumbles on the way and falls, it is believed that he will be sure to die within the year. In Upper Lusatia the figure of Death is constructed of straw and rags, and fastened to the end of a long pole, to be pelted with sticks and stones. Whoever knocks it off the pole is certain to live through the year. Afterwards the figure is either thrown into water, or taken to the boundary of the village lands and flung across it: its bearers then return home carrying green boughs or an entire tree, emblems of the springtide life which has taken the place of banished death. Sometimes the figure is dressed in white, as if in a shroud, and in one hand is placed a besom, in token of winter's sweeping storms, and in the other a sickle—one of the characteristic signs of the goddess whom the Old Slavonians represented as reaping the living harvest of the world. In Slavonia the figure is thumped with bludgeons, and then torn in twain, just as a somewhat similar puppet is treated in the middle of Lent in Spain and Italy. In Little-Russia a female figure is carried about, while springtide songs are being sung, and then is set on fire, the villagers singing, while it burns, joyous invocations to the Spring.

In many parts of Russia the 1st of March is the day still set apart in deference to old customs for the reception of the Spring. In the early morning the women and children go out to the highest places they can find, mounting the hills, if there are any in their neighbourhood, or climbing on the roofs of barns and other buildings, if the country around is utterly flat, and singing some of the numerous *Vesnyanki*,

Vesenniya Pyesni, songs appropriate to *Vesná*, the vernal season, such as,

> Spring, beautiful Spring!
> Come, O Spring, with joy,
> With great goodness:
> With tall flax,
> With deep roots,
> With abundant corn!

In some places the girls go into water up to the girdle, or, if the streams are still frozen over, take hands round a hole in the ice, and dance, and sing,—

> O healthful springtide water,
> To us also give health!

And sometimes sick persons are brought down to the banks of a river, and sprinkled with water, in the hope that it may restore them to health. In other places a similar custom prevails at a later period of the year, on the Thursday in Holy Week, or on the 1st of May. In the Government of Tula, for instance, the "Invocation of the Spring" commences with the first week after Easter. Before sunset the young people of a village go to the top of the nearest hill, turn towards the east, silently repeat a prayer, and then begin the circling dance and song of the Khorovod. The principal singer, holding a loaf in one hand, and an egg painted red in the other, begins

> "Beautiful Spring!
> On what hast thou come?
> On what hast thou ridden?"
> "On a plough,
> On a harrow."

Afterwards they all commence one of the choral songs :—

All the maidens are in the street!
All the fair maidens in the broad street;
One maiden is not there.
She sits in the upper room,
She embroiders a kerchief with gold,
She fastens a favour on a bridle.
Ah, a great sorrow!
By whom shall it be obtained?
It shall be obtained by my destined husband[2].

On March 9, the day on which the larks are supposed to arrive, the rustics make clay images of those birds, smear them with honey and tip their heads with tinsel, and then carry them about singing songs to Spring, or to Lada, the vernal goddess of love and fertility. The peasants have a springtide calendar of their own, according to which—on the 1st of March [o. s.] the *Baibak*, or Steppe Marmot, awakes from its winter's sleep, comes out of its hole, and begins to utter its whistling cry. On the 4th arrives the Rook, and on the 9th the Lark. On the 17th the ice on the rivers becomes so rotten that, according to a popular expression, "A Pike can send its tail through it." On the 25th the Swallow comes flying from Paradise, and brings with it warmth to the earth. On the 5th of April the Crickets bestir themselves; and on the 12th the Bear comes out of the den in which he has slept away the winter.

[2] Tereshchenko, v. 11.

Like the Greeks, the Romans, and the Teutons[3], the Old Slavonians seem to have greeted with special joy the return of the swallow, "the bird of God," as it is called in Ruthenia, "the Virgin Mary's bird," as the Bohemians name it, whose early arrival foretells an abundant harvest, whose presence keeps off fire and lightning, and the robbing of whose nest brings down terrible evils on the head of the robber, or at least brings out freckles on his face.

The cuckoo, also, is regarded with much respect in Slavonic lands. In the Old Polish Chronicle of Prokosz, quoted by Jacob Grimm in the *Deutsche Mythologie* (p. 543), it is stated that the people believed that the God Zywie, the Lord of Life, used to transform himself into a cuckoo, in order to address the faithful with ominous voice. This deity is the male counterpart of Jiva, the Slavonian Goddess of the Spring, whose name is a contracted form of Jivana, in Polish Ziewonia, that is, "the giver of life" (*jizn'*). Many of the other stories about the cuckoo and the swallow, mentioned by Mr. Kelly in his "Curiosities of Indo-European Tradition and Folk-lore[4]," are known to the Russian peasants.

The name of the cuckoo is associated with a singular custom of great antiquity. A few weeks after Easter—generally during the seventh week, the time of the Semik festival—the village women and girls meet together at some spot in the woods, and there fasten to a bough a figure made of shreds and flowers,

---

[3] Grimm, D. M. 723.
[4] Pages 97—101. See also Grimm, D. M. 1088.

and supposed to represent a cuckoo, and underneath it they hang the little pectoral crosses which all Russians bear. Sometimes, instead of this, they pull up by the roots the plant called "cuckoo-grass" (*orchis latifolia*), dress it up in a shift, and then bury it in the earth underneath two semicircles of wood [4] set crossways, which they cover with handkerchiefs, and on which they hang crosses. In the Orel and Tula Governments they place a small cross on the figure of the cuckoo itself, and sing,

> Gossips, darlings! (*kumushki, golubushki*) [5]
> Become gossips, love each other, make presents to each other!

This is called the "Christening of the Cuckoos" (*kreshchenie kukushëk*). When two girls have kissed each other under the decorated arch, and have exchanged crosses, they become "Gossips" for life, as intimately connected as if, at the christening of a child, they had become attached to each other by the spiritual ties of co-godmothership. On the Semik festival the villagers choose two young birch-trees in a wood, bend them down, and fasten their branches together into a circle, which they adorn with ribbons, handkerchiefs, and the like. Above this circle they place the figure of a cuckoo, or the dressed-up cuckoo-

---

[4] *Dugi.* The arch springing from the shafts of a Russian cart or carriage, above the head of the draught-horse, is called a *Duga*.

[5] The word *Kuma*, dim. *Kumushka*, is the French *Commère*, Scotch "Cummer," our own "Gossip," originally a connexion by common godmothership.

grass, and from the sides they hang crosses. Two girls then walk in different directions round the birch-trees, so as to meet at the leafy circle, through which they kiss each other three times, and give each other a yellow egg. Meantime the other women sing in chorus,

> O spotted cuckoo!
> To whom art thou a gossip?
> We will become gossips, O kumushka,
> We will become gossips, O golubushka,
> So that we may never be at variance.

They then exchange crosses, and divide the "Cuckoo" into two parts, one of which each of them keeps in memory of the occasion. Afterwards the whole party prepare and eat omelettes, and finish the day with dance and song. In the Orel Government, according to Tereshchenko, it is, or used to be, customary for men also to enter into the state of mutual cuckoo-gossipry[7].

The time set apart for the "Christening of the Cuckoos" coincides with that in which the souls of little children who have died unchristened appear under the form of small Rusalkas[8] seeking for the baptism which is necessary for their salvation. Coupling this fact with that of the soul being constantly represented as a bird, and remarking that the cuckoo is a common type in Russia of the orphan state, Afanasief suggests that the "Christening of the Cuckoos" ought, perhaps, to be regarded as a sym-

---

[7] Afanasief, P. V. S. III. 226—228. Tereshchenko, v. 41.
[8] See *supra*, chap. II. p. 144.

bolical rite having reference to the christening of such children as have died unbaptized, and are therefore obliged to fly wailing through the air. The baptismal idea must have originated during the Christian period of Russian history—perhaps about the time when, under the rule of Yaroslaf, the remains of the sons of Svyatoslaf, the heathen princes Yaropolk and Oleg, were exhumed for the purpose of being baptized, after which they were interred within a church; but the *kumovstvo*, or gossipship, is, in all probability, nothing more than a slightly altered form of the old *pobratimstvo*, or mutual brotherhood by adoption. To this day the Servians keep up a custom very similar to the Russian Cuckoo-Christening, held at Eastertide in memory of the dead, with kissings through willow circlets, and exchanges of red eggs, after which the men are called *Pobrati*, "adopted-brothers," and the girls "friends [9]."

In Lithuania, says Tereshchenko, at Eastertide, the young people of each village meet within some cottage. There they first sing various songs, and then they perform the cuckoo dance. A girl, whose eyes are bandaged, sits on a chair, round which the rest of the party dance in a circle. After each round the men come up to her, and taking her in turn by the hand, sing,

Queen Cuckoo—kuku, kuku!
She replies,
I am thine, brother—kuku, kuku!

[9] Afanasief, P. V. S. III. 229.

Eventually she uncovers her eyes, leaves her seat, and chooses three of the young men as her partners in the dance. Before parting she gives each of them a sash worked by her own hands, and they make her a present in return. Thenceforward she calls them her brothers, and they call her their sister. This custom is supposed to be founded upon the popular tradition of a sister who, in the olden days, felt so keenly the loss of her three brothers, who all fell in one battle, that she left her father's home and wandered about the forest weeping bitterly, until a compassionate deity turned her into a cuckoo. In one district the Lithuanian girls still sing,—

> Sister dear,
> Mottled Cuckoo,
> Thou who feedest
> The horses of thy brothers;
> Thou who spinnest
> Silken threads;
> Say, O Cuckoo,
> Shall I soon be married?

The length of time during which the girl will have to wait will be signified to her by the number of repetitions of the Cuckoo's cry [1].

Among many of the Roman Catholic Slavonians a feast, originally in honour of the Spring, is celebrated in the middle of Lent, and some traces of it are still to be found among them even in Holy Week, the day before Good Friday, for instance, being known to the Bohemians as *Green* Thursday. Palm Sunday is known

[1] Tereshchenko, v. 45—49.

in Russia as *Verbnoe Voskresenie*, Willow Sunday. The *verba*, or sallow, was made use of at this time of year long before it became likened to the palms or olive branches of Christianity, children and cattle being then, as now, beaten with its boughs, while such songs were probably sung as that which is still to be heard on such occasions in Little-Russia :—

> Be tall, like the willow;
> And healthy, like water;
> And rich, like the soil.

Even on Good Friday itself, in some places, the old pagan practices show signs of life. Before sunrise on that day it is customary for the Bohemians, says Orest Miller[2], to go into their gardens, and there, falling on their knees before a tree, to say,—

"I pray, O green tree, that God may make thee good,"—a formula which has probably been altered, under the influence of Christianity, from a direct prayer to the tree to a prayer for it. And at night they run about the garden, exclaiming,—

"Bud, O trees, bud! or I will flog you."

And on the next day, the Saturday in Holy Week, they shake the trees, while the church-bells are ringing, and go about the garden clashing keys. This they do under the impression that the more noise they make the more fruit will they get.

At Eastertide, according to a belief common to Germans and Slavonians, the Sun is accustomed to

---

[2] *Opuit*, etc. I. 48.

dance in the heavens, and so in Ruthenia the peasants rise before the dawn, and climb high places in order to witness the spectacle. In pagan times the gods were supposed to walk the earth at Springtide, and so the Russian peasant now believes that, from Easter Sunday to Ascension-day, Christ and His Apostles wander about the world, dressed in rags and asking alms. In the Government of Smolensk it is believed that Christ always visits the earth on Thursday in Holy Week, and so, in readiness for the heavenly guest, a particular kind of loaf is prepared in every house. In most of the villages of White-Russia songs are sung at this season in honour of the Virgin, of St. George and St. Nicholas, and of the Prophet Elijah, and eatables, adorned with green boughs, are provided. Among the viands generally figures a roast lamb or sucking-pig, the bones of which are afterwards either scattered about the fields to protect the crops from hail, or are kept in the houses to be burnt, during the time of the summer storms, as a preservative against lightning.

On Easter Eggs, much as is thought of them in Russia, it is unnecessary to dwell here at any length, as they are so well known elsewhere and so much has been written about them. But we may mention the epithet given to the Paschal week in Russia, that of *Svyetlaya*, "bright," one which [unless it is borrowed from the Greek *lampra*] may be derived from those heathen times in which our own ancestors worshipped the Goddess Ostara or Eástre, whose name, suggestive of the East and its brightness, has been preserved by us in that of Easter[3]. In Little-Russia it used to be the custom at Eastertide to celebrate the funeral of a being called Kostrubonko, the deity of the spring. A circle was formed of singers, who moved slowly around a girl who lay on the ground as if dead, and as they went they sang,—

> Dead, dead is our Kostrubonko!
> Dead, dead is our dear one!

until the girl suddenly sprang up, on which the chorus joyfully exclaimed,—

> Come to life, come to life has our Kostrubonko!
> Come to life, come to life has our dear one!

With the first week after Easter commences the festival of the *Krasnaya Gorka*, "the red, or bright little hill," the epithet referring, like the *red* colour of the Easter eggs, to the brightness of the spring, and the name of "little hill" being given to it because it was originally held, or at least inaugurated, on some high place. It lasts from Low Sunday till the end of June, and its chief feature is the *Khorovod*—the circling dance attended by choral song. The chief singer on these occasions is a woman, who holds in her hands a round loaf and a red egg—each an emblem of the Sun. Turning her face towards the east she begins one of the vernal songs, which is then taken up by the chorus, and in many places this is attended or followed by the destruction of the figure of Death, or Winter, to which allusion has already been made.

[3] Grimm, D. M. 268.

Many of the songs are addressed to the Goddess of Love, the presiding genius of the season, or at least have reference to her influence, and in some places it is customary to sing them under the windows of young wedded couples. But the dead also are remembered at this season of the year. The old pagan rites formerly performed in their honour are still kept up in some parts of Russia. The festival called *Rádunitsa*, held at the same time with, or just after, that of the *Krasnaya Gorka*, is chiefly devoted to the memory of the dead. In certain districts the women and girls still take food and drink to the cemeteries, and there "howl" over the graves of their dead friends and relatives. When they have "howled" long enough, they sit down and proceed to eat, drink, and be merry, deeming that the dead can "rejoice" with them. After their meal, the fragments which remain over are thrown to the evil spirits, in order to prevent them from troubling the repose of the dead, and with similar intent their flasks and drinking-cups are emptied over the graves[1]. Then they return home, dress themselves in holiday attire, and go out to the *Krasnaya Gorka*, to commence their songs and the games to which those songs form an accompaniment.

It has already been stated that the greater part of these songs relate exclusively to love, or to other subjects connected with social life, but there are also

---

[1] Tereshchenko, v. 17. For further information on this subject see *infra*, pp. 310—313.

some which may possibly have a mythical signification. In one of these a young man wanders with
uplifted hands in the space enclosed by the circle of
the Khorovod. The chorus sings,—

> Our bright Prince has gone,
> Has gone around his city,
> Has gone around his high city:
> Our bright Prince seeks
> His bright Princess.——
>
> . . . . .
>
> He goes, the Prince goes,
> Goes around the city.
> He cuts, he hews
> With his sword the gates.
> Shall we soon, O bright Prince,
> Find the fair maiden?

At this point the youth stands still, the chorus stops,
and he finishes the song as follows:—

> Wherever I shall find
> The fair princely maiden—
> To that princely maiden
> Will I give a golden ring.

In this dramatic poem, with the leading idea of
which may be compared the "Passage of the King
and Queen" among the Czechs and Servians, or the
German "Maigraf and Maigräfin," Orest Miller,
[*Opuit*, I. 51] sees evident reference to the idea of the
Sun, as a bright Prince, piercing with his beams, as
with a sharp sword, the icy obstacles by which Winter strives to keep him from his fair bride the Earth.

The most widely spread of the choral games belonging to the *Krasnaya Gorka* festival is that called

"The Sowing of the Millet," of which an account will be given in the chapter devoted to songs relating to marriage[5]. Of the rest we have already given several examples in the first chapter[6]. In the "Meeting," or "Coming together" (*Skhodbishche*), a number of girls go out into the meadows, where they are met by "the arrived ones"—the game belonging to the season at which the young men arrive in the villages after their winter sojourn in the towns. A circle of dancers is formed, in the middle of which a young couple take their places, and then the others move round them singing,—

> From one street comes a youth,
> From another comes a fair maiden;
> Close have they drawn near to each other,
> Low have they bent in greeting.
> Then thus speaks the brave youth:
> "Farest thou well, O beauteous maiden?"
> Smilingly the maiden answers,
> "Well do I fare, dear friend;
> How dost thou fare alone without me?
> Long is it since I have seen thee,
> Since that time when we two parted."

In the game called *Pleten'*, a word meaning a wattled fence, the dancers stand up in couples, and, with hands locked together after the manner of a fence, form in line. Their leader begins the following song:—

> Be twined together, O fence, be twined together!
> And do thou be coiled up, O golden pipe!
> Be folded up, O rustling damask!

[5] See *infra*, p. 283.   [6] See pp. 8—10.

> From behind the hills the maiden has driven out
> the ducks.
> Come away home, duckie!
> Come away home, gray one! . . .

When the chorus comes to an end the leading couple lift up on high their joined hands. Then, as in our own country-dance, the other couples pass under the arch so formed, while the chorus sings,—

> Untwine, O fence, untwine!
> Uncoil, O golden pipe!
> Unfold, O rustling damask!

The game called DON IVANOVICH is associated with an old popular tradition, according to which the rivers Don and Shat are the offspring of Lake Iván. Those who take part in it form a circle, and move around the leader, who is supposed to represent Don Ivánovich. As they go they sing a song, the changes in which he follows with suitable movements of his limbs. It begins—

> Now has our youth
> Come along the street to the end.
>   Ah! Don, our Don,
>   Don Iván's son!
> Ah! they have called the youth,
> They have called the bold one.
>   Ah! Don, *etc.*
> To feast at the banquet,
> To sit at the gathering,
> To take part in the games,
>   Ah! Don, *etc.*

Eventually the song and game resolve themselves into those already described (at p. 8), under the title of "The Murman Cap."

Here is one more of the songs sung at this time of year—a song specially worthy of notice on account of the hostile expressions it contains with respect to Byzantium, a city which, after the conversion of the Slavonians to Christianity, acquired a sacred character in their eyes.

> I will go up, I will go up,
> I will go up to Tsar-gorod.
> I will shatter, I will shatter,
> With my lance will I shatter the wall!
> I will roll away, I will roll away,
> A barrel of treasure will I roll away!
> I will give, I will give it
> To my harsh father-in-law!
> Be thou kind, be thou kind,
> Like unto my own father dear!
>
> . . . .
>
> I will bring out, I will bring out,
> A pelisse of fox's skin will I bring out!
> I will give, I will give it
> To my harsh mother-in-law!
> Be thou kind, be thou kind,—
> Like unto my own mother dear[7]!

In some of the songs which are now sung by the children only, but which used not to be confined to them alone, the rains which play so important a part at this season of the year are either begged to come, or entreated to go away. When the first spring shower falls the children thus address it,—

> Shower, shower!
> Get thyself ready to be seen.
> Shower, let thyself go well.
>
> . . . .

[7] Snegiref, R. P. P. III. 37—46.

> Pour, O rain,
> Over the grandmother's rye,
> Over the grandfather's wheat,
> Over the girls' flax,
> Pour in bucketsful.
> Rain, rain, let thyself go,
> Stronger, quicker,
> Warm us young ones.

And they make it promises, saying,—

> Dear rain, dear rain,
> I will cook thee some borshch [soup],
> I will put it on an oak.
> Three pigeons will come flying,
> They will take thee on their wings,
> Will bear thee to a foreign land.

The spring rain was supposed to produce a beneficial effect even upon the human body, and therefore it was customary to wash in it. Its efficacy was increased if it came attended by thunder. "St. Peter [evidently Perun's successor] lifts up his voice and gives us wine, that we may all drink our fill," says a Bohemian song. And in order to obtain that celestial wine from the clouds, not only were songs sung, but certain rites were observed.

Of such a kind are the well-known rites of Dodola kept up among the Servians to the present day. During a drought a girl, literally "in verdure clad," something like our own "Jack in the Green," but having no covering beyond one of leaves and flowers, is conducted through the village, her companions singing meanwhile " Dodola Songs," and afterwards the women pour water over her, she dancing all the time, and turning round and round. The people believe that by this means there will be extorted from the "heavenly women"—the clouds—the rain for which thirsts the earth, as represented by the green-clad maiden Dodola. The songs which are employed upon this occasion begin with a prayer for rain, after which they say,—

"We pass through the village, and the clouds across the sky. We go quicker, and the clouds go quicker, but the clouds have overtaken us, and have bedewed the fields." And again, "We go through the village, and the clouds across the sky, and see, a ring drops from the clouds!"

A custom exists in Russia of catching rain that falls during a thunder-storm in a basin, at the bottom of which rings have been placed; in the Riazan Government, water that has been dropped through a wedding-ring is supposed to have certain merits as a lotion; and at a Little-Russian marriage the bride is bound to give the bridegroom to drink from a cup of wine in which a ring has been put. In Dalmatia the same custom is kept up as in Servia, only instead of a girl called Dodola, it is a young unmarried man who is dressed up, and who dances and has water poured over him. He is called *Prpats*, and his companions, who are young bachelors like himself, bear the name *Prporushe*. In Bulgaria the same part is played by a girl, who must be just fifteen years old, and who is called *Preperuga* or *Peperuga*, and among the modern Greeks by a child of from eight to ten years old, who is called *Purpirouna*. In Wallachia the name has become Papeluga, as appears from the song which the children sing in time of drought—"Papeluga! Go into heaven, open the gates, and send rain from on high, that the corn may grow well!" In different parts of Germany similar customs used to prevail, and Jacob Grimm [D. M. 560—562] thinks that the Dodola and Purpirouna were originally identical with the Bavarian *Wasservogel* and the Austrian *Pfingstkönig*, whom he connects with old rain-preserving rites, although the custom of covering them with foliage, and then flinging them into a brook, has now degenerated into a mere practical joke played off upon the lazy.

The name of Dodola is by some philologists derived from *doït'* = to give milk, Dodola being looked upon as a bountiful mother, a type of teeming nature. Others connect it with Did-Lado, from the Lithuanian *Didis* = great, and Lado, the Slavonic Genius of the spring. From the mention of a ring made in the Dodola songs, and in others referring to storm and rain, it is supposed that a golden ring, in mythical language, is to be taken as a representation of the lightning's heavenly gold.

The 23rd of April is consecrated to St. George of Cappadocia, and is known as the *Yurief Den* (or *Yegorief Den*) *Vesenny*, i.e. Yury's (or Yegóry's) Day in the spring. On it a festival is celebrated of a national, as well as of an ecclesiastical character, and to it are devoted a number of special songs, which derive from it the name of *Yegoriefskiya Pyesni*. Their mythical character is, in many cases, apparent enough, serving to prove that the Christian hero, St. George, has merely taken the place of some old deity, light-bringing or thunder-compelling, who used to be honoured at this time of year in heathen days. It is not a slayer of dragons and protector of princesses who appears in these songs, but a patron of farmers and herdsmen, who preserves cattle from harm, and on whose day, therefore, the flocks and herds are, for the first time after the winter, sent out into the open fields. "What the wolf holds in its teeth, that Yegory has given," says a proverb, which shows how completely he is supposed to rule over the fold and the stall. Here is one of the songs :—

> We have gone around the field,
> We have called Yegory . . . .
> "O thou, our brave Yegory,
> Save our cattle,
> In the field, and beyond the field,
> In the forest, and beyond the forest,
> Under the bright moon,
> Under the red sun,
> From the rapacious wolf,
> From the cruel bear,
> From the cunning beast."

In Bulgaria a regular sacrifice is said to be still offered up on the occasion, a ram being killed by an old man, while girls spread grass on which the blood of the victims is poured forth. A White-Russian song represents Yegory as opening with golden keys —probably the sunbeams—the soil which has been hard bound all the winter.

Holy Yury, the divine envoy,
Has gone to God,
And having taken the golden keys,
Has unlocked the moist earth,
Having scattered the clinging dew
Over White-Russia and all the world[8].

In Moravia they "meet the Spring" with the following song:—

"Death Week! [The Fourth Sunday in Lent—the time of the expulsion of Death = Winter], what hast thou done with the keys?"
"I gave them to Palm-Sunday."
"Palm-Sunday! what hast thou done with the keys?"
"I gave them to Green Thursday [the day before Good Friday]."
"Green Thursday! what hast thou done with the keys?"
"I gave them to St. George. St. George arose and unlocked the earth, so that the grass grew —the green grass."

In White-Russia it is the custom on St. George's Day to drive the cattle afield through the morning dew, and in Little-Russia and Bulgaria the young people go out early and roll themselves in it.

Besides the springtide *Yurief Den*, there is another St. George's Day in the autumn, or rather winter, on the 26th of November. Upon that day, said a tradition which prevailed in Russia up to the sixteenth century, the people in a certain district by the sea [Lukomorie] used to die—to come to life again upon the corresponding Saint's Day, in April.

[8] Afanasief, P. V. S. II. 402.

Before temporarily giving up the ghost, they were in the habit of placing the wares they had on sale in a certain spot, from which the neighbours who wanted them took them away. The settlement of accounts took place as soon as the owners of the goods came to life again. This legend seems to be closely connected with that which Herodotus found himself unable to believe, of the people who lived beyond the bald-headed and goat-footed races, and who slept away six months of the year at a stretch—a story which Heeren supposed to have referred to the length of the Polar night, and which has also been explained as meaning that there were people who "lived indoors in comparative darkness half the year [9]."

The mythical character of Yegory the Brave becomes very apparent in some of the poems about him which have been preserved among the people by oral tradition. According to them he came into the world a strange child, for his arms up to the elbows were of gold, and his legs up to the knees were of silver, and his head was all of pearl. When the time of his martyrdom came, his pagan foe, King Demianishche, had him shut up in a deep dungeon, and gave orders "that he should not see the white light, nor perceive the red sun, nor hear the sound of bells or of church-singing." So Yegory lay in utter darkness for thirty years. Then "the red sun shone warmly, and there came a thunder-cloud, and the stormy winds arose," and swept away all the bolts

---

[9] See Rawlinson's Herodotus, III. 172.

and bars of the dungeon, so that Yegory was able to come out of it, and once more to see the white light. After that he fought many battles, including one with a fiery serpent, always coming off victorious, and finally he killed the heathen king, from whose veins poured forth such a torrent that Yegory stood up to his knees in blood. All this, says Afanasief, is nothing more than a poetic representation of the struggle which takes place in spring between Perun and the dark storm-clouds, which are crushed beneath his mace, or pierced by the shafts of his lightning. For a time the demon of wintry storms may hide the sun, keeping him, as it were, imprisoned, but the spring comes, the sunlight bursts out again in all its glory, and the thunder-god once more goes forth conquering and to conquer [1].

On the Thursday of the seventh week after Easter is held the feast called Semík (from sem = seven). In heathen times a number of rites were performed, and games were celebrated, during the month of May, in honour of the Goddess of the Spring: after heathenism had given place to Christianity, these games, and some remnants of their accompanying rites, were transferred with altered names to the festivals of Ascension Day and Whitsuntide. And in that way many of them have now become attached to the Semík

---

[1] Afanasief, P. V. S. I. 699—704. It should, however, be stated that the above-mentioned legend about Yegory has been preserved in certain poems, which some critics assert to be of a different origin from that of the songs to which the present chapter is mainly devoted. The question will be discussed on another occasion.

holiday, held upon the Thursday before Trinity Day, or Whit-Sunday. On that day the Russian villagers, and the common people in the towns, go out into the woods, sing songs, weave garlands, and cut down a young birch-tree, which they dress up in woman's clothes, or adorn with many-coloured shreds and ribbons. After that comes a feast, at the end of which they take the dressed-up birch-tree, carry it home to their village with joyful dance and song, and set it up in one of the houses, where it remains as an honoured guest till Whit-Sunday. On the two intervening days they pay visits to the house where their "guest" is; but on the third day, Whit-Sunday, they take her to a stream, and fling her into its waters, throwing their Semík garlands after her.

In the district of Pinsk, on Whit-Monday, the peasant girls choose the handsomest of their number, envelope her in a mass of foliage taken from birch-trees and maples, and—under the name of *Kust* (shrub or bush)—carry her about, just as the Dodola maiden is carried about in Servia. In the Government of Poltava, in Little-Russia, they take round "a poplar," represented by a girl with bright flowers in her hair. In the neighbourhood of Voroneje, at Whitsuntide, it was the custom in old times to construct a small hut in the middle of an oak copse, to adorn it with garlands and flowers and fragrant grasses, and to place inside it a figure made of wood or straw, and dressed up in a male or female holiday attire. To this spot the inhabitants of the neighbourhood would flock together, bringing their provisions with them, and would dance and make merry around the hut.

In these instances the Semík birch-tree, the "bush," the "poplar," and the Whitsuntide puppet, are all representatives of some Deity of the Spring whom the people worshipped in olden days, and whose memory still survives, although "the wearing of the green" has been adopted by the Church, and the birch-trees which once were put to pagan uses are now turned into the ornaments of Christian temples. All over Russia every village and every town is turned, a little before Whit-Sunday, into a sort of garden. Everywhere along the streets the young birch-trees stand in rows, every house and every room is adorned with boughs, even the engines upon the railways are for the time decked with green leaves. On the eve of Whit-Sunday the churches are dressed in green as ours are at Christmas, and the next day the women and children go to the morning service carrying posies, which they preserve during the rest of the year, deeming them a preservative against all sorts of maladies.

In many places, especially in Little-Russia, the young folks go out into the woods on Whit-Sunday, singing in chorus this song, in which there is a strange medley of Christian and heathen designations:—

> Bless, O Trinity,
> O Mother of God!
> We must go into the forest,
> We must weave wreaths,
> Ai Dido, Oi Lado!

We must weave wreaths,
And pluck flowers.

When the wreaths are ready they are exchanged between the youths and the maidens. The girls put them on their heads, the lads adorn their hats with them. In the evening, after the Khorovod games are over, or on the following day, they go to a stream, and throw their wreaths into it, singing the while—

I will go to the river Danube,
I will stand on the steep bank,
I will throw my wreath on the waters:
I will go afar off and see,
Whether sinks, or sinks not,
My wreath in the waters [2]. . . .

If the wreath swims steadily, without running ashore, its late wearer will marry happily and live long; if it circles around one spot, there is reason to fear some misfortune, a broken engagement, or an unrequited love; and its sinking is a very evil omen, foreboding that he or she who wore it will either die soon, or at least go down to the grave unmarried.

The songs which are sung in the Khorovods on these occasions frequently refer to a contest between two apparently mythical personages, and two mythical names are mentioned in them—those of Lado and of Tur. About Tur very little is known, but there seem to be reasonable grounds for identifying him with Perun or with Freyr [3]. Lado, or Did-Lado,

---

[2] Tereshchenko, VI. 169.

[3] See Afanasief, P. V. S. I. 662, 663. The word *tur* (cf. *taurus*) means an aurochs or bison.

as has already been observed, is generally supposed to be the solar deity, or the god of the spring and of love. One of the songs is as follows. A number of girls form a circle and sing,—
> Ah! on the grass, on the green turf,
> Around a great city,
> Strayed a bold youth.

While this is being sung, a girl, who wears a man's hat, walks with an air of pride around the circle. Then another girl, holding a handkerchief in her hand, goes inside the circle, the chorus singing meanwhile,—
> Oi, Tur, the bold youth;
> He from out of the great city.
> Has called the beauteous maiden
> To contend with him on the grass.
> Oi Did, Lado! to contend.

Then the girl with the kerchief comes out and deprives the other of her hat, and pretends to strike her, the chorus singing,—
> The beauteous maiden has come out
> And has overcome the youth;
> Has dropped him on the green turf,
> Oi, Did, Lado! has dropped him.

The conqueror goes away, and the song ends as follows:—
> The brave youth rising up,
> Hid his face in his hands,
> Dropped burning tears.
> His grief he did not dare
> To good people to tell.
> Oi, Tur! Did! Lado! to tell[4].

[4] Snegiref, R. P. P. III. 124.

The contest here described has been explained in various ways. Some commentators think it is the same as that mentioned in a Servian song, in which the Lightning-Maiden struggles with the Thunder-Youth and conquers him. Others, taking Tur to be the solar deity, refer it to the substitution for the daylight of the evening glow or the clear summer night.

Some traces of tree-worship may be found in the song which the girls sing as they go out into the woods to fetch the birch-tree, and to gather flowers for wreaths and garlands.

> Rejoice not, Oaks;
> Rejoice not, green Oaks.
> Not to you go the maidens,
> Not to you do they bring pies,
> Cakes, omelettes.
> Io, Io, Semík and Tróitsa [Trinity]!
> Rejoice, Birch-trees, rejoice green ones! . . .
> To you go the maidens!
> To you they bring pies,
> Cakes, omelettes.

The eatables here mentioned seem to refer to sacrifices offered in olden days to the birch, the tree of the spring. The oak, to which no sacrifice is offered, is the summer tree.

On the banks of the river Metch, near Tula, there stands a circle of stones. These, according to popular belief, were once girls who formed a Khorovod on this spot, and who danced on Whit-Sunday in so furious a manner that they were all thunder-smitten into stone.

In some of these songs reference is made to the bathing of a gaily-attired maiden, to whom is given the name of Kostroma, and sometimes not only the bathing but also the drowning of a "brave youth" is vaguely mentioned. These allusions connect them with the class of songs called *Kupalskiya*, which are sung at Midsummer, and which are evidently rich in mythical purport, though it is often difficult to ascertain their exact meaning, as they have come down to the present day in a very mutilated condition. In popular speech the St. Agrafena [Agrippina], to whom the 23rd of June is dedicated, is surnamed Kupálnitsa, and St. John the Baptist, who is honoured on the 24th, is known as Iván Kupálo. The rites which belong to these two festivals are also kept up on the Feast of All Saints, the first Sunday after Whitsuntide.

The word *Kupálo* has been explained in different ways, some philologists, for instance, connecting it with *kupát'* = to bathe, and others with *kúpa* = a heap—heaps of straw or brushwood being used for the bonfires which in Russia, as in many other parts of Europe, are the chief characteristics of these Midsummer festivals. Professor Buslaef points out the fact that the root *kup* conveys the idea of something white, bright, and also rapid, boiling, as it were, vehement—in Russian *yary*, whence seems to be derived the name of the similar mythical being Yarilo. Jacob Grimm [*Klein. Schrift.* II. 250] compares *kupa* with the German *Haufe*, and the Lithuanian *kaupas*, a heap, *kapas*, a mound, etc.

In some parts of Russia an image of Kupálo is burnt or thrown into a stream on St. John's night. In others no image is used, but fires are lighted and people jump through them themselves, and drive their cattle through them. In Ruthenia the bonfires are lighted by a flame-procured from wood by friction, the operation being performed by the elders of the party, amid the respectful silence of the rest. But as soon as the fire is "churned," the bystanders break forth with joyous songs, and when the bonfires are lit the young people take hands, and spring in couples through the smoke, if not through the flames, and after that the cattle in their turn are driven through it. In Little-Russia a stake is driven into the ground on St. John's Night, wrapped in straw and set on fire. As the flame rises the peasant women throw birch-tree boughs into it, saying,—

"May my flax be as tall as this bough!"

The Poles still keep up the customs which were described by a sixteenth century writer as being so diabolical that "the demons themselves took part in them." According to him the girls were in the habit of offering grass as a sacrifice to evil spirits, after which they wove wreaths out of it with which they adorned their heads, and then they lighted fires and "sang Satanic songs, and danced, and the Devil danced for joy with them, and they prayed to him and magnified him, and forgot God[5]." This picking

[5] Tereshchenko, v. 59.

of herbs and flowers on St. John's Day is common to various Slavonic peoples, as also is the habit of washing in dew on the morning of the festival.

Even at the present day, it is said, heathen rites are secretly observed in some of the remote districts of Russia. However this may be, it is well known that they prevailed in many places until a comparatively recent period, a fact which accounts for the significance attached to these Midsummer festivals in the eyes of the people. Of thoroughly heathenish origin is a custom still kept up on the Eve of St. John. A figure of Kupalo is made of straw, the size sometimes of a boy, sometimes of a man, and is dressed in woman's clothes, with a necklace and a floral crown. Then a tree is felled, and, after being decked with ribbons, is set up on some chosen spot. Near this tree, to which they give the name of Marena [Winter or Death], the straw figure is placed, together with a table, on which stand spirits and viands. Afterwards a bonfire is lit, and the young men and maidens jump over it in couples, carrying the figure with them. On the next day they strip the tree and the figure of their ornaments, and throw them both into a stream.

To equally heathenish times also must be referred the song which the peasants in White-Russia sing at sunrise on St. John's Day:—

> Iván and Márya
> Bathed on the hill:
> Where Iván bathed

> The bank shook;
> Where Márya bathed,
> The grass sprouted.

That is, says Afanasief, [P.V. S. III. 722] Perun and Lada bathed in the dewy springs on the hills of heaven. He shook the earth with his thunderbolts, she made the grass grow in the fields.

Both Kupalo and the similar mythical being called in the songs Yarilo appear to be intended at times for the Sun or the Spring, at times for Perun. According to a Bulgarian tradition, the sun, on St. John's Day, loses its way, and therefore a maiden appears who leads it across the sky, this maiden being the Dawn. The Bulgarians assert, also, that on the same day the sun dances and whirls swords about, that is, it sends forth specially bright and dazzling rays. In Lithuania it is supposed that on that day the Sun, a female being, goes forth from her chamber in a car drawn by three horses—golden, silver, and diamond—to meet her spouse the Moon, and on her way she dances and emits fiery sparks[6]. The Servians assert that the sun stands still three times on St. John's Day, and they account for its apparent pause at the time of the summer solstice by the fear which seizes on it at the thought of its downward career towards winter. The mixture of nuptial and funereal ideas connected with this Midsummer festival gives it a double nature; one set of its rites and songs being joyous, as if to exult

---

[6] Tereshchenko, v. 75.

over a marriage, and the other tragic, as if to lament for a death. In the former case it appears to be a mystical union between the elements of fire and water that is celebrated; in the latter the downward course of the sun towards its wintry grave. It is true that the feast of All Saints generally occurs some weeks before the summer solstice, and therefore it might at first sight seem difficult to explain as solar myths any allusions to decay or death that may be conveyed in its songs and customs, were it not well known that the Church arbitrarily altered the time of many popular festivals, and may therefore in this case have transferred to the week after Whitsuntide what were originally Midsummer ceremonies.

The custom of rolling a blazing wheel on St. John's Day, "to signify that the sun ascends at that time to the summit of his circle, and immediately begins to descend again[7]," common to so many lands, is observed also in some of the Slavonic countries— in Croatia, Carinthia, and Galicia[8]. To the same festival in all probability belonged in olden days the decidedly heathenish rites which in modern times have been celebrated either in the week after Whitsuntide, or on the Sunday after St. Peter's Day, June 29. The Bacchanalian character of those rites made the clergy anxious that they should not be observed

---

[7] Quoted by Kemble from a mediæval MS. See Kelly's "Curiosities of Indo-European Tradition and Folk-lore," p. 58, where a full account is given of similar customs in other countries.

[8] Grimm, *Deutsche Mythologie*, 590.

during the fast preceding that day, and so they have been transferred to a period a little before or after it. They bear the name of "The Funeral of Kostroma," or of Lada or Yarilo, and they evidently symbolize the decay and temporary suspension of the vivifying powers of nature as winter comes on. In the Governments of Penza and Simbirsk the "funeral" used to be represented in the following manner:—A girl was chosen to act the part of Kostroma. Her companions then saluted her with low obeisances, placed her on a piece of wood, and carried her to the bank of a stream. There they bathed her in the waters, while the oldest member of the party made a basket of lime-tree bark, and beat it like a drum. After that they all returned home, to end the day with games and dances. In the Murom districts Kostroma was represented by a figure made for the most part of straw, and dressed in female attire. This was carried to the water's edge by a crowd which divided into two parts, of which one attacked the figure and the other defended it. At last the assailants gained the day, stripped the figure of its dress and ornaments, trod it under foot, and flung into the stream the straw of which it was made. While this act of destruction was going on, the figure's defenders hid their faces in their hands, and seemed to deplore the death of Kostroma.

A similar custom prevails in the Sarátof Government, but the figure which is there escorted to the grave is supposed to represent the Spring. In

Voroneje the people used to meet in an open place, and decide who should represent Yarilo. Whoever was chosen for that purpose was fantastically clad, and had small bells fastened to his dress. Then, holding in his hand a mallet—an ancient emblem of the thunderbolt—he paraded around, dancing, singing, gesticulating; and after him followed a noisy crowd, which eventually divided into two bodies, between which a kind of boxing-match took place. In the town of Kostroma the people chose an old man, and gave him a coffin containing a Priapus-like figure representing Yarilo. This he carried outside the town, being attended on the way by women chanting dirges and expressing by their gestures grief and despair. Out in the fields a grave was dug, and in it the figure was buried amid weeping and wailing, after which games and dances were commenced, calling to mind the funeral games celebrated in old times by the pagan Slavonians. A similar custom used to prevail in Little-Russia, where, before the figure was buried, it was shaken, as if with the hope of awaking the dead Yarilo—the Slavonian representative of Adonis.

Some of the Russian archæologists see in the names Kostroma, Kupalo, and Yarilo, nothing more than the designations of as many summer festivals, and it cannot be denied that those names are of very uncertain derivation—*Kostroma*, for instance, meaning osier twigs, rods, etc., and *Kostér* being a name for certain weeds, such as tares or darnel [Kostër or Kostyór means a pyre]; whence it is supposed that the mythical being may have derived its name, inasmuch as its figure was made of straw mixed with weeds, twigs, etc. The general supposition, however, seems to be that expressed by Afanasief [P. V. S. III. 726], who says that the names conveyed to the popular mind the idea of living beings, similar to mankind, and that they appear to have originated at an exceedingly remote period.

During the night before St. Peter's Day, June 29, the people in some places do not go to bed at all, but spend the hours in games, or in sitting by a fire kindled on a high place and singing songs till the day dawns, and then they anxiously watch the sun as it rises, being under the impression that it dances in the sky on that day as well as on Easter Sunday. As soon as its first rays appear, the leader of the choir begins to sing, and after him all the others take up this song:—

> Oi Lado! Oi Lad! on the Kurgan
> The Nightingale is weaving its nest,
> But the Oriole is unweaving.
> Weave or not at thy will, O Nightingale!
> Thy nest will not be woven,
> Thy young ones will not be bred:
> They will not fly through the oak forest,
> Nor peck the spring wheat.
> Oi Lado! Oi Lado[9].

The 29th of July forms, in the popular calendar, the first autumnal festival. That day, it is generally

[9] Snegiref, R. P. P. IV. 67. *Kurgán* is a non-Slavonic word for a tumulus. The *Ivolga*, or Oriole, being golden-plumaged, may have been classed among the fire-bringing birds.

believed, cannot pass by without thunder. In olden times it was consecrated to Perun, the thunder-compelling deity; since the introduction of Christianity it has been transferred to Ilya, the Thunderer, as the Servians call the Prophet Elijah. But, except among the Bulgarians, there are no special songs devoted to Ilya's Day.

During the harvest-tide many customs of great antiquity are observed, most of which seem originally to have been rites performed in honour of the deities who were supposed to watch over the grain-crops. Corn is a holy thing to Slavonic eyes; they look upon it as "the gift of God." In the Christmas festivities the first song is sung in its honour: the peasant who is going to make a new loaf says, "Lord, grant Thy blessing!" as he takes the flour in hand, and he would consider as a great sin the uttering of "bad language" addressed to any sort of corn, and also the "messing" of bread, or the rolling of pellets made of it. Such conduct God punishes, he thinks, with death and famine. Moreover, if a man while eating bread lets pieces fall to the ground, they are collected by evil spirits, and if the weight of the heap thus formed ever becomes greater than that of the slovenly feeder himself, his soul, after death, will be forfeited to the devil[1]. On the other hand, he who shows fitting respect to his bread, eating it even when it is stale and mouldy, such a one will not be injured

---

[1] Afanasief, P. V. S. III. 763. A number of similar Bohemian traditions are given by Grohmann in his *Aberglauben und Gebräuche aus Böhmen* etc. pp. 102—104.

by the thunder, nor will water drown him, but he will live on, secure from poverty, to a green old age.

With the spring commences the season of field-labour, which is inaugurated by a religious service. Crosses, holy pictures, and banners, round which are twined festoons of green leaves and flowers, are carried in procession to the fields, and the priest blesses the soil, and sprinkles it with holy water, a ceremony which is repeated before the commencement of the hay and corn harvests. At Candlemas each peasant has a wax candle specially consecrated, and this he carefully preserves, in order to bear it to his plot of land at seed-time and harvest. On Lady-Day, and on the day before Good Friday, small loaves are consecrated, which are afterwards placed near, or crumbled up among, the seed-corn. When the sowers go into the fields to sow, they bend low towards the east, the west, and the south, uttering prayers each time, and flinging a handful of corn. Until this ceremony has been performed they do not begin their regular work of sowing.

In the Government of Vladimir there exists a custom called "Leading the Ears of Corn." About Trinity Sunday, when the winter rye is beginning to ear, the fields are solemnly visited by the peasants. The young people of each village meet together and draw up in two lines, linking their arms in such a manner as to form a kind of bridge, along which trips a little girl adorned with ribbons of various hues. The couples past whom she has gone run to the end of the lines and take up their places again, so that the bridge of arms is always renewed until the corn-fields are reached. There the girl jumps down, plucks a handful of ears, runs with them to the village, and throws them down close to the church. On their way to the fields the performers sing,—

> The Ear has come to the corn-field,
> To the white Wheat—
> Be thou produced abundantly
> O Rye with Oats,
> With Wheat, with Buckwheat.

Or,—

> The Ear is going to the young corn,
> To the white Wheat.
> Where the Queen has gone,
> There the Rye is thick.
> Out of the ear a measure,
> Out of the grain a great loaf,
> And of the half-grain a pie.
> Grow, grow,
> Rye and Oats—
> Flourish richly
> Father and Son.

When the crops have ripened, the mistress of each household goes out afield, bearing bread and salt and the Candlemas taper, and begins to reap the harvest. The first sheaf which she gathers is called the *Imyaninnik*[2], and is taken home and set in the place of honour near the holy pictures; afterwards it

---

[2] Imya = name; Imyanínui = name-day, day consecrated to the saint after whom a person is named. Imyanínnik, one who celebrates his name-day.

is threshed separately, and its grain is in part mixed with the next season's seed-corn, in part set aside as a preservative against evils. Its straw is used as a specific against diseases of cattle. In some parts of Little-Russia it is a priest who commences the reaping. At the end of the harvest the reapers go to the fields and collect any ears which may have been left uncut. These they weave into a crown, adorned with gold tinsel and with field-flowers, and place it on the head of the prettiest girl of their party, after which they visit the house of the owner or tiller of the soil, headed by a boy who carries a sheaf decked with flowers, and sing,—

> Open, O master, the new gates,
> We bring a crown of pure gold,
> O come out, even on to the balcony,
> O ransom, ransom, the crown of gold,
> For the crown of gold is woven.

In some Governments, as in those of Penza and Simbirsk, the last sheaf is dressed up in woman's clothes. In White-Russia the harvest-home feast is known by the name of Talaka[3], a name which is given also to a girl who plays the leading part in it, as may be seen from the following song:—

> Good evening, Talaka!
> Take, take from us
> This sheaf of corn,
> And put on, put on
> This fair crown with flowers.

[3] Toloká in some parts of Russia means the gathering of the hay or corn harvest by the united labour of a man's neighbours, and Tolók is a threshing-floor, or a corn-field left to lie fallow.

With these good things we will go
To the Lord and Master,
We will bring to him
Thy good fortune into his rooms.
He, the Lord and Master,
Will make ready for us the *Dojinok* [Harvest-home].

When the Talaka is brought in procession to a house, the master and mistress come out to meet her with low salutations, and the offering of bread and salt. Then she is invited indoors, and given the place of honour during the ensuing feast, at the end of which she takes off her crown, and gives it to the master of the house.

In olden times these customs were probably of a sacrificial nature—the sheaf, for instance, which is now taken home and placed under the *ikóna*, or holy picture, having originally been intended, in all probability, as an offering to the gods. A very evident trace of sacrifice is manifest in the custom of leaving patches of unreaped corn in the fields, and of placing bread and salt on the ground near them. These ears are eventually knotted together, and the ceremony is called "the plaiting of the beard of Volos," and it is supposed that after it has been performed no wizard or other evilly-disposed person will be able to hurt the produce of the fields. The unreaped patch is looked upon as tabooed; and it is believed that if any one meddles with it he will shrivel up, and become twisted like the interwoven ears. Similar customs are kept up in various parts of Russia. Near Kursk and Voroneje, for instance, a patch of rye is usually left in honour of the Prophet Elijah, and in another district one of oats is consecrated to St. Nicholas. As it is well known that both the Saint and the Prophet have succeeded to the place once held in the estimation of the Russian people by Perun, it seems probable that Volos really was, in ancient times, one of the names of the thunder-god[4].

Volos in olden times was known as the God of Cattle, and in that capacity he, together with Perun, is appealed to in the oath by which Svyatoslaf ratified his treaty with the Greeks. Various explanations of his name have been offered, Sabinin connecting it with that of Odin, which sometimes passed in the mouths of the people, through the form Woden or Wôde into that of Wôld or Wôl, and Prince Vyazemsky connecting Veles, one of the forms of the name, with the Greek βελιος, ἀβέλιος = ἥλιος. Afanasief considers that the name was originally one of the epithets of Perun, who, as the cloud-compeller—the clouds being the cattle of the sky—was the guardian of the heavenly herds, and that the epithet ultimately became regarded as the name of a distinct deity.

In Christian times the honours originally paid to Volos were transferred to his namesake, St. Vlas, or

[4] For a similar custom, anciently observed in Mecklenburg in honour of Woden, see Grimm's *Deutsche Mythologie*, p. 141. Dr. Mannhardt, in an article recently published (in Russian) by the Moscow Archæological Society, suggests that, in ancient times, the Slavonians may have plaited their beards in Assyrian fashion, and adduces in support of his suggestion the testimony of an urn found in a Wendish tomb near Dantzic in 1855, on which is represented the face of a man with a barred or chequered beard.

Vlasy [Blasius], who was a shepherd by profession. To him the peasants throughout Russia pray for the safety of their flocks and herds, and on the day consecrated to him [February 11] they drive their cows to church, and have them secured against misfortune by prayer and the sprinkling of holy water. At the same time they carry offerings of butter to the church, and place them in front of St. Vlas's picture—a custom which has given rise to the saying "Vlas's bread is in butter!"

In times of murrain, when the villagers are "expelling the Cow-Death" in solemn procession, they almost invariably carry with them the picture of St. Vlas, singing as they go a song which will be quoted in full hereafter, calling on the epidemic to depart, seeing that St. Vlas is going through the village,

> With incense, and with taper,
> And with burning embers.

The 1st of September is called *Semen Den'*, Simeon's Day, being consecrated to St. Simeon Stylites. He is popularly known as Simeon Lyetoprovodets, or year-leader, inasmuch as the Russian year formerly began with his feast. After Christianity had been introduced into Russia the 1st of March was for some time accepted as the commencement of the Ecclesiastical year, and the 1st of September as that of the Civil year. In 1348 a Council held at Moscow decided that the latter of these two days should be accepted, both by Church and State, as their New Year's Day, and accordingly it held that position, as has already been stated, until the year 1700 [5].

The first week of September bears the name of *Seminskaya Nedyela* or Simeon's Week, and it is also known as the *Bab'e Lyeto* or Woman's Summer. Some critics have derived the name from that of the cluster of stars called in Russia Baba [the Pleiades], which is apparent at that time of year; but it seems really to be due to the fact that, after the harvest is over, and all field-work is ended for the year, the babas, or women, betake themselves to what is called special "woman's work" (*bab'i rabotui*), such as spinning, etc. At this season the peasants predict what the coming winter will be like, judging by the abundance or rarity of the gossamer webs—the German *Alteweibersommer* [D. M. 744]—in the fields. By the Carpathian Slavonians this season of the year is called *Bab'in Moroz*—the *Woman's Frost*; and a legend is current among them of an old sorceress who was frozen to death on the heights, a story which may have been invented in order to explain the strange appearance of one of those stone female statues which used to stand by the roadside in some parts of Transylvania.

In the villages near Moscow the peasants extinguish all their fires on the eve of the 1st of September, and light them anew the next morning at sunrise, the kindling being performed by the "Wise Men" or "Wise Women" of the neighbourhood, who employ

[5] Tereshchenko, III. 10. See *supra*, p. 203.

special incantations and spells on the occasion. On this day the swallows are supposed to hide or bury themselves in wells. It is also set aside for a very singular funeral ceremony performed by the girls in many parts of Russia. They make small coffins of turnips and other vegetables, enclose flies and other insects in them, and then bury them with a great show of mourning [6]. An equally strange custom is the expulsion of tarakans [7], which takes place on the eve of St. Philip's Fast, when a thread is fastened to one of these obtrusive insects, and all the inmates of a cottage, with closed lips, unite in drawing it out of doors. While the " expulsion " is going on, one of the women of the family stands with dishevelled hair at a window, and when the tarakan nears the threshold she knocks and asks,—

" On what do ye feast ?" [before beginning to fast]; to which the reply is,

" On beef."

" And the Tarakan on what ?" she continues.

" The Tarakan on Tarakans," is the answer.

If this ceremony is properly performed, they think it will prevent the tarakans from returning. The " Old Believers," however, deem such acts of expul-

[6] It has been already mentioned that the soul was often represented by the heathen Slavonians as a fly, gnat, or other insect. See *supra*, p. 118.

[7] The Tarakans are a kind of cockroaches. They must not be confounded with some other insects of a sturdy nature, and not easily to be expelled, or in any way subdued, which the people call *Prusáki* or " Prussians."

sion wrong, thinking that the presence of such insects brings with it blessing from on high.

September is apt to be a gloomy month in Russia as far as the weather is concerned. And as the weather has its influence on the spirits, a number of proverbs are current with reference to the month, such as, "As surly as September," "September's spleen has seized him," or "He has Septembrian thoughts."

But a good deal of merriment takes place among the peasants, however ungenial the weather may be, this being the season for commencing such autumn games as the following, which is called "The Beer Brewing." The younger women of the village, followed by a festive rout, go from cottage to cottage, offering *braga*—millet-beer—first to the old, and then to the young. Afterwards the choir-leader commences the following song, during the singing of which the girls imitate the gestures of a drunken man :—

> On the hill have we brewed beer,
> Lado mine, Lado, beer have we brewed!
> For that beer shall we all meet together,
> On account of that beer shall we all part asunder:
> That beer will make us all bend the knee in dance,
> That beer will cause us to lie down to sleep.
> For that beer shall we stand up again,
> On account of that beer shall we all clap our hands.
> With that beer shall we all become drunken,
> Now on account of that beer shall we all take to quarrelling[8].

[8] Tereshchenko, v. 146.

With September begins also the threshing-season, The day on which a farmer begins to thresh his corn is looked upon, in many parts of Russia, as the nameday of his *ovín*. [The word, which is closely connected with the German *Ofen* and our oven[2], means the corn-kiln, or place in which the corn is dried before being submitted to the flail]. On the preceding evening he begins to heat the *ovin*, and next morning he calls together the threshers, and regales them with *kasha*. After the meal they stick a few ears into each corner of the barn or corn-kiln, in order that their labours may prove richly productive, and then they fall to work, usually commencing with the sheaf which was gathered the first at harvesttime. The *ovin* has always enjoyed a share of the respect paid to the domestic hearth. In olden days it seems to have been customary for the peasants " to pray under the *ovin*," for that practice is expressly forbidden, together with many other heathenish customs, by the " Ecclesiastical Ordinance" of St. Vladimir, and one of the old chroniclers says of the people that " they pray to Fire under the *ovin*." In the Orel Government it is still usual to kill a fowl in the *ovin* on the 4th of September; in some other places a cock is sacrificed there on the 1st of November. In the Government of Yaroslaf a peasant who feels a pain in his loins [*utín*], will go

---

[2] Ulfilas translates the Greek κλίβανος by *Auhns*, in Matt. vi. 30, where our version has " cast into the *oven*." The Salvonic equivalent used in the Ostromir Gospel (A.D. 1056-7) is *peshch*, the modern *pech*, a stove.

to the lower part (*podlaz*) of the *ovín*, rub his back against the wall, and say,—

Father *Ovín*, cure my *utín*.

Hence the old proverb says, "Churches are not like ovins: in them [i. e. the former] the holy pictures are all alike," i. e. it's all one whether you pray in your own parish church or in any other. But the old heathen worship of the domestic hearth, or of the *ovín*, was confined to such places only as belonged to each individual worshipper.

The 6th of September is one of the two principal days—the other being the 6th of December—set aside for the celebration of the *Bratchina*, or brotherly feast [*brat* = brother], held at the common expense. On each of those days the villagers go in a body to church, and there offer a large candle and have a service performed for the gaining of all things good. Afterwards they feast together and entertain hospitably their friends from the neighbouring villages. The relics of the meal are given to the poor, and any bread-crumbs that may remain undisposed of are tossed into the air, in order to propitiate the unclean spirits that might be tempted to destroy the trees or the cornfields.

Various other feasts of a similar nature are held after the harvest is over, such as the *Ssuipchina*, one to which the feasters contribute the necessary ingredients [*ssuipat'* = to pour in together]. On these occasions offences which may have been committed during the summer, such as trespassings and the like, are forgiven, and much good-will crowns the feast—unless it ends in a quarrel brought about by drink. Meanwhile the young people betake themselves to their circling dances, and sing such convivial songs as the following:—

> At the feast was I, at the gathering,
> Mead I drank not, nor small beer.
> Vodka delicious I drank, I drank.
> Not in a cup, nor a glass,
> But a bucketful I drank, I drank.
> Home I went without wandering,
> But to the yard when I came, there I staggering
> Clung to the posts of the door.
> Oaken door-post of mine,
> Hold me up, the drunken woman,
> The drunken woman, the tipsy rogue[1].

The 8th of September, in the year 1380, was a memorable day for Russia, for on it the great victory was gained at Kulikovo by Dmitry Donskoi over the forces of the Tartar Khan Mamai. In memory of the Christian warriors who fell upon this occasion a solemn festival was instituted by the conqueror, and was held for many years between the 18th and the 26th of October. In 1769 Catherine II. ordered the day of its celebration to be changed to that of the commemoration of the beheading of St. John the Baptist, August 29. The battle of Kulikovo having been fought on a Saturday, the day of its commemoration has received the name of *Dmitriefskaya*

[1] Tereshchenko, v. 149—152.

Subbota, Dmitry's Saturday—a name now given by the peasants to the autumnal festival they hold every year in remembrance of their ancestors and dead relatives. If at that time a thaw follows the first frosts of winter, the people say, *Roditeli otdokhnut,* " the Fathers enjoy repose," for they hold, as will be seen in the chapter on Funeral Songs, that the dead suffer from cold, as well as from hunger, in the grave. On the day of the commemoration the peasants attend a church service, and afterwards they go out to the graves of their friends, and there institute a feast, lauding amidst many tears the virtues and good qualities of the dead, and then drinking to their eternal rest. So important a feature in the ceremony is this drinking, that it has given rise to a proverb, " One begins for the repose of the dead, and one goes on for one's own pleasure." It is customary on such occasions to hand over a portion of the articles provided for the feast to the officiating ecclesiastics and their assistants, a fact to which allusion is made in the popular saying, " It is not always Dmitry's Saturday with priestly children."

During the part of the winter preceding that Christmas festival of Kolyada with an account of which the present chapter commenced, the principal amusements of the younger members of a village community are found in the Posidyelki which have already been described. It is to a great extent at these social gatherings that the courtship of young Russians of the agricultural class is carried on—courtship which, in the great majority of cases, leads to a marriage, some day after the cares and toils of harvest are over. How many relics of the past are still preserved in the customs attendant upon a Russian marriage, and how rich it is in old songs, the next chapter will attempt to show.

CHAPTER IV.

MARRIAGE SONGS.

HAVING formed some idea of the various other divisions of the *Obryádnuiya Pyesni*, or Ritual Songs—many of them relics of pagan worship or mythical doctrine which, after having undergone a more or less serious change, have come down to our own times, and still live in the memories and on the lips of the Russian peasantry—we will now proceed to glance at that mass of popular poetry which is closely connected with the social life of the people, specially consecrated to days of family joy or mourning. The principal occasions on which songs of this kind may be heard are those of a wedding or of a burial, and therefore it is mainly to the marriage and funeral customs of the Russian people that this chapter and the next will be devoted. The Marriage Songs alone are numerous enough to form a bulky volume; but all that can be done here is to attempt, in a hasty sketch, to convey some idea of their nature and their worth.

Before introducing the songs themselves, it will be necessary to give some account of the marriage customs and rites which they, for the most part, accompany and illustrate. These customs differ somewhat in the various districts of Russia, but their purport is always the same, however much their form may have been warped by time or accident. Tereshchenko has devoted to the subject a volume of 618 pages, giving a detailed account of the mode of conducting a marriage in nine distinct Russian provinces, as well as in Little-Russia, White-Russia, and Lithuania. In the rapid sketch of a peasant wedding in the present day which I am about to give, I shall partly rely upon the animated picture drawn by Ruibnikof [III. 347-409] of a marriage in the neighbourhood of Lake Onega, and partly upon that contained in the eighth chapter of Tereshchenko's exhaustive treatise.

In the districts to which Ruibnikof's account refers, "the marriage ceremony has developed," he remarks, "into a complete scenic representation," of which, in order to understand it aright, it is necessary to be familiar with this list of

DRAMATIS PERSONÆ.

The *Knyaz* [Prince],   i. e. The Bridegroom.
The *Knyazhná*, or
   Knyagínya[1] [Princess], i. e. The Bride.
The *Tuísyatsky*[2] [Captain
         or Chief], i. e. The chief of the Bridegroom's party.
The *Druzhki* [*drug* = friend], i. e. The Groomsmen.

[1] In Russian an unmarried princess is called *Knyazhná*, a married one *Knyagínya*.
[2] *Tuísyacha* = 1000.

The *Boyáre*[3] [Lords], i. e. The male members of the bridal cortége, called also *Poyezzhane* [*Poyezd* = cortége].

The *Boyáruini* [Ladies], i. e. The female members of the cortége, called also *Bryudgi*.

The *Voplénitsa*[4] [Wailer], i. e. The mistress of ceremonies, who directs the whole course of the wedding, so far as what takes place in the bride's house is concerned.

These are the principal characters, but besides them there are also the *Svat* and *Svakha*, the male and female match-makers, and a number of youths and maidens who attend upon the bride and bridegroom. In some districts, it should be observed, the *Voplénitsa* is unknown.

The bride and bridegroom, in the districts of which Ruíbnikof speaks, have generally become acquainted at the gatherings called Besyedas, and have glided into a sort of informal engagement, during which they have been known as a *parochka*, or pair. At last, having ascertained that the girl's family will not object, one autumn or winter day the lover has begged his father or godfather to go to her

---

[3] This term is also applied to all the members of the bridal party.

[4] *Vopit'* = to wail or sob. She is also called the *Plakalshchitsa*, (*plakat'* = to cry). More will be said about her in the next chapter.

parents and ask for her hand. So the envoy has set out on the *Svátanie*, or match-making, attended by various other members of the bridegroom's family.

They always start at night, and they choose a byeway, so as not to meet any one, for a meeting would be an evil omen. Having arrived at the house of the bride's father, they knock at the window and ask for admission. *Milosti prosim*, " Do us the favour," is the ordinary reply. When they have come in they are asked to sit down, but they refuse. " We have not come," they say, " to sit down, nor to feast, but to ask in marriage. We have a *Dóbry Molodéts**, a brave youth ; you have a *Krásnaya Dyevítsa*, a fair maiden. Might not the two be brought together ? " The parents of the bride return thanks for the compliment, on which the visitors take off their caps and sit down to a meal. When it is over the matchmakers ask for a final answer. The parents at first plead for delay, but, if they see no objection to the match, eventually give their consent. Upon this a candle is lighted and placed before the holy picture, and the contracting parties, having crossed themselves and uttered a prayer, strike hands on the bargain, and settle the matter. After the *Rukobitie* [*ruká*, a hand; *bit'*, to beat] the girl generally begins to lament, and to entreat her relatives to break off the engagement. Let them do what else they will with

---

* This is the stereotyped term in the songs for their heroes. Dóbry = good ; Molodéts = (1) a youth ; (2) a young bachelor; (3) a gay, daring, brave young spark or springald : in this sense the word is often accentuated *Mólodets*.

her, she cries, she will be their faithful servant; only let them not send her away into a land of strangers, and so forth ; or perhaps her wailing takes a narrative form :—

Not two ravens have flown together in the dark forest,
Nor have two warriors ridden together in the open plain,
But two match-makers have met within my home,
In the chief, the revered corner, the place of honour.
The first of them is my father dear,
The second is a match-maker from the abode of strangers.
They have taken close counsel together,
They have lighted candles of pure wax
Before the wonder-working picture,
And have crossed their bright eyes,
And have struck hand upon hand . . . [6].

In the districts of which Tereshchenko speaks, the *Svátanie* is performed somewhat differently. Very often it is the girl's family which makes the first move, its members sending a *Svakha*, or female match-maker, to suggest the idea of the marriage to the youth's parents. They receive her as if in total ignorance of her designs, and she at first pretends to have dropped in accidentally. Presently, however, she proceeds to business. If the idea proves acceptable, the youth's parents in their turn send a *Svat* to carry on the parleying. An agreement is soon arrived at between the two families, and then the young people make each other presents, and their

[6] Ruibnikof, III. 350.

engagement is celebrated by a feast, at which only cheerful songs are sung, such as

> The nightingale flew
> To the coppice green,
> To the birchwoods bright.
> To a spray, without heeding,
> The nightingale flew.
> That spray so alluring,
> That verdure enchanting,
> The nightingale pleased,
> The songster delighted:
> He will not depart from it now.

And so—the song goes on to say, introducing the names of the youth and the maiden—Luka Ivánovich, without any settled purpose, came to Efim's house, and then saw the fair Prascovia Andreevna, and, having seen her,

> Part from her he cannot,
> But wed her he will [7].

Two days after the hand-striking, continues Ruibnikof, begins the ceremony of *poruchénie*, elsewhere called *obruchénie*, or betrothal. During the interval the bride, as she may now be called, visits her relatives, attended by half a score or a score of other girls, with whom she sings various songs and *zapláchki*, or laments.

Towards the end of the second day arrive the bridegroom and his friends. The *Tuísyatsky* and groomsmen lead the way, and, having left the bridegroom and the rest of his escort at some house in the village, go straight to the bride's house, where they

[7] Tereshchenko, II. 117—124.

entreat her friends to get her ready as soon as possible. This being promised, after a fee has been paid to the *Voplénitsa*, the recognized directress of the ceremony, the bridegroom arrives with his festive train, and the whole party sit down to a table covered with a white cloth and provided with bread and salt.

Meanwhile the bride has been adorned in wedding apparel, with a *fatá*, a sort of veil, on her head and covering her face. When she is ready her friends form a procsesion, and bring her in state to the table at which the guests are seated. In front, together with the *Bozhatka*, or Godmother, go the *Peredovshchiki* and *Peredovshchitsui*, the "Foremen" and "Forewomen" [*pered* or *pred*=before]. The bride follows, leaning on the arms of two girls called *Pristavlenitsui* [*Pristávit* = to set over, *etc.*] When the procession draws near to the table, the leaders open out on both sides, and the bride is led up to it, while the chorus of girls, standing in one of the corners, sings what are called *Pripyeval'nuiya* songs [*pripyév* = accompaniment of song, or refrain; *pripyevát'* = to accompany with singing].

The Tuísyatsky then asks the bride's relatives to unveil her, saying, "We have come to see not a veil, but a bride." They comply, and the unveiled bride bends low to the bridegroom's relatives in general, and to the Tuísyatsky and the "Young Prince" in particular. "Is the young Princess *lyubá* [pleasing] to you?" ask the "Foremen." The bridegroom expresses his satisfaction by a silent inclination of the head, but his escorters cry loudly

"*Lyubá, Lyubá*" [She is, she is pleasing]. "But ask the young Princess," they continue, "if our young Prince is *lyub* to her." The bride replies by a low bow or salaam (Russian peasant women do not curtsey, but bow low as the men do, in oriental fashion), but her attendants exclaim "*Lyub, Lyub*" [He is, he is pleasing].

The bridegroom now rises from the table, and hands to the bride a tray with two glasses of vodka, the Russian whiskey. She takes them round—the bridegroom filling them as they are emptied—first to her own relatives, then to those of the bridegroom. When all have been served, the young people help themselves, and, having signed a cross over their eyes, strike their glasses together, the bridegroom trying to lift his glass highest, so as to pour some of its contents into the bride's glass, his friends exclaiming, if he is successful, *Ai-da mólodets*, "There's a fine fellow!" After this the bride retires from the table, and the *Voplénitsa* intones a song beginning,

> Grant Thy blessing, O Lord God,
> On the holy, and happy hour,
> On the prosperous time and season. ...

Meanwhile the bride sits on a bench, and the women of her family lament over her, bewailing her impending departure to "the land of strangers." When they have finished, the bride herself begins to sing sadly,

> No leisure have I to be sitting here,
> To be talking and chattering.

The season for work has come,
The mowing time and the haymaking. . . .

Then she rises, takes the tray with glasses, and again makes the round of the guests, whose praises meanwhile the *Voplénitsa* sings, ending with those of the bridegroom, who is helped last, describing how—

He sits there bright as a burning taper;
When he speaks it is like the giving of roubles.

. . . . . .

His ruddiness is taken from the sun;
His fairness from the white snow.

. . . . . .

His cheeks are like the crimson poppy,
His bright eyes are the eyes of a hawk,
His brows are black with the blackness of a sable. . . .

Then comes the *poruchénie*, the act of betrothal. "Its essence," says Ruibnikof, "consists in this, that the bridegroom, having lifted a glass of vodka to his lips, should take the hand (*ruká*) of the bride, and press it." After this the glasses are removed from the table, and the bridegroom offers to the bride a casket of presents. She takes it away from the table, but immediately brings it back, remarking that the key does not accompany it. The *Voplénitsa* addresses the bridegroom, singing,—

Thou hast given a coffer of metal work,
Now give the golden key.

The bridegroom unlocks the casket, and the bride carries it off, inspects the gifts, and then usually returns her thanks in song :—

Wherefore, O young son of thy father,
Hast thou given me a coffer of metal-work?
No Priest's child am I,
No Deacon's child am I,
But the child of a simple peasant.

After this she again offers spirits to the bridegroom's relatives, who soon afterwards, having been feasted and presented with various gifts by her family, retire to their homes. When they have left, the bride goes the round of her own relations, serving them with drink, and receiving gifts from them—from the men ribbons and kerchiefs, and from the women shifts and pieces of different stuffs, and the like.

After the betrothal come two or three *Vecherinki*, or social gatherings, of which the last, on the eve of the wedding, is the most important. In the central provinces of Russia this is known as the *Dyevíchnik*, [*dyéva, dyevítsa* = a maiden]. Of this "girls' party" we will now give a description, following the account given by Tereshchenko [II. 126—130]. The day before the wedding the bride's unmarried friends meet at her house, and spend the evening with her, bewailing her coming departure, consoling her in her grief, and inspecting her wedding-dress and presents. When it grows dark a number of candles are lighted, and *Khlyeb-sol'*, bread and salt, and *Karavaí*, a particular kind of cake, are placed on the table. The girls then lead the bride to a raised seat, and group themselves around her in a ring. One of their number wraps the bride's head in the wedding-veil, and leads the songs, in which, accompanied with many tears, they describe her impending departure from among them, and the altered form of life which she will have to adopt. After a time they take off the bride's veil, and begin combing her "ruddy tresses." Unmarried Russian girls wear their back hair hanging in a long, single plait, adorned with ribbons and sometimes, especially in Little-Russia, with flowers. This plait, called *kosá*[8] is a maiden's chief ornament, the cherished object of her care, the principal source of her girlish pride. Its unplaiting is a sign of the change which is coming upon her, for married women do not wear the *kosá*. Their back hair, if it is not cut short, is worn in two plaits, which are generally wound round the head, and concealed under a kerchief.

During the unplaiting of the *kosá* the girl who superintends the operation begins to sing,—

> O my plait, my plaitling,
> My dear plait,
> Ruddy and golden!

And the girl who is assisting her replies,—

> Early is it to unplait thee,
> And for the long journey,
> The long one to prepare thee!

When the bride's tresses have been combed out, and her *kosá* is about to be plaited anew, she sings,—

> Not for gold do I mourn,
> Nor mourn I for bright silver.
> For one thing only do I mourn.
> For the maiden beauty
> Of my ruddy *kosá*.

---

[8] *Kosoi* = slanting, bent. *Kosá* has several meanings, signifying, for instance, a scythe, a curved spit of land, etc.

To which one of her friends replies,—

Weep not, weep not, dear Prascovia,
Make not unhappy the fair maidens,
Stain not with tears their white faces,
Nor break the strength of their hands!
Not for ever shall we remain unmarried,
Singing of our maiden freedom.

While the *kosá* is being replaited the chorus sings,—

O thou my dear, my ruddy *kosá*!
O thou my dear, my silken *kosník*[9]!
Do thou plait, O my bride,
Plait thy braid, ever so finely,
Tie the knots, ever so tightly!

When the plait has been braided as tight as possible, and tied with blue laces, the bridegroom's brother, the *Svakha*, or some other personage deputed for the purpose, arrives, and begins bidding for it. To the sale of the *kosá* a great many songs are devoted, such as,

It was not a horn that in the early morning sounded;
It was a maiden her ruddy braid lamenting.
Last night they twined my braid together,
And interweaved my braid with pearls.
Luká Ivánovich—Heaven requite him!—
Has sent a pitiless *Svakha* hither.
My braid has she begun to rend.
Tearing out the gold from my braid,
Shaking the pearls from my ruddy braid.

The intending purchaser stands at the door, and bows to the company. Then he tries to get at the *kosá*, but the girls keep him off, while the bride weeps and sobs. Turning to her brother, or to one of the girls who represents him, she entreats him to

---

[9] The *kosník* is the bunch of ribbons at the end of the *kosá*.

defend her, and not to sell her *kosá*, or at all events not to sell it cheaply. The girls sing,—

> Stand to it, brother!
> Brother, hold out!
> Sell not thy sister
> For a rouble, for gold.

The brother replies,—

> Dear to a brother is a sister,
> But dearer still is gold.

Then in chorus the girls exclaim,—

> Tartar of a brother!

The purchaser now goes up to the bride, and lays hold of her *kosá*, throwing money on the table as a sign that it has been sold and bought. This sale, in the north-east districts to which Ruibnikof's account refers, takes place the next day, just before the bride goes to the church.

After the sale of the *kosá* has taken place, the girls sit down to table, and sing the *Karavaí* [cake] song,—

> The *Karavaí*
> For all the family is fit.
> Let the young Princess,
> Taste it to-morrow;
> Then will the young Prince
> Love the young Princess.

In some places it is believed that if the bride tastes the cake on the eve of the wedding her husband will not love her. After the cake song, a number of others are sung, their tone being generally in accordance with the feelings displayed by the bride.

One of the most poetic of the ideas to which the ceremonies of this girls' party gives expression, is the division by the bride of her *krásota* among her maiden companions. The word usually means "beauty," but, on this particular occasion, it is applied to "a kind of crown made of ribbons and flowers," which is placed on the table before the bride. It is intended to represent the ornaments which she used to twine in her braided hair in her girlish days, and so to typify the maiden liberty which she is about to exchange for the subjection of married life. Of the songs devoted to this subject, the number of which is very great, the following is a fair example:—

 O my friend, beloved companion,
 Whither shall I send my beauty?
 Shall I let it go into the woods?
  Soon will it lose its way.
 Shall I let it go into the meads?
  Long will it wander about.
 Shall I let it go down to the stream?
  There will its feet be set fast.
 I will give my beauty
  To my dear companion,
 To that sweet fair maiden,
  Dear Olinka.
 With her my beauty
  Will find a shelter;
 The darling one will be lapped in ease.
 A mother of her own has she,
  A father of her own;
 Brothers has she, bright falcons,
  Fair swans are their wives[1].

[1] Tereshchenko, II. 323.

After supper the girls retire for the night, to return the next morning and prepare the bride for the marriage ceremony.

We will now proceed with Ruibnikof's account. Part of the day preceding the marriage, he says, is spent by the bride in paying farewell visits to her relatives. To her godfather she addresses the following *zaplachka*, or lament:—

> I have come to thee, O my bright Sun,
> Beloved parent—Godfather,
> I, the young one, have come to thee,
> To bend low my forehead, and bow down.
> Do thou forgive me, father dear!
> I have been a giddy girl; . . . .
> Bless me, father dear,
> With an enduring benediction!

And before her godmother she sings,—

> Farewell, my own,
> Thou never-enough-to-be-looked-on Sun!
> Bless me, O my mother,
> Bless, and be not angry;
> Remember not, my own,
> My girlish follies,
> My careless words!

Some of the bride's relatives spend the night before the wedding in her father's house. In the morning she awakes them with laments devoted to that purpose. Afterwards she addresses one of her married friends, asking her what parting with one's kith and kin (*rod-plemya*) is like. The reply is that—

> Hard is it to part
> From one's kith and kin,
> From one's father and mother.

Hard is it to become accustomed
To another family,
To another father and mother . . . .

Presently the *Svakha* begins to unplait her braided hair for the last time, amid much wailing song. When the operation has been performed, the bride is arrayed in wedding attire. Meantime, in some places, the bridegroom and his friends—or the friends only, the bridegroom having gone on to the church—have come to the house, and are waiting in the *Syeni*[2] at the open doors. They beg that the bride may be brought to them, and at last, after their request has been many times repeated, the " Princess " appears, attended by her relatives and attendants, but stops short at the door. Again the bridegroom's friends demand the bride, but are told first to " Cleanse the threshold; then will the young Princess cross the threshold." On this the bridegroom's friends place some copper coins in a bowl, and offer them to the bride's relatives, who take a *grosh* or two apiece, and then open their ranks, and let the bride pass through into the *Syeni*. There they all "pray to God," and then—if the bridegroom is present—lead the young people up to each other. The bridegroom places one hand on the bride's head, and with the other turns her round three times " as the sun goes," while in

---

[2] This word is a very difficult one to translate. In the houses of the " gentry " it means the antechambers, or rooms through which admission is gained to the reception-rooms. In a peasant's house it represents the space not devoted to the " keeping-rooms." I have sometimes translated it by " the passages."

doing so, if he is adroit, he gives her a kiss. Then they enter the "living-room," and sit down to table, after the bridegroom has given a present to the children of the family, who have previously occupied all the places, in order to induce them to give up their seats. About this time, in the districts of which Ruibnikof speaks, takes place the sale of the bride, which, in the province referred to by Tereshchenko, occurs at the girls' party on the previous evening. The Tuísyatsky makes the purchase, handing money to the bride's female relatives till they pretend to be satisfied, on which the groomsmen cry, "Ye have sold the bride: she is yours no more." After this they prepare to go to church, but not before the bride has received her mother's last blessing. This is conferred at various times in different districts, but always in the same manner. The mother takes the holy image from the corner of honour, and blesses her daughter with it. To this ceremony the last lines refer in the following song. The word *Sudáruinya*, which occurs in it, is an abbreviation of *Gosudáruinya*, lady or mistress:—

"Mátushka! what is that dust on the plain?
Sudáruinya! what is that dust on the plain?"
"My child, the horses have galloped about:
My darling, the horses have galloped about."

"Mátushka! guests to our courtyard have come!
Sudáruinya! guests to our courtyard have come!"
"My child, do not fear, we will not give thee up:
My darling, fear not, we will not give thee up."

"Mátushka! now they are mounting the steps!
Sudáruinya! now they are mounting the steps!"

"My child, do not fear, we will not give thee up;
My darling, fear not, we will not give thee up."

"Mátushka! into the house[3] have they gone!
Sudáruinya! into the house have they gone!"
"My child, do not fear, we will not give thee up;
My darling, fear not, we will not give thee up."

"Mátushka! at the oak table they sit!
Sudáruinya! at the oak table they sit."
"My child, do not fear, we will not give thee up;
My darling, fear not, we will not give thee up."

"Mátushka! down has the picture[4] been taken!
Sudáruinya! down has the picture been taken!"
"My child, do not fear, we will not give thee up;
My darling, fear not, we will not give thee up."

"Mátushka! see, they are blessing me now!
Sudáruinya! see, they are blessing me now!"
"My child! may the Lord be ever with thee!
My darling! may God be ever with thee[5]!"

As soon as the young couple arrive in the church, says Tereshchenko, the priest begins the wedding service. Over the heads of the bride and bridegroom the groomsmen hold crowns [*vyentsui*, whence the rite is called *vyenchanie*, or crowning]. The crowns must be allowed to press to some extent on the head, for if, in order to prevent the bride from being wearied, her crown is kept actually above her head, the peasants augur ill for the happiness of her

---

[3] The *novaya gornitsa*, literally, "the new apartment," but the epithet has no real meaning.

[4] The *obraz*, or icona—the sacred picture—taken down from the wall, in order to be used in the maternal benediction.

[5] Tereshchenko, II. 134.

married life. But if it is allowed to drop on her head, terrible misfortunes are expected. Omens are looked for also in the burning of the tapers which the young people hold in their hands.

When the nuptial benediction is pronounced the priest puts the wedding rings on their fingers, and then, having joined their hands with a piece of white linen, he leads them round the reading-desk. Afterwards he three times gives them red wine to drink, and tells them to kiss each other. The ceremony is over[6].

The bridegroom now leads his bride, says Ruibnikof, to his home. On the top of the steps leading into the house his father and mother meet the young couple, and bless them with bread and salt, while some of the other relatives pour over them barley and down, and give them fresh milk to drink; the first that they may live in harmony and happiness, and the second "that their children may be not black, but white." The young people enter the house and sit down on a bench, the Princess [now no longer called *Knyazhná* but *Knyagínya*, as being a married woman] hiding her face from sight with a handkerchief. Then comes her mother-in-law, or an aunt, takes away the handkerchief, divides her loosely hanging tresses into two parts, and sets on her head the *Povoínik*, or married woman's headdress. After that begins the *Knyazhenetsky Stol* or "Princely Table," the "wedding-breakfast" of Russian pea-

[6] Tereshchenko, II. 136—137.

sant life, which is celebrated with great mirth and spirit. Towards the end of it the young couple retire to their chamber, round which, in old times, one of the party, called a *Klyetnik*, used to watch.

The next day, after having taken a bath, the young wife makes presents to the relations of her "Prince," and to the *Tuísyatsky*, and a little later her husband goes to his mother-in-law's house, where she offers him an omelette. It is customary for him to make a hole in the middle of the omelette, into which a groomsman pours *maslo*—butter, or oil—and then breaks the pot from which the *maslo* was taken.

Some days later a dinner is given by the bride's mother to all the relatives on both sides, at the end of which a number of presents are made. And at the end of a week the bride's family are entertained by the bridegroom. Finally each of the persons who took part in the wedding invites the young couple either to a dinner or an evening entertainment.

[Ruibnikof asked how much the poorest peasant would have to pay when his daughter was married, without counting church fees, and the following list of expenses was made out for him:—

For entertainments, etc.	8 to 10	roubles
For 1 or 2 *vedros* of spirits	8 ,, 16	,,
(The *vedro* being about 2¼ gallons).		
To bridegroom's father, 3 shirts and 3 towels .	2 ,, 5	,,
To bridegroom's mother, 6 shifts and 10 towels	4 ,, 7	,,
To bridegroom's parents, a counterpane each .	½ ,, 1	,,
For presents to *Tuísyatsky*	1 ,, 1½	,,
To the *bryudgi*, a shift each .	2 ,, 6	,,
To others, towels and shirts .	2 ,, 6	,,
	27½ ,, 52½	,,

Or from about 4*l*. 8*s*. to 8*l*. 6*s*. of our money.

So much is this tax felt by the poorer peasants, that in some cases, says Ruibnikof, they allow their daughters to make "run-away marriages," in order that the expense of a regular wedding may be avoided. In such cases the marriage is formally solemnized in a church, but the domestic rites are omitted.]

This sketch of the nuptial customs of the present day will, I hope, assist in rendering more intelligible than they would otherwise have been, the specimens of marriage songs which will follow. Some of them are specially interesting and valuable, inasmuch as there may be discovered in them traces of the habits and customs of the heathen Slavonians with respect to marriage, a subject on which no great amount of direct light has been thrown by history.

The earliest of the chroniclers of Old-Russia, the monk Nestor, writing towards the close of the eleventh century—he died about A.D. 1114—states that very different ideas, with respect to wedlock, prevailed in heathen times among the various Slavonic tribes in the neighbourhood of the Dniester.

There were the Drevlyane, he says, who were unacquainted with marriage, but who " carried off girls at the water," probably taking advantage of their coming out to the river for water [7]. Among several other tribes, he remarks, such as the Syeveryane, for instance, a milder custom prevailed. Their young men were in the habit of carrying off their brides, it is true, seizing upon them during the religious festi-

[7] Solovief thinks that the words "among them there was no marriage," merely mean that the Drevlyane paid no attention to the wishes of the families from which they took their wives.—*Ist. Ross.* I. 74.

vals which they celebrated from time to time in the villages, but then the capture or abduction was performed with the consent of the girls themselves. The Polyane, on the other hand, had regular marriages, on the occasion of which a dowry was paid, namely, a sum of money given to the bride's parents in return for their consent. For if the bride was not captured, at all events she was purchased. This custom is supposed to be typified in the game and choral song called "The Sowing of the Millet." The singers form two choirs, which face each other and exchange winged words. This song, it is as well to remark, belongs to the class of those devoted to vernal rites, a fact which may account for the invocation of Lado, the deity of the Spring and of Love, which is repeated after every line of the original.

The first chorus begins,

> We have sown, we have sown millet,
> Oi Did-Lado, we have sown!

To which the other replies,

> But we will trample it, trample it,
> Oi Did-Lado, will trample it.

Then they sing alternately,

1. But with what will ye trample it?
2. Horses will we turn into it.
1. But we will catch the horses.
2. What will ye catch them with?
1. With a silken rein.
2. But we will ransom the horses.
1. What will ye ransom them with?
2. We will give a hundred roubles.

1. A thousand is not what we want.
2. What is it then ye want?
1. What we want is a maiden.

On this one of the girls in the second choir goes over to the first, the two sides singing respectively, "Our band has lost," and "Our band has gained." The game lasts until all the girls have gone over from one side to the other[8]. In a corresponding Servian song the winning side says in plain terms, "If ye will not give us a maiden, we will take one by force."

To the forcible carrying away of the bride seems to refer, says Orest Miller, "a long series of nuptial songs from all parts, not only of Russia, but of the whole Slavonic world." In them the bridegroom is spoken of as a foreigner and a stranger, who has been wafted, Heaven knows whence, by a black cloud, and who is surrounded by brave companions, hostile to the bride. Even among the Czekhs, whose ideas have been considerably modified by foreign influences, the arrival of the bridegroom is still announced by the words, "The enemy is near at hand." "The bridegroom, that evil thief, has come," says a Vologda song. In Russia he is often called, also, after the invaders of the land, the Tartars or the Lithuanians.

In order to get at the bride the bridegroom has "to batter down the walls of stone," to "let fly the arrow of pearl," to "shatter the guarding locks." She

[8] Sakharof, I. iii. 27.

looks upon him as her destroyer, for whom she must unplait her maiden braid, by whom her girlish beauty will be ruined. One of the many acts in the long drama, as it were, which is performed at every peasant wedding, consists in a representation of the attack and defence of the bride. Thus, in Little-Russia, when the bride's tresses have been unplaited, and the cap is being put on her head, she is bound to resist with all her might, and even to fling her cap angrily on the ground. Then the groomsmen, at the cry of "Boyars, to your swords!" pretend to seize their knives and make a dash at the bride, who is thereupon surrounded by her friends who come rushing to the rescue[9].

In some parts of Russia, on the eve of the marriage, all the doors of the house and the gates of the yard are closely shut, and when the bridegroom comes they are not opened until after long parleys, which evidently refer to the purchase of the bride, Numbers of the songs refer to such bargains. One of them, for instance, tells how the "match-makers" arrived, and how, taking aside the bride's father,—

---

[9] "The hurling of old shoes after the bridegroom among ourselves *may be* a relic of a similar custom. It is a sham assault on the person carrying off the lady, and in default of any more plausible explanation, and we know of none such, it may fairly be considered as probable that it is the form of capture in its last state of disintegration." For an exhaustive account of "the origin of the form of capture in marriage ceremonies," see the erudite book from which this somewhat doubtful suggestion is taken, Mr. J. F. McLennan's "Primitive Marriage." Edinburgh, 1865, 8vo.

They began to inquire about the white swan,
Began to fix the price of her dear unfettered freedom.

Then thus does the father fix the terms,—

"Let her freedom be set at a hundred roubles,
And her ruddy tresses at a thousand,
But the beauteous maiden is beyond all price."

On hearing this the chief of the match-makers begins to brag, and promises the father shall receive "towns with their suburbs, and villages with their surroundings." Finding this of no avail, he tries the effect of flattery, praising the residence of the stubborn father, and the gait and speech of his young son. But, continues the fair cause of the bargaining,—

Not on that account would my father give way,
Nor would he barter away my dear unfettered freedom.
But cunning was the evil one, the chief manager of the marriage.
Close up to my father did he press,
Low before him did he bow down,
Promising him, once and again,
Forty measures of green wine,
Forty casks of mighty beer.
On that my parents did give way,
And bartered away my freedom and liberty
For that sweet green wine,
For those small wine cups.
Ruinously did they drink away their possessions,
And squandered my freedom on debauchery[1].

[1] Ruibnikof, III. 353—354.

In the olden days, to which these songs are supposed to refer, women were not thought worthy of any great respect, and if the bride's parents were unwilling to part with her it may have been because they did not like the idea of losing a useful servant, or of transferring to other people " a living broom or shovel"—to make use of a popular Slavonian definition of a woman. In those patriarchal times a daughter was utterly at the mercy of her parents, and they might even sell her if it so pleased them. And in one sense it may be said that it did please them so to do, only the girl's purchaser was her future husband, and the purchase-money formed a species of dowry—for their benefit.

But although her parents have treated her cruelly in thus bartering away her liberty for money, yet the bride mourns bitterly at having to part from them. They may have betrothed her during her infancy, swinging her away from them in her cradle—the Russian cradle being suspended instead of being placed on rockers—according to the expression used by a young wife in the following song:—

   O my Father!
   O my Mother!
   When did ye ruin me?
   Then did ye ruin me,
   When my mother bare me,
  And having borne me, laid me in the cradle,
   And three times swung me.
   The first time, alas!
    To an unknown land.

> The next time, alas!
> To an unknown father.
> The third time, alas!
> To an unknown mother [2].

But it grieves her to have to leave her old home, to give up her maiden liberty for a wife's state of subjection, and to pass from among kindly and familiar faces into a circle of unfriendly strangers. Such are the expressions used in one of the numerous songs of which some account has already been given, those sung during the unplaiting of the bride's *kosá*, or plait of hair:—

> In the house of my own father,
> In the house of my own mother,
> I used to comb you, O ruddy tresses
>   Amidst the oaks afield.
> I used to wash you, O ruddy tresses,
>   In fountain water cool.
> I used to dry you, O ruddy tresses,
> On the steep red steps in front of the house,
> In the rosy light of the rising sun.
> But now in that unknown, far off land,
>   In the house of my husband's father,
>   In the house of my husband's mother,
> I shall have to comb you, O ruddy tresses,
>   Within a curtain'd recess.
> I shall have to wash you, O ruddy tresses,
>   In the wave of my bitter tears.
> I shall have to dry you, O ruddy tresses
>   In the longing of my grief [3].

[2] Orest Miller, *Chrestomathy*, I. 20. Quoted from a Pskof collection.

[3] Orest Miller, *Chrest.* I. 21. Quoted from a Perm collection. I have taken the liberty of turning the *kosá* into "tresses."

When she thinks of the family into which she is about to marry, the bride (in what are supposed to be the older songs) shudders, looking upon its members as "bears," or as "piercing thorns and stinging nettles." On the other hand, she is looked upon by them in an unfavourable light, being considered a "she-bear," a "cannibal," a "sloven," and so forth. In one song, for instance, a girl complains as follows:—

> They are making me marry a lout
>   With no small family.
> Oh! oh! oh! oh dear me!
> With a father, and a mother,
>   And four brothers
>   And sisters three.
> Oh! oh! oh! oh dear me!
> Says my father-in-law,
>   "Here comes a bear!"
> Says my mother-in-law,
>   "Here comes a slut!"
> My sisters-in-law cry,
>   "Here comes a do-nothing!"
> My brothers-in-law exclaim,
>   "Here comes a mischief-maker!"
> Oh! oh! oh! oh dear me[4]!

She complains bitterly of the conduct of her father and mother. In a Siberian song a daughter says that her parents have "locked up their stony hearts in a coffer, and flung the keys into the blue sea; and in a Galician song a young wife says that her wishes have been utterly set at nought by her relatives, for,

[4] Shein, I. 331.

> He whom I love truly
> Stands there outside.
> To one whom I have never seen
> Have they given my hand.

Better would it have been for her, she says, if her father had taken his sharp sword and struck off "her ill-fated head," than that he should have condemned her to captivity in an unknown land; for whither she is going she knows no more than a leaf driven before the wind. In some of the Bohemian nuptial songs a very sombre future is held up before the eyes of the bride. "Wait a little, dark-eyed maiden," they say to her; "thou art destined to weep without ceasing. After the first week of married life not a day will pass without tears. And when a month has gone by, thou wilt weep even more." No wonder that the bride, finding all her appeals to her parents fruitless, turns to her brother, and, as we have already seen, entreats him to help her.

In some places, as has been mentioned before, during the betrothal ceremonies a present of money is made to the bride's brother. In Galicia, when he accepts it the chorus sings,—

> Thou Tartar, brother, thou Tartar!
> To sell thy sister for a thaler,
> Her ruddy hair for a piece of six,
> Her fair face for nothing at all.

Sometimes, however, the bride takes a more business-like view of the transaction, as, for instance, in the song which (in the Saratof Government) her companions sing while the bargaining with the brother is going on :—

> It is dark, dark out of doors,
> But darker still in the upper chamber.
> The Boyars have seized the gates,
> They bargain, bargain for Dunya.
> > Bargain, bargain, brother,
> > Do not sell me cheaply!
> > Ask for me a hundred roubles,
> > For my maiden tresses ask a thousand,
> > But my beauty is beyond appraising.
> > Enter Boyars!
> > Enter Boyars!
> > Long have we expected you[5].

While the trading is going on, the bridegroom, in many districts, stands outside the door, even if it be in the depth of winter, and must not come into the house till the bargain is struck.

Finding her appeals to her father and brother useless, the bride indulges in imprecations against the *Svatui*, and *Svakhi*, the male and female arrangers and managers of the marriage. In one song she entreats her father to take the *Svat* out of doors, " and comb his head with a harrow;" in another she begs her attendant maidens to fasten a sharp knife in her hair, so that when the *Svakhi* come to unplait it they may cut their fingers. And in return for the service the chief *Svat* has done her she hopes there may be

> To him forty sons,
> And to him fifty daughters.
> That the sons may never get wives,
> And the daughters may find no husbands.

[5] Tereshchenko, II. 344.

Sometimes these imprecations are uttered, not by the bride, but by the friends of her girlhood, who, on the eve of her wedding, assemble at her house for the *Dyevichnik*, or girls' party, of which a description has been given. Among the numerous songs sung on that occasion, bewailing the approaching loss of the bride's "maiden freedom," and the "beauty" with which that freedom is associated, is one[6] in which a being called the "White Kika" threatens to destroy the bride's maiden beauty, the *Kika* being here most likely a type of married life, for that word means some sort of head-covering in many Slavonian dialects.

The songs about maiden freedom convey a favourable impression of the manner in which the Old Slavonians used to treat their daughters. Not only her mother is constantly spoken of by the bride in terms of warm affection, but her father also. "Where hast thou grown up, Kalinushka," asks a Galician song [the Kalina being the guelder-rose], "that thou hast become so slim and tall, and that thy foliage has spread so widely?" "In the meadows beside the fountain, beside the cool waters, away from the wild winds, and from the scorching sun."

"Where hast thou grown up, O maiden, that thou hast become so beautiful?" "In my father's house, in the pleasant shade."

"Whatever the father-in-law may be like," says one song, "he never can be the same to you as your

---

* A Vologda song.

born father;" or as another more poetically expresses it, "However warm the winter may be, yet for all that it is not the summer." But the songs which most graphically depict the affection existing between parents and their daughters are those which have special reference to the case of an orphan bride. In them she grieves bitterly at the thought that she has no parent to bid her God-speed on her new path in life, but she is not without some hope that her father or mother will stand beside her in ghostly shape on the day of her wedding, if not to give her away, at least to bestow a blessing upon her.

> O my brothers! ye bright falcons!
> Enter into the church of God!
>   Strike three times on the bell!
> Split open, damp mother earth!
> Fly asunder ye coffin-planks!
> Unroll, O brocade of gold!
> And do thou rise up, O father, bátyushka!
> Say farewell, and give me thy blessing!
>
> . . . . . .
>
> I am borne away by my own, my brothers,
> Give me thy blessing, father, bátyushka [7].

In one of the Little-Russian songs a dead mother transforms herself into a rain-cloud, and pours a fruitful shower over the village in which her daughter is about to spend her married life. It seems from the songs, says Orest Miller [*Opuit*. I. 114], as if the severity with which parents treated their daughters in the old "patriarchal" days, and the

[7] Ruibnikof, III. 363.

state of dependence in which they held them, had become greatly altered as time passed by. In what some commentators suppose to be the oldest relics of Slavonian nuptial poetry, the bride is purchased from her relatives by a stranger, whom she is compelled, much against her will, to follow to his home; and there she is treated by his family in a manner which makes her look back with fond regret to the relatives she has left behind. But in another group of wedding songs, later in date than the first it is supposed, but still ancient, the bride is represented as being allowed to choose a husband for herself, and she looks forward to being treated by his relatives as kindly as by her own.

In the songs which are now sung by the bride, or addressed to her, at the time of her wedding, the old complaints are still kept up, but they are for the most part conventional, and have but little or no real meaning. The bride is still expected to weep and wail at the idea of leaving her father's house, and the bridegroom still, by deputy, goes through a form of bargaining for her, but these customs are but symbols, survivals from a period of sterner domestic relations.

The following account of how her mother counselled Máryushka Efímovna [Mary, the daughter of Euthymus] may be taken as a specimen of the nuptial songs which refer to the brides's right of selection, and which are more in accordance with modern sentiment than most of the marriage poems:—

> Her mother has counselled Máryushka,
> Has given counsel to her dear Efímovna.

"Go not, my child,
 Go not, my darling,
Into thy father's garden for apples,
 Nor catch the mottled butterflies,
 Nor frighten the little birds,
Nor interrupt the clear-voiced nightingale.
 For should'st thou pluck the apples
 The tree will wither away;
 Or seize the mottled butterfly,
 The butterfly will die.
And should'st thou frighten a little bird,
 That bird will fly away;
Or interrupt the clear-voiced nightingale,
 The nightingale will be mute:
 But catch, my child,
 My dear one, catch
The falcon bright in the open field,
 The green, the open field."

 Máryushka dear has caught,
 Caught has the dear Efímovna,
The falcon bright in the open field,
 The green, the open field.
 She has perched him on her hand,
 She has brought him to her mother.
 "Mother mine, Gosudáruinya,
 I have caught the falcon bright[8]."

In another song her mother leads Máryushka from the terem, or women's chamber, into the room in which the guests are sitting, "the young men in bright array," and there makes her sit down by her side, saying,—

 "Choose, my child,
 My dear one, choose,

[8] Sakharof, I. iii. 124.

Out of unknown guests a known one,
Out of the youths a youth in bright array.
For with that youth thou hast to lead thy life,
To lead thy life, and me, thy mother, to forget."

Then the maiden chooses, and tells her mother on whom her choice has fallen, ending with the words,

With him, dear mother, will I lead my life,
But thee, my mother dear, I never will forget [9].

Sometimes a girl who is awaiting her lover's visit, sings thus :—

Go down, O ruddy sun!
But rise, thou gleaming moon!
And shine through all the night,
Through all the dark night shine,
On all the road, on every path!
So may'st thou yield thy light to my betrothed,
To my dear love Iván;
That so he may not miss his way,
Nor have to turn again,
Nor wander in the forest lost,
Nor in the river drenched;
So that no evil men on him may fall,
No savage dogs may drive him far away.
Away from him my life is weary,
Away from him my life is sad [1].

When her lover leaves her for a time he gives her a golden ring [*pérsten'*, a signet-ring, or one set with gems, from *perst*, a finger], and receives from her a gold ring in exchange [*Kol'tsë*, a plain

---

[9] Sakharof, I. iii. 125.   [1] Sakharof, I. iii. 123.

circlet, like our own wedding-ring, from *Kolo*, a circle].

It is not a falcon flying across the sky,
It is not a falcon scattering blue feathers,
But a brave youth galloping along the road,
Forth from his bright eyes pouring bitter tears.
   He has parted from his home,
   The Lower-River track, through which
   In all her beauty Mother Volga flows.
   He has parted from the maiden fair,
   And with her as a token left
     A costly diamond ring ;
   And from her has he taken in exchange
     A plighting ring of gold.
And while exchanging gifts thus has he spoken,
   Forget me not, my dear one,
   Forget me not, my loved companion.
Often, often gaze upon my ring ;
Often, often will I kiss thy circlet,
Pressing it to my beating heart,
   Remembering thee, my own.
If ever I think of another love,
The golden circlet will unclasp :
Should'st thou to another suitor yield,
From the ring the diamond will fall [2].

Sometimes she tells her companions that their turn will come, and lovers even better than her own will be theirs, but that she shall not envy them, so contented will she be with her lot. She does not now look on her suitor as her enemy, or her purchaser. He is her loved one, who showers gifts on her relatives. And those relatives, instead of regarding her as a mere "living broom" to be sold into cap-

[2] Shein, I. 303.

tivity, prize her, and mourn at having to part with her. When she goes to her new home her father-in-law shows himself in the light, not of "an evil bear," but of a loving parent. So happy is she that she prefers drinking water with her husband to indulging in mead with her mother.

> Beyond the hill Khveklunka is weaving wreaths;
> Her mother sends messengers after her.
> "Come, Khveklunka, to drink mead."
> "I will not come, mother, to drink mead.
> To me to drink mead, is drought,
> But to weave wreaths, is beauty."
> Beyond the hill Khveklunka is weaving wreaths;
> Samuska sends messengers after her.
> "Come, Khveklunka, to drink water."
> "To thee will I come, Samuska, to drink water.
> With thee to drink water, to me is beauty;
> Without thee to weave wreaths, to me is drought[3]."

In a number of Little-Russian songs, indeed, she finds her lover far kinder than her parents, for they refuse to help her when she is drowning.

> As the maiden sank,
> She called to her father,
> "O father dear!
> Do not let me drown..."
> "My dear child,
> I cannot swim,
> I dare not go into the river."

Then she appeals to her lover, who immediately replies in the most prompt as well as sensible manner,

> "My dear girl!

[3] A White-Russian song. Tereshchenko, II. 561.

I dare go into the water,
And I know how to swim,"

and then proceeds to save her.

As soft and romantic a sentiment as breathes in some of the Great-Russian songs which have been quoted, makes itself felt also in the corresponding utterances of the other Slavonic nations. In one of the Moravian songs a mother, who is vexed at her daughter's readiness to get married, paints a very gloomy picture of the husband who is awaiting her, and of all his family, constantly remarking " It was you yourself who would have him." To which the girl replies, " Yes, I chose the rose blossom for myself. That betrothed of mine is dearer to me than all the world beside." So much in Bohemian songs does many a girl love her betrothed, that for his sake she willingly parts with her green wreath—the type of maidenhood—being ready to place it in his hand "if only he will always love and cherish her till death itself." In one of the Servian songs a bride is asked if she does not grieve at leaving her mother. " Why should I grieve ?" she replies. " In my loved one's house, I am told, I shall find a still better mother." In another a mother is represented as bitterly grieving over the daughter who is about to leave her, but the daughter herself feels little sorrow, she longs so to be with her bridegroom.

We have seen from some of the songs that among the Russian peasantry considerable liberty of action, with reference to the choice of a husband, has long been conceded to girls. In this respect the despotism of fathers has greatly altered since the patriarchal times, to the severe tone of which so many of the wedding songs bear witness. And the seclusion of women which was practised by the Boyars during the "Moscow period," a custom introduced by them from the East, and borrowed from them by the merchant class, seems scarcely to have been known to the peasantry. Among what may be called the higher and middle classes, it used to be customary for a bridegroom not to see the face of his bride until after the nuptial as well as the betrothal ceremonies had come to an end, but the young people of the lower classes seem never to have had to submit to any such restrictions on their elective privileges. For a long time, at all events, there has been full freedom of intercourse between the young men and maidens of the Russian villages. The houses of the peasants are not, as a general rule, large enough to allow their women much seclusion, and as it is customary for men and women to work together in the fields, the barriers between the sexes, which it would be difficult to maintain at home, cannot well be set up out of doors. But the occasions on which the young people in Russia most easily form acquaintance with each other are the summer Khorovods and the winter Posidyelkas which have been described in the introductory chapter. At these, as has already been remarked, the youths and maidens have every opportunity of falling in love, and of commencing a courtship which, as a general rule, terminates in a marriage.

Of the numerous songs referring to such love-matches one specimen has been given at p. 31. Here is another of the same kind. It is supposed to be sung by a chorus of girls, in honour of a bridegroom who rejoices in the name of Andrei Polikarpovich, the bride's name being Avdótya Nikoláevna.

As from her nest,
Her warm little nest,
A young bird has fluttered forth,
And down from the apple-tree bough
Has flown away to the open fields,
The green fields, the grassy meadows;
There has plucked up by the roots a blade of grass,
Then flung the blade of grass aside;
But afterwards has cropped, the little bird has cropped,
  Has plucked a poppy blossom;
And, having plucked, has fallen in love with it.
So from the terem, the terem,
From the fair, the lofty terem,
The fair, the lofty, the bright,
From under her mother's care,
Has come forth the fair maiden,
Has come forth, has hastened out,
The sweet fair maiden, Avdótyushka.
Out into the wide courtyard
Has gone the sweet Avdótyushka,
Into the green garden and grove of cedars.
The dear Nikoláevna has sat down
At the new, the oaken table,
Has looked round at the guests, the new arrivals,
All the new arrivals, strangers to her.
And she has chosen herself a bridegroom.
Not a single one of those there was to her liking.
Avdótyushka has chosen for herself,
Nikoláevna dear has chosen for herself,

Has chosen thee Andrei, our master,
Thee Andrei Polikárpovich.
And now, having chosen, she has fallen in love,
Fallen in love with him, grown proud of him.
"Oh! how fond I am of him!
Oh! how dear he is to my heart!
Oh! how I can never be tired of looking at him!
Oh! how I can never gaze at him enough!
Oh! how I never want to part with him[5]!"

The right of choosing their husbands, which is at least partially enjoyed by Russian peasant girls, is claimed by their sisters in other Slavonic lands. Even among the Slovenes, who are said still, as of old, to call their young girls "shovels" and "brooms," and among whom a bride is obliged, the day after her marriage, to do all the menial work of the household herself—even among them a girl is seldom called upon to marry an utter stranger. As a general rule her hand is asked for by some young man who has made her acquaintance at the games in which both sexes take part. One of the marriage customs still kept up among the Slovenes serves to prove that women were anciently looked upon by them as the servants of their husbands, but also shows that the wife's position became improved at some later period. After a marriage the bride is obliged to take her husband's boots off—a custom which prevails in Russia also—but having done so she hits him over the head with one of his boots, by way of a protest against the idea

[5] Sakharof, I. iii. 122.

of inferiority implied in the function which she has just fulfilled. If a Slovene bride, indeed, contrives to reach the church porch before her husband, after the marriage-service is over, she hopes that she will enjoy a life-long supremacy over him—an idea which is shared by brides in many lands. In Russia the struggle between young married people is as to which of the two shall be the first to tread on the cloth laid down for the bride and bridegroom to stand on. But the idea of a wife's possible supremacy over her husband would be impossible, one would suppose, among people who took so low a view of the social status of women as appears to have prevailed among the heathen Slavonians. In every land a young wife is liable to the distaste for her new home, the longing after that of her girlish days, which is expressed in the following song. The first two lines are what is technically called a *Pripyevka*—something which accompanies the song, generally a refrain, here a prelude. Like the *Prískazka*, which often stands at the head of the *Skazka*, or tale, it usually has neither meaning of its own, nor connexion with what follows.

> Through the currant bushes
> There flowed a stream,
> What time my mother
> Bare me, the unhappy one.
> Having chosen unwisely,
> She gave me in marriage,
> To go to a distant,
> Unknown home.
> My father-in-law

Scolds me for nothing;
My mother-in-law,
For every trifle.
I will flee, dart away;
In a cuckoo's shape:
I will fly to my home,
To my father's home.
In his garden green
Will I take my place,
On the apple-tree
My mother loves.
I will cuckoo cry,
I will sadly wail,
Till my wailings sad
Make all eyes weep,
Till the garden is drowned
In bitter tears.

Through the passages
My mother speeds;
Her daughters-in-law
She rouses up.

"Up, up! in haste,
My daughters dear!
What bird is that
In our garden there?"
"I will shoot it dead,"
Cries her eldest son.
"I will drive it away,"
Cries her second son.
Says the youngest son,
"I will go and look
If it may not be
Our sister sad,
From among strange folk,
From her far-off home, strange folk among."

MARRIAGE SONGS. 305

"Come, come, sister,
Into our chamber come.
Tell us about your sorrows,
Ask us about ours [5]."

It must not be supposed that all the Russian marriage songs are of this mournful cast of thought. Here, for instance, is one of happier tone, intended to be sung in honour of the husband's father (Iván Ivánovich) and mother (Anna Ivánovna):—

Our young Boyáruinya has strolled through the rooms,
In her hands she held an embroidery frame.
On the frame was stretched a piece of rose-coloured velvet.
Three patterns has the Boyáruinya embroidered.
The first pattern she embroidered—
The morning dawn with the white light.
The second pattern she embroidered—
The bright young moon with the stars.
The third pattern she embroidered—
The red sun with its rays.
The morning dawn with the white light,
That is love and agreement with one's wife,
Great love from all one's heart.
The bright young moon with the stars
Is Iván with his sons,
Dear Ivánovich with his falcons.
The red sun with its rays
Is Anna with her daughters
Dear Ivánovna with her swans [6].

---

[5] Shein, I. 339. In another version of the same song it is not her brothers who make such harsh observations, but her sisters-in-law, while her "born sister" comes to her aid.

[6] Quoted from a Perm collection by Orest Miller, *Chrest*. I. 27.

X

And here is another in which a very poetic view is taken of the relative positions of husband and wife :—

" Little did I, the young one, slumber at night,
Little did I slumber, but much did I see in sleep.
Just as if in the middle of our courtyard
There grew a cypress tree,
And another sugar-sweet tree;
And on the tree were golden boughs,
Golden boughs, and boughs of silver."
Then spake the head of the household, the master.
" I, my soul, will explain to thee thy dream . . .
The cypress tree—that is I who am thine,
The sugar-sweet tree—that is thou who art mine:
And the boughs on the tree are the children who
   are ours,
Our children, children dear⁷."

In the olden time the celestial divinities were supposed to be favourers and protectors of marriage, and the first nuptial crown was attributed to that heavenly framer of all manner of implements who forged the first plough for man. And so in some of the songs—one of which has been quoted [p. 198]—a prayer is offered up to a mysterious smith, beseeching him to construct a golden nuptial crown, and out of the fragments of it to make a wedding-ring, and a pin with which to fasten the bridal veil.

In another song a divine being is asked to come to the wedding, and to forge such a marriage as may be firm, strong, long enduring, eternal—one on which

⁷ O. Miller, *Chrest.* I. 28, from the Perm collection.

the wind may blow without scattering it, and the rain may beat without washing it away, and which the sun may dry without turning it into dust.

In one of the songs mention is made of a golden-horned stag—one of the forms, perhaps, of the solar deity—who promises to be present at a marriage, and to light up the whole courtyard with his antlers. But the mythic personages who are usually invited to a wedding, with a view towards reaping the benefit of their powers as metal-workers, are the saints Cosmas and Demian—the Christian heroes who, as we have seen, have usurped the place occupied in heathen times by the Slavonic Vulcan. Here is one of the songs in which their names occur:—

Kuzma and Demian, Oi Lado! Oi Lado!
Give us to drink to the wedding, Oi Lado, Oi Lado!
From Khalimon's to Peter's court
Lead three foot-paths.
Along the first path
Goes Kuzma with Demian.
And along the second path
The most Holy Redeemer Himself.
But along the third path
Has gone Khvatei with Alinya.
He takes her by the right hand,
And leads her to the court of God,
To the court of God; to the wedding [8].

Thus do Christian and heathen names still clash in the wedding songs of the Russian peasantry, just as, in the funeral songs to which we are now about

[8] From the "Ethnographical Collection" published by the Russian Geographical Society. Pt. vi. *Bibliog. Ukaz.* 13.

to direct our attention, ideas founded on the Christianity of the present will be found strangely confused with those belonging to the heathenism of the past.[9]

---

[9] Kavelin thinks that many of the wedding songs now preserved among the common people were, in all probability, originally composed for and sung at the weddings of Princes and Nobles. Many of the allusions in the songs seem to him to point to such an origin ; among others the frequent mention of the *terem*, the upper room set apart for the women of the family, which is generally supposed to have derived its name from the Greek word *teremnon*, a room. Some of the marriage customs, he suggests, are relics of ancient religious rites. Of such a nature, for instance, is the progress around a fire, outside the house, often performed when the bridal procession returns from church. But those which are connected with ecclesiastical ceremonies, it should be stated, probably come from Christian Greece, the Russian *vyenchanie*, or crowning, for example, answering to the Greek *stephanôsis*.

As regards the complaints of the modern bride about the "far-off land" into which she is about to be carried, when, perhaps, she is not going to leave her native village, Kavelin remarks that in olden times marriages seem not to have been contracted between members of the same community, who were looked upon as all forming one family ; and therefore girls really had to go far from home when they married. And as each community looked upon all others as possible foes, so the bride who married into a different clan might fairly consider that she was going among not only strangers but enemies.

CHAPTER V.

FUNERAL SONGS.

FROM the gaiety of the epithalamium we now abruptly pass to the melancholy of the dirge. Marriage and death were often brought into strange fellowship by at least some of the Old Slavonians. Strongly impressed with the idea that those whom the nuptial bond had united in this world were destined to live together also in the world to come, they so sincerely pitied the lot of the unmarried dead, that, before committing their bodies to the grave, they were in the habit of finding them partners for eternity. The fact that, among some Slavonian peoples, if a man died a bachelor a wife was allotted to him after his death, rests on the authority of several witnesses, and in a modified form the practice has been retained in some places up to the present day. In Little-Russia, for instance, a dead maiden is dressed in nuptial attire, and friends come to her funeral as to a wedding, and a similar custom is observed on the death of a lad. In Podolia, also, a young girl's funeral is conducted after the fashion of a wedding, a youth being chosen as the bridegroom who attends her to the grave, with the nuptial kerchief twined around his arm. From that time her family consider him their relative, and the rest of the community look upon him as a widower. In some parts of Servia when a lad dies, a girl dressed as a bride follows him to the tomb, carrying two crowns; one of these is thrown to the corpse, and the other she keeps at least for a time[1]. And so the ideas of the Old Slavonians about the grave were not always of a sombre nature, nor are those of the Russians of the present day. A proof of this is afforded by the strange combination of grief and rejoicing which characterizes the festival of the *Rádunitsa*. This is held soon after Easter, the tenth day after Easter Sunday being generally devoted to it in North-east Russia. At that time of year the dead "Fathers" are supposed to feel some relief from the cold of the long winter, and from the idea of their "rejoicing" most etymologists derive the name of *Rádunitsa* [*radost'* = joy, *rádovat'sya* = to rejoice].

This seems doubtful[2], but thus much is certain, that the festival has always been one of a partly mirthful nature. In olden days it seems to have commenced with heathen rites, after which the relatives of the dead wept and wailed for their loss. Then a feast

[1] Kotlyarevsky, 58, 231.

[2] Kotlyarevsky, in his excellent work "On the Funeral Rites of the heathen Slavonians," compares the name of *Rádunitsa* with a supposed Sanskrit word *radanh* = sacrifice, offering, from the root *rádh*, to complete, sacrifice, *etc*. But on this M. Lerch remarks that no such word as *radanh* exists in Sanskrit. (Perhaps *rádhana* may have been intended.) The author, he says (as quoted by Afanasief, P. V. S. III. 796), probably meant the Zend word *rádanh*

was celebrated over the graves, on which were scattered and poured some portions of the viands and the drinks, and revels commenced which lasted long. All these features are to be distinctly traced in the festival celebrated by the modern Russians, only Christian have been substituted for heathen rites at its commencement. On the second Tuesday after Easter, crowds flock early in the morning to the cemeteries, carrying with them small bundles, and there celebrate the commemoration of their dead. He who does not have a *Panikhída*, or requiem, sung in honour of his departed " Fathers," is held to commit a grievous sin, for the omission is the cause of great pain and distress to their sad ghosts, who would have attended the service, and have received from it much solace. Moreover, it is generally believed that if the end of the world shall at any time happen to coincide with the performance of one of these requiems, the souls to whom the service refers will go straight to Paradise, along with those of the persons at whose request it is being performed.

After the service the mourners visit their ancestral graves, and wail there, uttering loud invocations to the dead. Then they eat and drink to their repose, moistening the earth with beer, meal, or spirits, and strewing crumbs of their viands over it. Among

to which a Sanskrit *râdh-as* might correspond. But the guttural *n* before *h* in Zend has nothing in common with the sound *n* in the syllable *ni* of *Rádunitsa*. He thinks, however, that both *rádunitsa* and *rádovat'sya* may spring from the same root as *râdanh* and *râdh-as*. [Doctrinally, though not etymologically, the *Rádunitsa* may possibly have been linked with the Indian *Srâddha*.]

other things thus offered to the dead are coloured Easter Eggs, and on that account some of the peasants call the act of commemoration their *Khristósovanie* with their departed relatives: for when people meet at Easter they kiss each other joyfully three times, one of each couple saying, " Christ is risen !" and the other replying, " He is risen indeed !" and to perform this rite, which is often attended with the presentation of Easter eggs, is called *Khristósat'sya*[3]. Newly-married couples frequently take such eggs with them at this time, and visit the tombs of their respective parents, in order to ask for the parental blessing upon their union.

After this, in Little-Russia,—where, as well as in White-Russia, says Tereshchenko, the joyous nature of the festival is most clearly seen,—singers of a semi-ecclesiastical nature, seminarists and the like, are invited to chant "spiritual songs" to funereal strains. Thereupon the mourners take to weeping, and wailing piteously. Then the senior of the party calls on the secular minstrels who are in attendance to perform. They begin with funeral songs, on hearing which the grief of the mourners bursts forth anew. All of a sudden the musicians strike up a lively tune. In a moment all sorrow is forgotten, merriment takes its place, and the rest of the day is devoted to songs, dances, and strong drinks. "Beer was drunk at the Carnival," says a proverb, "but it was after the Rádunitsa that heads ached." The memorial cakes,

---

[3] See "Russia in 1870," by W. Barry, p. 171; a book containing a great deal of useful information about the Russian peasantry.

MODERN FUNERAL RITES. 313

it should be remarked, must be supplied in odd numbers, in threes, fives, and so forth, and must be eaten without sauce. If any one is too poor to provide them for himself, his richer neighbours are expected to furnish him with what is necessary [4].

Before speaking about the relics of old poetry relating to the dead which have been preserved in the memories of the Russian peasantry, it may not be amiss to say a few words with respect to the heathen rites celebrated at funerals by the Old Slavonians, and to point out such traces of the influence of those rites as are to be found in the customs still kept up at funerals among the modern Slavonians, especially among the Russians. This subject has been so exhaustively treated by Kotlyarevsky in the erudite work to which we have already referred, that little more is required than to give a summary of his conclusions. We will begin with the customs which are still observed on the occasion of a death in a Slavonic village. They vary, of course, to a certain extent, according to the nationality and the religion of the villagers, but still a marked similarity is to be found in the descriptions which have been written of them, whether the describer had in view the inhabitants of Great, Little, or White-Russia, the various Slavonic subjects of Austria or of Turkey, or such scattered fragments of the stock as the Kashoubes of the Baltic and the Wends of Lusatia. It need hardly be observed that, under the influence of modern ideas,

[4] Tereshchenko, v. 27—30.

old customs are fast dying out in all much-frequented neighbourhoods, and that, when it is said in the following sketch that such and such practices occur, it is not always meant that they are of notorious and constant occurrence.

When the course of a Slavonic peasant is evidently all but run, those who are in attendance on the sufferer do their best to mitigate his dying agony. For this purpose they often take the patient from his bed, on which they think he would "die hard," and stretch him on the floor, sometimes on the bare earth, sometimes on a couch of straw. This practice is common to nearly all the Slavonic peoples, among several of whom there prevails also the custom of clearing the way for the departing spirit. Thus in some parts of Ruthenia they make a hole in the roof over the sufferer's head, and in Bulgaria they sweep off the dust and cobwebs, and all else that is attached to or hanging from the ceiling. Some of the Slovaks also fumigate the dying person with burning grass, under the impression that his soul will fly away together with the smoke, as with something of a kindred nature.

When all is over, the window is immediately opened, and sometimes a cup of water is set on the sill for the use of the departing soul. Some Slavonians place bread there also, and others set apart a chair as a resting-place for the spirit. As a general rule a lighted candle is placed by the side of the corpse, or in its hand.

Within the house in which the dead man lies all labour ceases, so that his rest may not be disturbed.

Some of the family prepare the body "for its long journey;" others go round with the tidings of death, or engage themselves in completing any thing that the defunct may have left unfinished. The Western Lusatians still keep up an old custom which used to be general among the Baltic Wends, of announcing a death by passing a black wand from hand to hand through the village. Among the Polish Mazovians, as soon as a peasant is dead, it is customary for his heir to make the round of his homestead, and announce the change of ownership to its buildings, its trees, and its live-stock, saying, "Your former master is dead. I am your new one now." The Lusatian Wends make a similar announcement to their bees also.

The body is generally washed after death, but in some parts of Ruthenia and Carniola this must be done while the dying person is still alive. In some places a burial garment, a *Sávan*, or shroud, is put on at once, but in others, among the South Slavonians for instance, this dressing is deferred till a later period. Great care is taken to provide the dead man with what he requires on his long journey, especially with a handkerchief or towel, which is tied round the neck or waist, and with a coin, which is placed in the hand of the corpse, or wrapped in the handkerchief. The Russian peasants say that the dead man will require the handkerchief to wipe his face with after his long journey, and the coin for the purpose of buying a place in the other world; but the money, if not the handkerchief, was undoubtedly intended for the ghostly ferryman, the Charon of the Slavonic spirit world. The custom of providing money for the corpse has always been universal among the Slavonians, but practice varied with regard to the disposal of the coins, which were sometimes used for the purpose of closing the eyes of the dead, sometimes thrown into the grave at the burial. The practice of furnishing the corpse with the parings of human and other nails, to be used by the climbing spirit, has already been mentioned. [See p. 110.]

In all Slavonic countries great stress has from time immemorial been laid on loud expressions of grief for the dead. These was formerly attended by laceration of the faces of the mourners, a custom still preserved among some of the inhabitants of Dalmatia and Montenegro. The keening begins immediately after a death, continues until the body has been laid in the grave, and afterwards breaks out afresh at certain intervals.

As a general rule a wife laments for her husband, a daughter for a parent, a mother for a son, and a sister for a brother. If there is no relative to perform the duty, it devolves upon a stranger. But in some places the lamenting is done by deputy, a professional mourner being called in for the purpose. This may be in accordance with the idea, prevalent among so many different nations, that a man's relatives must not mourn for him, that their tears would cause him discomfort or even pain. At the present day, however, the Russian *Plakal'shchitsa,* or Public

Wailer, is generally employed at a funeral merely because she is better acquainted with the conventional expressions of grief than the relatives of the dead person can be expected to be. All Slavonic peoples are rich in stores of the wailings used on such occasions, but it is among the Little-Russians and the Servians that they flourish most luxuriantly. After the dead man has been properly dressed, his body is set in some appointed place, and all who are present kiss him and say farewell to him, and drink to his prosperous journey. Liquor is provided for this purpose, and with it is brought bread, for bread (or corn) plays a considerable part in the funeral rites. The Pinsk peasantry, for instance, when they take the corpse from the bench on which it is usually laid, strew corn on the place it has occupied, and set bread on the spot which its shoulders have pressed.

Among most Slavonian peoples at the present day the corpse is put into a coffin, but the practice is not universal. Neither the Bulgarians nor the Montenegrines use regular coffins, but they employ planks in their graves. The Russian word for coffin, *grob*, [Lithuanian *grabas*, Gothic *graban*,] did not originally bear that meaning, but signified something dug out.

The old heathen Slavonians commonly placed their dead in hollowed-out trunks of trees. Such a trunk is called *kolóda*, and by that name a coffin is known in many of the provincial dialects of Russia. The Slovenes used these trunk-coffins up to the beginning of the present century, and to this day the Raskolniks of the Chernigof Government still inter their dead in them.

The corpse was often carried out of the house through a window, or through a hole made for the purpose, and the custom is still kept up in many parts. Among some of the Hungarian Slavonians it was customary to tap three times with the coffin at the corner of the *izba*, or at the threshold of the doors, and the Czekhs used to shake the bier above the threshold, or sign a cross with it. For under the threshold live the domestic deities, the guardians of the family, the souls of ancestors. In some places the old custom is still observed of placing on the threshold an axe, or some other implement, the axe corresponding to the hammer to which, in Scandinavian mythology, a consecrating influence was so often attributed. When the corpse of a rustic proprietor is being carried out, it is customary in some parts of Poland to let loose all his cattle, that they may take leave of their old master.

In some places, after a man's body has left the house, his widow takes a new pitcher, and breaks it to pieces on the earth, and afterwards strews oats over the ground traversed by the funeral procession.

In former times the corpse is said to have been conveyed on *sani*, a sledge; whence comes an old Russian phrase, "to sit in a sledge," meaning "to be at the point of death." But by the term *sani* was probably meant, not the modern sledge, which is used only in winter, but a light sort of vehicle employed at all seasons of the year. A mare was seldom used for the conveyance of the corpse, for fear she might prove barren for the future.

The funeral rites have always been performed before sunset. The sun had to show the disembodied spirit the way to its future abode. After dark the ghost would have been obliged to wander about, painfully seeking its way. Among some of the Croatians it is customary to open the coffin before it descends into the tomb, in order that the sunbeams may warm it.

As regards the ceremonies performed at the grave itself, we will pass over them for the moment, to recur to them when we are dealing with the old burial customs of heathen times, and will now proceed to those which follow the actual interment, and in the first place to the rites of purification. Of these no written evidence exists; their nature can be gathered only from the customs of the people, among which are the following:—The bed on which the dying person lay is carried out of the house, the straw of which use has been made is burnt, and the cottage itself, or its principal room, is strewed with corn. Among the South Slavonians the mourners, on their return from the funeral, are met by an old woman, who carries a vessel containing live coals. On these they pour water, or else, having washed their hands, they take a live coal from the hearth, and fling it over their heads. In Ruthenia they look steadfastly at the stove, or place their hands on it. In olden times the Bohemians, when returning from a funeral, avoided looking back, and were accustomed to throw sticks and stones behind them. The Lusatian Wends still make a point of placing water between themselves and the dead as they return from a burial, even breaking ice for the purpose if necessary.

Among the Servians neither the spades which dug the grave, nor the cart and horses which conveyed the coffin, are brought into the farm-yard, but the horses are turned loose into the pastures, and the other accessories of the burial are left for the space of three days outside the gates; otherwise they might introduce death into the homestead.

After the purification comes the funeral banquet, the partakers of which eat and drink to the memory of the dead. This is the descendant of the ancient *Strava*, which will presently be described; but that meal was held either on the grave or near it, whereas its modern representative generally takes place in the house in which the death occurred. The Bulgarians, however, still celebrate it near the grave, and in the Pinsk Government some of the funeral party are in the habit of rising from table in order to finish the meal above the tomb.

With this feast the funeral rite may be said to close. But the departed one is not soon forgotten. In olden days a memorial banquet was held in his honour on the third, sixth, ninth, and fortieth day after his death, and on its anniversary, and he was remembered also in the feasts celebrated at springtide in memory of the Fathers, the collective family dead. To these feasts it was customary to invite the dead, standing before the open door. Silently the living sat down to table, they ate without using knives, and they threw portions of the food under the table for their spirit-guests. What fell by accident was the share of orphan souls who had no friends to nourish them. After a time the unseen banqueters were escorted out, and their hosts turned their attention to drink and merriment.

The customs of the present day are of an equally heathenish nature; some of them, indeed, seem to be even older than those just described. In the Government of Pinsk the peasants at their memorials cover a table with a white cloth, and in the middle of it place a vessel in which *vodka*, or whiskey, is set on fire. They also throw salt on burning coals, and listen to its crackling. When the memorial cakes are ready the oldest of the party walks round the house, gazes at the family graves, and invites the ancestors to the feast. On his return the rest of the party stand silent for a time, as if listening to spiritual accents, and then begin to eat, taking care to pour out for the dead the first three spoonfuls of each dish.

But even stranger than this custom is one kept up in some parts of the Government of Olonets, in which the inhabitants of a village sometimes celebrate a joint festival in honour of their collective dead. Having chosen a house for the purpose, they spread three tables, one outside the front door, one in the passage, and one in the *izba* itself. Then they go out of doors as if to meet their unseen guests, and

Y

return escorting them into the house with the words, "Ye are tired, our own ones; take something to eat." After sitting down to the first table they pass on to the second, and then enter the *izba*. There the master of the house says to the ghostly visitors, "Doubtless ye have grown cold in the moist earth, and on the road, perhaps, it was not warm. Warm yourselves, our own ones, at the stove." Thereupon the living guests take their seats at table. Just before the end of the repast, when the *kisel* (a sort of pudding) is served, the host "opens the window, and lets down into the street the linen in which the dead had been lowered into the grave," and then the whole party begins to escort the unseen visitors from the stove into the outer air, saying, "Now it is time for you to go home, and your feet must be tired: the way is not a little one to travel. Here it is softer for you [i. e. along the linen]. Now, in God's name, farewell!" And the dead are supposed to descend by means of the linen, just as, on the day of their burial, they had been let down into the grave[5].

From these interesting specimens of survival, we will now turn to the rites of which they are fragments, those with which the Old Slavonians, while yet heathens, celebrated the burial of their dead.

Though the subject is one of great interest I do not purpose to enter at all deeply into it, for the evidence which its Russian investigators have

[5] Tereshchenko, III. 123. Taken from Dashkof's "Description of the Olonets Government."

brought together with regard to it is almost entirely derived from foreign and well-known sources, and my main object in the present work is to render intelligible to the general public the speech of exclusively Slavonic witnesses. It will be sufficient, therefore, merely to allude to what has been said about Slavonic funerals by Greek, Arabian, Teutonic, and other writers—to mention how the Emperor Maurice [† A.D. 602] in his *Strategica* explained why the wives of Slavonian warriors refused to survive their husbands; that Theophylactus, early in the seventh century, relates how the Roman General Priscus penetrated into the Slavonic territory, and captured "the king of the Barbarians," one Mousokios, who had been celebrating a brother's funeral with too many wine cups—a piece of evidence which is valuable, and would have been still more so had it been clearly stated that Mousokios was really a Slavonian; that the statement of Theophylactus was copied by Theophanes and by Anastasius the Librarian [about A.D. 886]; that Saint Boniface [A.D. 755] testified, that among the Slavonic *Winedi*, or Wends, the marriage tie was so strong that wives killed themselves when their husbands died, a passage which has given rise to much discussion; that during the first half of the tenth century the Arabian travellers, Ibn Dosta, Masudi, and Ibn Fozlan, gave full accounts of Slavonic burials, including some sensational descriptions of the sacrifices which attended them, some of which accounts were afterwards incorporated into his own work by Leo the Deacon; that

Dithmar, Bishop of Merseburg [A.D. 1018], wrote on the subject, and made one remark in particular to which reference will presently be made; that Otto, Bishop of Bamberg [A.D. 1125], has left behind him some valuable pieces of evidence in his letters forbidding burials in woods and fields, and other heathenish customs; that from the writings of Cosmas of Prague, who died in 1125, copious information is to be gained; and that the Latin poem by Klonowicz, called *Roxolania*, published at Cracow in 1584, contains a graphic sketch of a funeral among its pictures of Ruthenian life in the sixteenth century. The testimony borne by Menetius, or Meletius, in 1551, in his letter *De sacrificiis et ydolatria veterum Borussorum*, and repeated by Lasicius in his work, "*De Diis Samogitarum*," is too well known to require more than a passing reference [6].

Having thus alluded to some of the chief authorities on the subject, we will pass to the consideration of a few of the most important facts which their evidence appears to substantiate, such as the following:—that the old Slavonians sometimes buried and sometimes burnt their dead; that, in some cases at least, human sacrifices were offered on the occasion of a burial, and that it was not an uncommon occurrence for a man's widow to kill herself, or allow herself to be killed, at his funeral; and that the burial was followed always by a feast, and sometimes by martial games, in honour of the dead.

[6] Kotlyarevsky, pp. 42—153.

The question as to whether the Old Slavonians disposed of their dead by interment or by cremation has given rise to much discussion, and a great amount of writing has been bestowed upon the adverse theories of Dobner and Anton; the first of whom asserted that the Slavonians buried, whereas the Teutons burnt, while the second maintained an exactly opposite opinion. Some writers, moreover, have explained that the Slavonians, while Nomads, used to burn their dead, but took to burying them when they accepted a settled form of life. Others have divided the heathen Slavonians into two religious sects, each of which had its own ideas about burial. Others, again, have held that the Slavonians used to burn their dead so long as they were heathens, but gave up the practice on becoming Christians; and a fourth set of scholars have suggested that rich Slavonians used to be burnt, while poor ones could only get buried. After duly weighing all these arguments, Kotlyarevsky arrives at the conclusion that there never was any general rule, but that some Slavonians buried without burning, while others first burnt their dead, and then buried their ashes, acting in accordance with old family traditions. In excavating, it is not uncommon to find traces of both customs in the same tomb: near the remains of a corpse interred without cremation lie the ashes of one which has been calcined or at least partially burnt.

As regards the spots in which they deposited either the bodies or the ashes of their departed relatives, various customs seem to have prevailed. Sometimes hills, and especially caves in hills, were chosen as burial-places. In very remote times it is possible that they may have buried the remains of their dead within their dwellings, under the threshold, the spot still selected by many of their descendants for the burial of unchristened babes. The Baltic Slavonians and the Czekhs are known to have chosen fields and forests for this purpose. General cemeteries do not seem to have been known (except for strangers) among the heathen Slavonians, for no ancient word for such places occurs in any Slavonic dialect[7]; and the excavations which have been made in Slavonic lands bear out this idea, the tombs having almost always been found to stand either singly or in family groups.

Whether the Slavonians ever sent their dead afloat on an actual sea it is impossible to say, but the geographical position of most of them renders such an idea improbable, so far as the European period of their history is concerned. The term *nav'* for a dead person is supposed by some writers to imply ideas connected with navigation, and there seems to be reason for supposing that boats, or at least boat-shaped cases, were used for the reception of corpses at funerals, but these boats may merely have been intended to allude to the (atmospheric) sea which the soul had to cross after death.

From the accounts of the foreigners who have written on the subject it may be gathered that it

---

[7] Kotlyarevsky, p. 227.

was customary among the old Slavonians to place the boat, or other wooden case containing the corpse, on a pyre, which, after the family had taken a last farewell of the dead, was lighted by one of their number. It has been supposed, but it is not certain, that a particular kind of wood was always used on such occasions—that, namely, of the thorn, one of the trees connected with the lightning.

Together with the corpse various objects were burnt, or buried. The dead took with them to the other world, according to the popular belief, their favourite horses and other animals, their dress, their arms, and their ornaments, and many other things which were likely to conduce towards their comfort and happiness in the grave. Of certain material aids to the aspiring soul, such as leather thongs, ladders, and nail-parings, mention has already been made. But by far the most important among the companions of the dead were the human beings who either killed themselves, or were put to death, upon the occasion of a funeral.

The fact that, in Slavonic lands, a thousand years ago, widows used to destroy themselves in order to accompany their dead husbands to the world of spirits, seems to rest on incontestable evidence; and at an earlier period there can be no doubt that "a rite of suttee, like that of modern India," prevailed among the heathen Slavonians, the descendant, perhaps, as Mr. Tylor remarks of "widow-sacrifice" among many of the European nations, " of an ancient Aryan rite belonging originally to a period even earlier than the Veda[8]." According to Ibn Dosta, in some places it was customary for the dead man's favourite wife to hang herself, in order that her body might be burnt with that of her lord; in others she was expected to allow herself to be buried alive with his corpse. To this practice there are many allusions in the songs and the customs of the people. Among the latter may be reckoned the so-called "marriages" between the living and the dead, which have already been mentioned, and among the former those Moravian songs in which the dead are described as rising from their graves, and carrying off their wives or their betrothed, the Builina in which the dead Potok is buried together with his living wife, and some other poems of a similar nature.

In addition to being accompanied by his widow, the heathen Slavonian, if a man of means and distinction, was solaced by the sacrifice of some of his slaves. The fullest description of what occurred on such an occasion is that given by Ibn Fozlan, who declares that he was an eyewitness of what took place. According to him, when one of the "Russian" merchants, with whom he became acquainted in Bulgaria, died, "they asked his girls which of them would die with him. One answered that she would," whereupon she was handed over to the care of the two daughters of an old woman who had the appearance of a "yellow, wrinkled witch," and who bore the

---

[8] E. B. Tylor's "Primitive Culture," I. 421; where the subject is discussed at length.

name of "The Angel of Death." They kept watch over her till the final moment in which "the woman called Death's angel fixed about her neck a twisted rope, which she gave two men to pull," and at the same time drove a knife in between her ribs, so that she died. Her dead body was then placed beside that of her lord, in a ship which had been taken from the river for the purpose, and which was propped up by four trees and surrounded by "wooden images of men and giants." With the human corpses were placed those of a dog, two horses, and a pair of fowls, and finally the ship was set on fire. Just before the girl was killed, says Ibn Fozlan, she cried out three times, saying, "Look! there do I see my father and my mother!" and again, "Look! I see all my relations sitting together there!" and finally, "Look! There is my lord! He sits in Paradise. Paradise is so green, so beautiful! By his side are all his men and boys. He calls me: bring me to him!" And after all was over the "Russians" scoffed at their Arabian friend as belonging to a race who buried their dead, and so gave them as a prey to worms and corruption; whereas they themselves burnt their dead at once, and so obtained admittance for them without delay into Paradise. The whole of the narrative is remarkably interesting, but unfortunately it is not quite clear who these "Russians" were. Ibn Fozlan describes them as the filthiest people he had ever seen, and Rasmussen repudiates them as Scandinavians on account of the want of modesty attributed to their king; but some Russian critics think they must have been Varangian traders[9].

Above the spot on which the funeral rites were celebrated, a mound was heaped. Ibn Dosta says that the ashes of the dead were collected the day after the cremation, and placed in a memorial urn, which was set up on the mound. Ibn Fozlan, on the other hand, states that the mound was piled above the funeral pyre. In some of the tombs which have been explored, vases have been found containing bones which showed traces of fire; in others, the remains have been discovered of bodies which seem to have been interred, and then to have had mounds piled above them. In olden days every one who was present at a funeral deemed it a religious duty to assist in the erection of the mound, just as now every bystander throws a handful of earth *into* the grave.

Upon the mound, it is supposed, a memorial was set up in the shape of a tent, or small wooden house, in which not only the soul might find rest and shelter when visiting the body in which it used to abide, but also the relatives of the dead when they came to mourn over his remains. Traces of this custom are still to be found in Russia. In the

[9] Ibn Fozlan's narrative was published in 1823 by the Russian Academy of Sciences, with a German translation by C. M. Frähn. Rasmussen had previously translated it into Danish, and an English rendering of his version appeared in the 4th vol. of "Blackwood's Magazine." Ibn Dosta's work was published for the first time in 1869, at St. Petersburg, with notes and a Russian translation by the editor, Prof. Chwolson.

Government of Chernigof, for instance, the White-Russians still, in spite of ecclesiastical prohibitions, erect over graves a kind of log-hut. Such a construction is known in some other districts as a *Golubets*, a term sometimes applied to the roofed cross commonly set up over a grave.

Among most of the Slavonic tribes, directly after the funeral rites were over came the *Strava*, the memorial feast, held above the grave, or close beside it. According to Jacob Grimm[1], the name *Strava* is one of Gothic origin, and means a funeral pyre [from *straujan* = *sternere*]. But Kotlyarevsky claims it as a Slavonic word.

Among some of the Slavonians was celebrated the solemn rite of parting with the dead, called the *Trizna*. Its name and its nature are both involved in some uncertainty, but the former is supposed to be akin to *terzanie*, laceration; and, as regards the latter, we know that it took the form of a meal of some kind, followed by games and contests, horse-races and personal combats. It was a form of honouring the dead which could only have prevailed among a warlike people—such as in a like manner honoured a dead Patroclus or Beowulf—and therefore it does not seem to have been known to all the Slavonians. Those of the south were partially

---

[1] *Kleinere Schriften*, II. 239. The words in which Jornandes describes a part of the ceremonies performed at the burial of Attila are well known. "Postquam talibus lamentis est defletus, stravam super tumulum ejus, quam appellant ipsi, ingenti commessatione concelebrant."—*De Getarum Origine*, cap. 49.

acquainted with it, and it is known with certainty to have existed among the Russians. With the course of time it passed into the form of the *Strava*, and now lives in the memorial meal which follows a Russian funeral.

After the tomb had closed over the body or the ashes of the dead, it did not always remain intact. From time to time it was opened for the reception of new tenants, for the heathen Slavonians often buried in one such receptacle the remains of many generations, their respect for it increasing with the number of protecting "Fathers" whose abiding-place it became. This custom has been kept up in some Slavonic countries till the present day; and sometimes a corpse which has not lain long in the ground has to make way for a new comer. Csaplovics states that he was himself an eyewitness of the following occurrence:—A Slovene, whose mother had died, dug up the corpse of his father, collected his bones, washed them with red wine, tied them up in a clean white towel, placed the bundle on his mother's coffin, and then buried the remains of his two parents together[2]. A similar practice prevails in Bulgaria, where, it is said, if no relative dies within the space of three years, the family tomb is opened, and any stranger who happens to expire is buried in it—a custom due to the lingering influence of the old idea, that the grave required a victim.

That of the rites celebrated every spring by the

---

[2] *Slavonien*, I. 184, as quoted by Kotlyarevsky, p. 252.

Old Slavonians in memory of their dead, many traces are still to be found in the customs of their descendants, has been shown in the account given of the *Rádunitsa*, and of such entertainments as the Olonets villagers offer to their family ghosts. To these descriptions may be added one more, that of the old Russian practice of burying, at the commencement of every spring, the bodies of the unknown and uncared-for dead which had accumulated during the winter in the *Ubogie domui*—"poor-houses" set apart for the reception of the bodies of friendless strangers, or of persons who had been murdered or who had died suddenly, and, in fact, for the remains of all the waifs and strays of humanity. During the winter these corpses lay in pits dug within the "poor-houses;" in the spring charitable people met together, took the dead bodies from their temporary resting-place, and buried them decently in consecrated ground. There was a cemetery near Moscow called the "Potter's Field"—in allusion to that which was bought with the thirty pieces of silver "to bury strangers in"—to which the charitable citizens were wont to resort on the seventh Thursday after Easter, there to dig graves for the bodies, and to have divine service performed for the souls, of the friendless dead. They did not know the names of those for whom they prayed, says Karamzin, but they trusted that God would know, and would let their prayers be of good effect.

And now let us turn to the poetry itself—to the complaints, funeral wailings, or keens, uttered at the death or the burial of a relative, or, at a later period, over his grave—*pláchki, zapláchki, etc.* [*plakat'*, = to cry], or *Prichitan'ya* [*prichitát'* = to read beside, to complain]. The songs with which a bride bewails the loss of her girlish freedom are called *Prichitan'ya*, and so were those in which mothers used to lament the departure of their sons to the army. At times, as has already been shown, these *zapláchki* are improvised on the spot, but most of them have been handed down by tradition from a very remote age. Such, for instance, are those in which the lightning is represented as rending graves open, and the spirits of the dead as manifesting themselves to mortal eyes in the form of birds. The following will serve as a specimen of this class:—

> From the side of the East
> Have risen the wild winds,
> With the roaring thunders,
> And the fiery lightnings.
> All on my father's grave
> A star has fallen, has fallen from heaven . . . .
> Split open, O dart of the thunder,
> The moist mother Earth!
> Do thou fall to pieces, O mother Earth,
> On all four sides!
> Split open, O coffin planks,
> Unfold, O white shroud,
> Fall away, O white hands,
> From over the bold heart,
> And do ye become parted, O sweet lips!
> Turn thyself, O my own father,
> Into a bright, a swift-winged falcon;
> Fly away to the blue sea,
> To the blue sea, to the Caspian.

Wash off, my own father,
From thy white face the mould.
Come flying, O my father,
To thy own home, to the lofty terem;
Listen, O my father,
To our songs of sadness![3]

It was generally a friendly ghost that thus revisited the earth beneath the pale glimpses of the moon, being usually the spirit of a parent who sympathized with a child, and longed to do it good service. But there were cases, also, to which the *Skazki*, or stories, bear frequent witness, in which the dead assumed a baleful shape, and, as vampires, or werewolves, ran riot through the world, thirsting for human blood. It was generally a wizard, or witch, or some other disreputable character who behaved in this manner after death, but even the spirits of persons who had led blameless lives might be induced, if proper respect was not paid to them, to revenge themselves on their forgetful survivors. The spirit invoked in the *zapláchki* is usually that of a parent, who is entreated to be present at the wedding of an orphan bride, or at least at the time when the bride and bridegroom are betrothed by the joining of hands, and the parental blessing is bestowed on her: such is the case, for instance in the following lament:—

There are who will give me to eat and to drink,
But to bless me, the young one, there is none;
Neither the father dear who nourished me,
Nor the mother dear who bare me.

[3] Quoted by Orest Miller, *Chrest.* I. 11, from a Perm collection.

See, O my sunlight, my own brother,
If from the Nikolsk oak-wood
Comes not the father dear who nourished me.
For my father dear promised,
At the moment of swift death,
In his very last hour,
To be at the striking fast of hands,
At the last farewell,
At the life-long blessing [4].

The same complaint, the same longing for the parental blessing, is heard in the wailings of a girl who, in rude and untutored language, laments a mother's death:—

There stands a green oak on the hill,
There is no wind, and yet it shakes,
There is no rain, but it is wet.
Many, many on the green oak,
Many a branch and spray is there,
Many a green branch;
Only the green oak
Has no golden top,
No gilded vane,
Such as now it ought to have
At this very time,
Or in the summer fair,
Or in the ample spring.

Much has the fair maiden,
Much wealth of kin,
Many and many a relative,
Many a close friend,
Many a near neighbour.
Only the fair maiden
Has no mother dear,
Such as she now needs,

[4] Ruibnikof, III. 423.

At this very time,
For the great marriage-blessing.
There are who will give her to eat and drink,
But to bless her there is none[5].

The next *zapláchka*—also a very unpolished one—gives utterance to the grief of a mother who bewails the death of a young child.

I will sadly go
To my own, my loved one,
My own heart's love. . . .
Now on this day
The sun burns not as in summertide,
Warms not as in the spring.
With what a fall have I let fall,
With what a loss have I lost!
I will go this day,
In sorrow and tears,
To my loved beloved.
" Tell me, my loved,
" Why hast thou deserted
" Thy mother forlorn?
" Not a word can I gain,
" Not a single secret word,
" To my careworn heart!
" Oh listen, my loved one,
" My own, my darling child!"
Now am I indeed a mother ill-fated!
A cuckoo ill-starred in a green pine-wood,
Such am I, ill-fated, unhappy[6].

But the most remarkable among the group of "complaints" from which we have been quoting, that collected by Ruibnikof in the neighbourhood of Lake Onega, are the two which are intended to be sung at the funeral of the father of a family. One of

[5] Ruibnikof, III. 423. [6] Ruibnikof, III. 417, 418.

them, at least, seems worthy of being translated in full, although it runs to some length. The language in which it is written proves, say Russian critics, that it is of great antiquity. I have rendered it word for word, without attempting to trim it.

After the body has been washed and dressed, it is placed upon a table, and the relatives gather around it. Then, turning to the widow, they address her in song. In the case of poor people the following form is used:—

> Wert thou sitting by the painful bedside,
> Wert thou present at the parting of the spirit,
> When the soul was divided from the white body?
> And how did swift Death come to thee?
> Came she as a beggar-woman, a wandering cripple,
> Or as a brave youth, brisk and burly?
> Or as a stout burlák from Petersburg[7]?

The widow replies:—

> Had I been living in a rich and ample state,
> Then I should have been sitting by the painful bedside,
> And I should have seen swift Death.
> Had she come as a wandering cripple
> I would have spread the hospitable table,
> I would have fed the wandering cripple,
> And she would have left me my wedded spouse.
> And if she had come as a brave youth, brisk and burly,
> I would have clothed her in coloured vestments,
> And would have shod her with goatskin boots,
> And would have given her a silken girdle.
> If she had come as a stout Petersburg burlák,

[7] The *burlák* is here a man who goes up to the city to work for wages.

I would have given her uncounted wealth of gold,
And she would have left me my wedded spouse.
But as I live in an accursed and unhappy condition,
With little children dear, the cause of many cares,
In our house there is no hospitable table,
In our house are no sweet dainties,
Neither are there clothes for youth,
Nor goatskin boots for the feet,
Nor uncounted wealth of gold.
So I did not see my lawful spouse,
When the soul was divided from the white body.

Too great for the peasant-woman's strength is her toil,
Too great for her mind are her accursed cares.
Well nigh all the thoughts in my head are in confusion,
The untimely light fades from my eyes.
How shall I bring up my dear little ones
Without my wedded spouse?
Shall I lose myself in the dark forest,
Or fling myself into some round lake,
Or drown in a swift brook,
So as to get rid of my great misery?
If I become a wandering beggar,
And rid myself of my great misery in the open field,
Then from my great misery
Would spring up thick forests:
No room would there be there for my misery:
The neighbours living around would forbid it,
For their fertile corn-fields would be covered over.
If I were to get rid of my great misery
In a glorious wide lake,
There would be never-moving rocks under the waters of the lake,
And on the meadows stones that never gave way:
So there would be no room for my misery;
It would become an obstacle to the fishermen.
Were I to get rid of it in the whirling river Svir,

Roaring cataracts would become fixed there ;
There too would be no room for my misery,
For stagnant would become the spring waters in
    the rivers.

I will take my dear children [and see],
Whether moist Mother Earth will not split open.
If moist Mother Earth splits open,
Straightway will I and my children bury ourselves
    in it,
So hateful is it to me, the miserable one,
To remain in this home life.
Do thou forgive me, O my wedded spouse!
Thou and I have taken counsel together,
But never didst thou speak to me about this swift
    death.
I would not have given thee up, O my wedded
    spouse,
I would have given up my dear children,
And so have preserved my wedded spouse.
Split open, moist Mother Earth,
And be thou open, O new coffin-planks,
And come flying from heaven, Angels and Arch-
    angels,
And set the soul in the white breast,
And speech in the wise head,
And white light in the clear eyes !
And do thou arise, my wedded spouse;
I have won-thee-by-asking from the Lord God.
Make the sign of the cross, according to what is
    written,
Bow low, according to the fashion of the wise,
Pay me greeting !
Not alone have I invited thee,
But with me I bring thy dear children :
And let us return to our home life,
For now has this life become weariness.
It is plain that my wedded spouse remains angry
With me, on whose head are many miseries.

I have remained in my husband's house,
Bread and salt have I not set eyes on,
And my misery have I not diminished but increased.
Clearly this thing cannot be,
That one dead shall return from the grave:
An orphan must I be without my husband [8].

The companion song is of a similar nature, but is intended to be employed in well-to-do households. It is one which I would fain translate at equal length with its predecessor, but I fear to trespass on the patience of my readers, to whom I can convey but little idea of the merit of the original, depending as that does to a great extent upon the charm of its simple, unaffected, but archaic language, in which so much expression is conveyed by daring diminutives which would be utterly void of meaning to our minds were an attempt made to translate them, and upon the measured verse in which it moves, moulded in a form which holds together and sustains without cramping, and strengthens without impeding.

The preservation of poems so lengthy as are these widows' wailings is, for the most part, due to the jealous care of the professional mourners. In some parts of Russia their profession is unknown, and there the songs are dying out most quickly, but in the remote districts in which Ruibnikof made his collections, in the neighbourhood of Lake Onega, the *Plakal'shchitsa*, or *Voplénitsa* [*vopít'* = to sob or wail], the professional " Crieress "—is a personage of no small importance. She it is, says Ruibnikof, who " watches over the genuineness of social rites;

[8] Ruibnikof, III. 410—413.

it is she who guides the course of marriages, funerals, and memorial feasts." On the day of betrothal, the *Plakal'shchitsa* attends the bride, and sings *zapláchki* expressive of the sorrow a young girl feels at leaving her family and going into "a strange and far-off land;" and during the whole course of the ceremonies preceding that which takes place in church, she settles every detail, and intones almost every song. At a funeral, also, she renders invaluable aid, by seeing that all the traditional ceremonies are observed, and by supplying the sad songs in which the relations of the dead are expected to express the grief they feel at their loss. It was from the lips of an excellent specimen of her class, a *Plakal'shchitsa*, who was so celebrated for her *zapláchki*, that she was frequently invited into outlying districts—and even into one, the natives of which were famous for their knowledge of such lore, and their faculty of improvisation—that Ruibnikof gathered some of the best of his nuptial and funereal laments.

It is chiefly at the time of the *Pomniki*, or commemorations of the dead, in the arrangement of which also the *Plakal'shchitsa* in some districts takes a leading part, that the *Prichitaniya*, or lamentations for the dead, of which we have already spoken, are to be heard. On those occasions it is customary for women to go out to the graves of their relatives, and there to wail or keen, or, as the Russians express it, *golosít* [*golos* = voice]. Throwing themselves on the grave, says Tereshchenko, they first shake their heads over it for a few minutes, and begin whimpering, then they take to wailing a little, and at last, throwing both arms about the mound, they press their bosoms to it, raising their voices all the time, louder and louder still, until they may be heard over the whole of the cemetery. Here is a specimen of a *Prichitanie*, intended to be recited over a grave on the twentieth of April, early in the morning. These lamentations, it should be observed, though of a decidedly poetical nature, do not assume a metrical form.

"O ye, our own fathers and mothers! in what have we angered you, our own, that you have no welcome for us, no joy, no parental charm? O thou sun, bright sun! Rise, rise at midnight, make bright with joyous light all the graves, so that our departed ones may not sit in darkness, nor languish in woe, nor endure endless longing.

"O thou moon, bright moon! Rise, rise at eventide, make bright with joyous light all the graves, so that the departed may not in darkness consume their bold hearts, nor in the darkness go sorrowing about the white world, nor in the darkness pour forth burning tears to their dear children.

"And, O wind, wild wind! do thou arise, arise at midnight, bring to our dear departed the welcome tidings, that for them all their kinsmen are painfully longing, that on account of them all their kinswomen are steeped in sorrow [9]."

And here, by way of conclusion, is a specimen of an orphan's wailings above her mother's grave:—

"O mother dear that bare me, O with sadness longed-for one! To whom hast thou left us, on whom are we orphans to rest our hopes? From no quarter do warm breezes breathe on us, we hear no words of kindness. Good folks turn away from us,

---

[9] Quoted by Orest Miller from Sakharof, II. vii. 23.

our kinsfolk renounce us; rust eats into our orphaned hearts. The red sun burns in the midst of the hot summer, but us it heats not: scarcely does it warm us, O green mother-grave! Have a care for us, mother, dear, give us a word of kindness! No, thou hast hardened thy heart harder than stone, and hast folded thy uncaressing hands over thy heart.

"O my white cygnet! for what journey hast thou prepared and equipped thyself, from which side may we expect thee?

"Arise, O ye wild winds, from all sides! Be ye borne, O winds, into the Church of God! Sweep open the moist earth! Strike, O wild winds, on the great bell! Will not its sounds and mine awaken words of kindness¹?"

---

[1] Quoted from Dashkof by Tereshchenko, III. 102, 103. An interesting description of a Russian cemetery on one of the "Parents' Days" is given by Madame Romanoff in her "Rites and Ceremonies of the Greco-Russian Church," p. 247.

There is a striking resemblance between the Russian *zaplachki* and those *myrologia* of the modern Greeks, of which Fauriel gives so interesting an account in the introduction to his *Chants populaires de la Grèce Moderne*. The *myrologion*, he says, "is, in the full sense of the term, a poetic improvisation inspired by grief." Almost all Greek women possess the faculty of improvisation to some degree, but excellence is of course rare, and a good "myrologist" holds in her own village a distinguished position. In Asiatic Greece and in the Islands there are professional myrologists whose functions are very similar to those of the Russian "wailers." The Myrologia are now sung by women only, but in olden times men also sang them. Several specimens are given in Passow's *Carmina popularia Græciæ recentioris*. See also Tozer's "Researches in the Highlands of Turkey," II. 241.

CHAPTER VI.

SORCERY AND WITCHCRAFT.

THE ideas which were prevalent among the heathen Slavonians with respect to the life beyond the grave, and their belief in the close communion of mortals with the inhabitants of the spiritual world, are of themselves sufficient to account for the wide-spread and deeply rooted belief in the supernatural powers of necromancers and other dealers in magic, the remains of which are to this day very plainly manifest in Russia. But when, in addition to these causes, we consider the great influence which the Finnish races have had upon the Slavonic in the Northeast of Europe—the Finns being, of all European peoples, the most addicted to conjuring—we ought not to wonder at the fact that the Russians used to be no less remarkable for a steadfast faith in the powers of sorcery and witchcraft than were our own forefathers. Nor is it unintelligible—the isolation of villages, and the dearth of education being taken into account—why their descendants, the peasants who now till the soil of Russia, should be as prone to superstition, as responsive to the influence of the imagination, as obedient to the impulse of a morbid fancy, as those benighted Orientals of whom Mr. Tylor tells us, who still believe in spirit-rappings, and planchette-writings, and wizard-elongations[1]. Much time and space would be needed by any one who should undertake to describe the relics of the magical arts of their ancestors which the Russian peasants still preserve. At present I propose to give merely the briefest possible sketch of the history of witchcraft in Russia, as illustrative of some of the songs sung by the people, and of a branch of Russian folk-lore which is closely connected with the popular poetry, the *zagovórui*, or spells—prefacing it with a few remarks upon the *zagádki*, or riddles, in which the people delight so much, and to which in old days a high degree of importance was attached.

Except at one period of the year, the propounding or guessing of riddles is looked upon merely as an amusement by the Russian peasantry, but during the *Svyatki*, the Christmas festivals, it resumes something of its old dignity, and to some extent claims to be performed as a duty of an almost religious character. For in olden times the *zagádka*, the " sense riddle," as Mr. Tylor calls it [*gadát'* = to guess], was, in the Slavonic, as in other lands, an enigma fraught with mythical meaning, an oracular utterance, clothed in dark language, but full of enlightenment to those who rightly understood it. And therefore the *zagádki* which have come down to our time, corrupt and mutilated as their present forms in many cases are,

---

[1] " Primitive Culture," I. 131—141.

frequently serve to throw light upon the mythological ideas of the old Slavonians, often yield us fragments of their mythological language. For to many of the *zagádki* may be applied the expression used by Professor Max Müller in speaking of certain proverbs, that they are "chips of mythology." They originally were condensed myths, as it were, or at least mythical formulas, and by their means a number of cosmical myths have been preserved in compact forms, unnoticed by the casual observer, but easily to be recognized by the experienced eye. In them an illiterate peasantry have unconsciously preserved the views about " God's world " current among their remote ancestors, the questions which daring speculators in far-off ages had asked and had tried to answer with reference to the great forces of nature[2]. It was on account of this close connexion between the *zagádka* and the myth, that the propounding of riddles was attributed by the Slavonians to such mythical beings as the Russian Rusalkas or the Servian Vilas; all of whom were supposed to be thoroughly versed in enigmatical lore, and who treated the unfortunate mortals who could not read their riddles aright with as scant courtesy as was shown by the Sphinx to the travellers who preceded Œdipus.

The oldest *zagádki* seem to have referred to the elements and the heavenly bodies, finding likenesses to them in various material shapes. In some of what appear to be the most ancient of their number,

[2] Afanasief, P. V. S. I. 25.

the sun is compared to a dish of butter, which suffices for the whole world; or the crescent moon to "a crust of bread hanging in a larder, which the dogs bark at but cannot reach;" or the stars to "peas scattered about a mat." In a Lithuanian *zagádka* the sky is likened to "a sieve full of nuts;" and the same idea is found in one of its Slovak cousins, in which there is also mentioned one very big nut which is the moon. Of a more poetic nature are those Russian *zagádki*, in which the stars are likened to a fiery inscription on the surface of the sky, as, for instance,—

"There is inscribed a writing on blue velvet, and to read that writing is given neither to priests nor to deacons, nor to wise moujiks[3]."

Equally poetic is that Slavonic version of "Humpty Dumpty," in which a golden ship [the moon], sailing across the [heavenly] sea, crumbles into fragments [the stars], which neither princes nor priests can put together again. A somewhat similar idea is conveyed by the tradition shared by the Russians with many other nations, that God uses the old moons to make stars of.

Among the animals which figure in the *zagádki*, the horse and the cow occupy prominent places. Sometimes [as the moon] the horse traverses the [celestial] sea without wetting its hoofs; sometimes [as the thunder] it tears along, making the earth

[3] Afanasief, P. V. S. I. 52. An interesting account of the riddle among savages is given by Mr. E. B. Tylor, "Primitive Culture," I. pp. 81—85.

tremble beneath it. A black cow frequently represents the night, and a white one the day, as in the following instance:—

"A black cow has overthrown the whole world but a white cow has set it up again."

Birds also are frequently mentioned. Sometimes the night, as—

"A bird has waved her wing, and shut out all light with a single feather."

Sometimes the stars move like "a bevy of swans," or the sun stands afar off in the heavens, as—

"Sits on an ancient oak a bird which neither king nor queen nor maiden fair can seize."

And sometimes fire appears in the guise of "a red cock"—an idea expressed also in the popular saying, "to set the red cock free," i. e. to light the fire.

But perhaps the most interesting of the mythical *zagádki* are those in which the sun and moon, the dawn, the thunder, and the storm, are likened to human beings. In some of them the dawn [*Zaryá*] is represented as a fair maiden who has lost her keys. The moon takes no notice of them, but the sun picks them up. The keys are, of course, the dew, which the moonlight does not affect, but the sunbeams dry up. In one variant they are lost by the Zaryá when she shuts the [heavenly] gates. In this case she probably is the after-glow of sunset, which is called in Russian the *vechérnaya* (or evening) *zaryá*.

Here is one of the many forms of this *zagádka* :—

"The fair maiden, the Dawn, went wandering through the forest, and dropped her keys. The moon saw them, but said nothing. The sun saw them, and lifted them up."

Sometimes the moon is a shepherd and the stars are his sheep, or they are goats which hide when they see the dawn :—

"There were goats crossing a bridge. They saw the dawn, and plunged into the water."

The following about fire, earth, and water, is a fair specimen of a large but common-place class :—

"There are three brothers. The first eats, and is never full. The second drinks, and is never satisfied. The third plays, and is never tired of playing."

The next is a poetic, though not a novel personification of day and night :—

"A sister goes to pay a brother a visit. But he hides himself from his sister."

An idea closely akin with that of the dialogue in the Rig Veda, in which the Night implores her brother [the Day] to make her his wife, but he refuses, saying, "They have called it sin that a brother should marry his sister[4]."

Finally, we may quote an enigmatic description of death, which, in its allusions at least, is thoroughly Slavonic :—

[4] See Prof. Max Müller's "Lectures on the Science of Language," Second Series, p. 510.

In the ocean-sea,
On the island Buyán,
Sits the bird Yustritsa.
She boasts and brags
That she has seen all,
Has eaten much of all.
She has seen the Tsar in Moscow,
The king in Lithuania,
The elder in his cell,
The babe in his cradle.
And she has not eaten that
Which is wanting in the sea[5].

Of the *zagádki* which do not seem to have any claim to be considered mythological, many may appear, at first sight, nonsensical; but that is generally either because their readers are unaware of the similarity between certain objects mentioned in them which was apparent to their framers, or because, in the course of time, some of their words have been unconsciously altered by their reciters. For instance, it would be difficult to find the meaning of this dark saying,—

" The ox in the cattle-shed has a haycock on his horns, but his tail is out of doors in the woman's hands,"

did we not know that the *ukhvat*, or oven-fork, is often spoken of as "the horned one." In this instance a woman is holding it by the handle, while its horns support a pot taken from the oven.

The same difficulty would be met with in comprehending the following enigma:—

[5] Sakharof, I. ii. 91. For *Buyán*, see *infra*, p. 374.

"The bay mare went about the field, came to us
—is come into our hands,"

were we not aware that the sieve therein alluded to
is made of horsehair, and that a part has been taken
by the enigmatist for the whole.

As specimens of verbal corruption may be quoted
the following riddles about a besom, and a comb.
The *vyenik*, a whisk or besom, is supposed to be
described in the words,—

"Hither Mitya, thither Mitya, and went under
the bench."

There seems to be no sense in calling a besom
Demetrius [*Dimítry*, dim. *Mítka* and so *Mítya*], but
the saying is made reasonable by reading—

"Hither swept [*mete* or *metyó*], thither swept, and
went under the bench."

One of the uses of a comb—one to which the Russian peasant, unfortunately, too often has good reason
for turning that instrument—is alluded to in the
saying "Tsar Kostyantin [Constantine] drives
horses across a fence." The metaphor is, in other
respects, only too intelligible, but why should a
comb be named Constantine? The explanation is
clear when the Little-Russian variants are consulted, as for instance the enigmatical statement
that "The toothed *kostyan* drove pigs over a hill"—
kostyan, or *kostyanoy*, meaning "made of bone"
[*kost'* = bone], and so being an epithet thoroughly applicable to a comb. In the Great-Russian riddle for the
rational *kostyan* has been substituted the like-sound-

ing but quite meaningless name of *Kostyantin*, (dim. *Kostya*) Constantine[6].

Among the Russian peasantry these riddles have always enjoyed great popularity. Khudyakof has printed a collection of them, 1705 in number, in the sixth volume of the "Ethnographical Collection [*sbórnik*]" of the Russian Geographical Society, and has prefixed to it a valuable essay containing much information on the subject. Among other things, he mentions that, in the Government of Pskof, on the occasion of a marriage, the bridegroom and his friends are not allowed to enter the bride's cottage until they have answered all the riddles her friends propound to them; and in one of the villages in the Yaroslaf Government, on similar occasions, a bargain, of which the bride is the subject, is concluded between the *Druzhka*, or groomsman, and the "seller of the bride"—riddles, answered by gestures instead of in words, taking the place of coin.

The Oriental tales about riddles, which spread so widely during the middle ages, were fully appreciated in Slavonic lands; many of them, indeed, so impressed the popular mind, that to this day the Russian peasants retain among their own stories some of those which they borrowed, centuries ago, about such foreign personages as Solomon and the Queen of Sheba, or the Sultan whom a Croatian version of a familiar tale represents as ordering a supposed Abbot to solve three problems—the last being

[6] Afanasief, P. V. S. I. 23.

"What am I thinking," to which the answer is, "You think I am the Abbot, but I am really the cook." Of more interest than such avowedly borrowed stories are those in which, not Oriental potentates, but Russian historical characters, such as Iván the Terrible or Peter the Great, are introduced. In one of these, for instance, a number of tribute-bearing kings and princes propound certain riddles to Iván the Terrible, offering to pay him twelve barrels of gold if he finds them out, on the condition that if he is unable to solve them he is to lose his throne. By the aid of an old man, to whom he promises one of the barrels, the Tsar is enabled to give the requisite answers, but he afterwards cheats his benefactor by filling two thirds of the barrel with sand. His device is at once seen through by the sage, who says to the dishonest monarch, "Thou hast introduced treason into orthodox Russia, and thou wilt never be able to root it out[7]."

Still more interesting are the riddle-stories belonging to the class of old Slavonic skazkas, tales which have formed part of the heritage of the people from time immemorial. In a Russian version of a wide-spread story, a princess says to her father, "Permit me, my father, to guess riddles: if I guess any one's riddles, let his head be cut off."

Her request being granted, various suitors set conundrums, and lose their heads. At last the inevitable Iván-Durák, Iván the Foolish, the Slavonic

[7] Afanasief, *Skazki*, VIII. 455—459.

"Boots," the youngest of the stereotyped "Three Brothers," enters the perilous lists. On his way to the palace he sees a horse in a cornfield, and drives it out with a whip, saying "Here's a riddle!" A little farther on he kills a snake with a lance, and makes a similar observation. When he is confronted with the princess he says to her, "As I came to you I saw by the roadside what was good; and in the good was good, so I set to work and with what was good I drove the good from the good. The good fled from the good out of the good." The puzzled princess pleads a headache, and postpones the unriddling till the next day. It arrives, and Iván favours her with his second enigma.

"As I came to you, I saw on the way what was bad, and I struck the bad with a bad thing, and of what was bad the bad died."

Whereupon the Princess accepts Iván[8].

In a manifestly mythical story a Slavonic Penelope [the Earth?] who is constantly annoyed by suitors, is sitting at table with them one day, when she sees the glasses every now and then dashed from their lips by an unseen hand. She guesses in a moment that her Ulysses [the Sun, or the Thunder-god, whom winter has long kept away?] has returned, wearing the invisible-rendering cap which she had given him. Looking out of window, she sees that "in the garden all the tree-tops are budding," and so, feeling sure that her surmise is

[8] Afanasief, *Skazki*, II. No. 20.

correct, she immediately propounds a riddle to her suitors.

"I had a self-acting casket with a golden key. I lost the key and despaired of finding it, but now that key has come back of its own accord. Whosoever guesses this riddle, him will I marry."

The "Tsars and Tsaréviches, Kings and Princes," long rack their "wise heads" over the *zagádka*, but they cannot make it out. Then the Queen exclaims, "Show thyself, my dear love!" and her husband doffs his cap, "takes her by the white hands, and kisses her sweet lips."

"Here is my riddle," then cries the Queen : "The casket am I, and the golden key is my true husband." So the suitors had to drive away home[9].

By way of conclusion I will give one of the numerous songs, the theme of which is the *zagádka*.

A maiden fair was strolling in a garden,
Gathering rosy flow'rets was the maiden.
By that way a merchant's son came driving.
"Now may God be with thee, beauteous maiden,
God be with thee, rosy flow'rets gathering!"
"Many thanks! O merchant's son! Thanks many!"
"Shall I ask thee riddles, beauteous maiden?
Six wise riddles shall I ask thee?"
"Ask them, ask them, merchant's son,
Prithee ask the six wise riddles."
"Well then, maiden, what is higher than the forest?
Also, what is brighter than the light?
Also, maiden, what is thicker than the forest?
Also, maiden, what is there that's rootless?

[9] Afanasief, *Skazki*, VIII. 147.

Also, maiden, what is never silent?
Also, what is there past finding out?"
"I will answer, merchant's son, will answer,
All the six wise riddles will I answer.
Higher than the forest—is the moon,
Brighter than the light—the ruddy sun.
Thicker than the forest—are the stars.
Rootless is, O merchant's son, a stone.
Never silent, merchant's son, the sea,
And God's will is past all finding out."
"Thou hast guessed, O maiden fair, guessed rightly,
All the six wise riddles hast thou answered.
Therefore now to me shalt thou be wedded,
Therefore, maiden, shalt thou be the merchant's wife[1]."

The *zagádka* has now completely lost the venerable character it once possessed, being degraded from the lofty realm of mythological philosophy to the humble field of popular amusement; but time has not dealt so hardly with the relic of heathenism to which we will next turn our attention, the *Zagovór*, the Slavonic Spell, Rune, or Incantation. The riddles belonged to the people in general, and no one had any special interest in maintaining their accuracy, and handing them down to posterity intact. But the spells were the peculiar property of a small body of sorcerers, who watched over them with jealous care, and delivered them to their successors as precious heirlooms from which nothing was to be taken away, for the whole virtue of the *zagovór* depended upon its absolute correctness. If any change was made in its wording its pronouncer became as power-

[1] Quoted by Prof. Buslaef as a song heard in Moscow.—*Istor. Ocherki*, I. 33.

less to kill or to cure as was Groa when, in her joy at recovering her husband, she forgot the Runes which would have loosened the stone from Thor's head [2], or as the Finnish deity in the Kalewala, Wäinämöinen, when he was unable to remember the magic words that would have stanched his flowing blood [3], and so was obliged to bleed on till an old wizard with a stronger memory came to his aid. In order not to be placed in so unpleasant a predicament the Russian sorcerers—of whom more will be said farther on—used frequently to commit their spells to writing. Some of these manuscripts still exist, but none of them, it is said, can be referred to an earlier period than the eighteenth century; for, until the time of Peter the Great, the Church and the State agreed in strongly objecting to sorcerers, and when they burnt them they unfortunately burnt their manuscripts also [4].

Among the old Slavonians, as among all other peoples, spoken words were supposed to possess certain magical powers. In their figurative language the lips and the teeth are often spoken of as locks, of which the key is the tongue. When that has once unloosened them, out shoots the word, like an arrow from a bow, and it is capable of flying straight to, and acting directly upon, the object at which it is aimed by its utterer. "A word is not a sparrow," says a Russian proverb; "once let it fly out, you will

[2] *Deutsche Mythologie*, 348, 1197.
[3] Castren, *Finnische Mythologie*, p. 249.
[4] Afanasief, P. V. S. I. 45.

never catch it again[5]." In olden times countless magical formulas, for good or for evil, seem to have been known to those persons who were originally styled " Wise Men" and " Wise Women," and afterwards wizards and witches. Many of these spells have come down to our times—for the sorcerer's occupation is not yet gone in Russia, though his class only exists now where it formerly flourished—and large collections of them have been formed by various careful gleaners in the field of folk-lore.

The name under which these spells are generally known is that of *zagovórui*. As " *sprechen, singen*, become *besprechen, besingen, schwören beschwören*, jurare *conjurare,* cantare *incantare, etc.*[6]," so the Russian *govorít'*, "to speak," becomes *zagovorít'*, one of the meanings of which is to conjure, to utter a spell or *zagovór*—a form of words in which, though now written as prose, there is always rhythm, and sometimes rhyme. In primeval times the *zagovórui* may have been mere prayers [*mólvit'* = to speak, *molítva* = a prayer], which, as years went by, degenerated into spells. At first sacred hymns bless and implore the gods; at a later period they demand from them (*zaklinayut*) what their utterers desire, and are known as spells, *zaklinániya* or *zagovórui*[7].

These spells were no doubt originally preceded by

---

[5] Afanasief, P. V. S. I. 404.   [6] *Deutsche Mythologie*, 1173.

[7] Afanasief, P. V. S I. 414, who refers to Prof. Kuhn's remarks, [*Herabkunft des Feuers*, p. 147], as to how the power of prayer as a personification in the Brahmanaspatis takes Indra's place, and the personified worship destroys dragons, etc.

rites, but the rite long ago stiffened into a verbal formula. The *zagovór* generally begins with a narrative, in which often occur highly poetic descriptions of nature. The utterer goes forth "in the early morn" to "the open field;" there he bows to all four quarters, but eventually turns his face "to the eastern side;" he washes himself in the morning dew, dries himself in the sunlight, and becomes "clothed with the clouds," and "girdled with the countless stars." Sometimes he strikes the stars, which are represented as silver nails, or covers himself with the brazen heaven. Then he addresses himself to the elements, asking the earth—Mother Earth, bright with flowers and full of vigorous life—to make his life bright and vigorous; asking the strong blue sea to strengthen him, and the wild winds to brace his courage, and the stars—the eyes of heaven—to make his eyesight keen[8].

As regards the world-wide custom of turning towards the east before praying, it will be enough to say that it still prevails in many parts of Russia among the peasantry, who are also of the opinion that it is from the East that sick people must look for alleviation of their complaints. In Bohemia it used to be required of persons who were about to take an oath, that they should do so looking eastward, appealing, as it were, to the rising sun. And a similar idea lay at the root of the custom of pronouncing the *zagovór*, in most cases, at the hour of

---

[8] Orest, Miller, *Opuit.* I. 75.

sunrise. Sometimes, however, these spells were probably intended to be uttered at other hours, at moonrise, for instance. To this day the Russian peasant, when he sees the new moon, will say,—
"Young moon! God give thee strong horns and me good health!"

As the stars, also, are frequently addressed in the *zagovórui*, it is very likely that some of the spells were spoken at night, and others may have been meant to accompany the sunset or the gloaming.

The spells were originally uttered in a loud, clear voice. Now-a-days many of them are always whispered, a practice which may have been derived from the Finnish sorcerers, who have had so great an influence on Russian superstition, or it may have gradually crept in as the subject of conjuring assumed more and more the character of something secret and forbidden. The addresses to the elements, the celestial luminaries, and the various forces of nature, which they contain, were of old the prayers with which the heathen Slavonian worshipped his elementary gods, and were meant to be, as it were, "spoken on the house-top," not whispered in the secrecy of the closet. And so still in the muttered speech of the rustic who desires to be freed from some trivial annoyance, or to be gratified by some small gain, may be heard the echo of the words with which his far-off pagan ancestor greeted the return of day, or watched the sinking of the western sun, or "blessed the kindly light" of the "gleaming moon" and the "many stars," or acknowledged the past aid, and implored the future assistance of those heavenly beings whom he adored —beings to whom, perhaps, in immemorial times, when what are now the many Aryan nations formed but one people, his and our ancestors offered their simple worship somewhere far away in Central Asia.

"Dost thou hear, O Sky? dost thou see, O Sky?" cries the peasant of to-day, addressing the Svarog, the Ouranos, the Varuna of old religion. "O ye bright Stars! descend into the marriage-cup, and in my cup let there be water from a mountain spring. O thou fair Moon! bow down to my *klyet'*, [kind of store-room]. O thou free Sun! dawn upon my homestead. O ye Stars! deliver me, the servant of God so and so, from drink! O Moon, turn me from drink! O Sun, draw me from drink!"

"O righteous Sun! do thou in my foes, my rivals, my opposers, in the powers that be, and public officials, and in all people of godly mouth and heart, parch up evil thoughts and deeds, so that they may not rise up, may not utter words baleful for me!"

Or, addressing the *zaryá*, the dawn and gloaming,

"Ho, thou morning *zaryá*, and thou evening *zaryá*! fall upon my rye, that it may grow up tall as a forest, stout as an oak!"

"Mother *zaryá* [apparently twilight here] of morning and evening and midnight! as ye quietly fade away and disappear, so may both sicknesses and sorrows in me, the servant of God, quietly fade and disappear—those of the morning, and of the evening, and of the midnight!"

Here is an address spoken by a lover to the winds. "In the ocean sea, on the island Buyan [i. e. in the cloud-island sailing over the heavenly sea?] there live three brothers, three winds: the first northern, the second eastern, and the third western. Waft, O winds, bring on the servant of God (such and such a maiden) sorrow and dreariness [*sukhota* = dryness], so that without me she may not be able to spend a day nor pass an hour!"

The force of the *zagovór* sometimes depends upon the assistance of the heavenly and other bodies adjured, as may be seen from the following spell to prevent swarming bees from wandering afar [9].

"I take a bee, I place it in the hive. But it is not I who place thee there; the white stars place thee; the horned moon, the red sun, they place thee and keep thee still."

When heathenism was dethroned by Christianity, these ancient adjurations were so far altered, that for the names of the elementary deities were substituted those of the Saviour, the Virgin Mary, the Apostles, and various saints and martyrs. Sometimes the old and the new names occur together, as we have seen is often the case in the mythical songs; but there are also instances in which, while the archaic form of the *zagovór* is preserved, its tone has become to all appearance thoroughly Christian; so that it has even found its way, under the heading *Molítvui*, or prayers,

[9] Zagovórs about bees are very common. In the *Deutsche Mythologie*, 1190, J. Grimm says that as he has met with no German *Bienensegen*, he will quote a Latin one.

into the church books called *trebniki*, both Russian and Servian, of the 15th—17th centuries [1]. This is a different case from that of the well-known poem of the Merseburg MS., in which a spell intended to cure a lame horse is preceded by an account of how, as Baldr rode through a wood in company with other Teutonic deities, his horse met with a sprain; a poem which, in this instance, has preserved its heathen complexion intact, although it figures in a copy of "*Hrabani expositio super missam*," but is generally found in as Christian a tone as that of the Norse—

   Jesus reed sig til hede, *etc.*,

or our own—

   The lord rade,
   And the foal slade, *etc.*[2]

The copyist in the case of the Merseburg MS. may have wished to stand well with the old powers as well as with the new, but in many of the variants of the spell its heathen character had probably been forgotten. The mixed nature of these superstitious formulas is best shown, perhaps, in some of those preserved by the wilder sects which discredit the Russian *Raskól*, or general body of dissenters from the Established Church, and are too often carelessly identified with the respectable though bigoted body of Old Believers, the Russian Nonconformists. Here is a specimen of the strange adjurations in

[1] Afanasief, P. V. S. I. 420, from whose pages the greater part of this account is condensed.

[2] *Deutsche Mythologie*, pp. 1180—1183.

use among the *Skoptsui*, the most fanatical, in all probability, of the Raskolniks who now exist in Russia :—

"Forgive me, O Lord; forgive me, O holy Mother of God; forgive me, O ye Angels, Archangels, Cherubim and Seraphim, and all ye heavenly host! Forgive, O sky; forgive, O damp-mother-earth; forgive, O sun; forgive, O moon; forgive, ye stars; forgive, ye lakes, ye rivers and hills; forgive, all ye heavenly and earthly elements³!"

In this case it is easy to see that the alteration which has taken place is one of heterogeneous combination, not of corruption or decay.

After the old prayers had passed into spells, their magical properties were often supposed to be automatic, no longer depending on the aid of the divinities they invoked, but acting, for good or for evil, by the force of their own inherent attributes. *Zagovórui* of this nature generally end with the phrase, "My word is firm!" or "My word will not pass away for ever!" or,—

"May my words be sticky and tough, firmer than stone, stickier than glue or resin, salter than salt, sharper than a self-cutting sword, tougher than steel. What is meant, that shall be fulfilled⁴!"

It has already been mentioned that the mouth is defined in metaphorical language as a lock—the

---

³ Quoted by Afanasief from Nadezhdin's *Report on the Skoptsui Heresy*, one of the many valuable documents, it may be worth remarking, reprinted in London by the late Alexander Hertsen at the "Free Russian Press."

⁴ Afanasief, P. V. S. I. 420.

Russians use padlocks to a great extent—of which the tongue is the key. That idea is expressed in the following termination of a *zagovór* :—

"For these words of mine [my] lips and teeth [are] a lock; my tongue, the key. And I will fling the key into the sea [but] remain thou lock in the mouth!"

Here is one of a slightly different nature :—

"I, the servant of God,[5] will make fast thrice nine locks. I take out from the thrice nine locks the thrice nine keys. I fling those keys into the clear ocean-sea; and from that sea will come out a golden-finned, copper-scaled pike, and will swallow my seven-and-twenty keys, and will sink into the depth of the sea. And no one shall catch that pike, or find out the seven-and-twenty keys, or open the locks, or do hurt to me the servant of God[6]!"

The range attributed to the force of the *zagovór* is as wide as that with which the *Lieder* and *Runen* used to be credited, and the Russian spell was supposed to be fully capable of performing most of, if not all, the actions of which, in speaking of its Teutonic equivalents, Jacob Grimm has given so long a list[7], or which

---

[5] In these spells the words "servant of God" are intended to be followed by the name of the utterer, or of some other person.

[6] *Loc. cit.* p. 422. With these Zagovór-terminations may be compared the ending of a Parsee *Patet* from the Khordah-Avesta (Bleek's translation, p. 171)—"This heavenly Patet (or confession-formulary) shall be a fast brazen wall like as the earth is broad, the mountains high, the heavens strong, that it may keep the gate of hell fast in bonds," *etc.*

[7] *Deutsche Mythologie*, p. 1176.

used to be claimed as the effect of the songs of Odin. These were, apparently, mythical in their origin, but the figurative language of the spell has been interpreted literally at a later period. In some of the Russian zagovórs, however, remarks Afanasief, their mythical character is still plainly visible, and he quotes, in illustration, two spells against toothache. The first is as follows :—

"O thou young moon! test the dead and the living: the teeth of one who is dead, do they ache? Not at all ache the teeth of one dead, [whose] bones are tanned, [whose] teeth are mute .... Grant, O Lord, that the teeth of me, the servant of God, may become mute, may never ache!"

The other spell must be three times pronounced by its utterer while he bites at the portal of the church :—

"As this stone is firm, so may my teeth also become stony—harder than stone!"

In the first spell, says Afanasief, the sufferer, who wishes his teeth to be mute as in death, addresses the moon, remembering the ancient character of a ruler in the land of the dead, which it, as the nightly luminary, used to bear. In the second, his appeal to the stone of the church portal is supposed to be a reference to that of which in older days the stone was a symbol, the hammer of Thor or Perun, which could turn all things into stone—the hard-hitting thunderbolt[8]. But all this seems very doubtful.

[8] P. V. S. I. 426.

But in order to convey an idea of the peculiar nature of the *zagovórs*, it will be necessary to give some specimens of those among their number which are of the greatest length, and which contain most mythical allusions—those for which the Russians proudly claim a greater fulness and a more poetic colouring than is generally to be found in the Teutonic Runes. Before doing so, however, I will quote the following short spell, in order to introduce, in connexion with each other, two names about which some remarks must presently be made, the "island Buyan," and the "white stone Alatuir." Here is a specimen of the numerous *zagovórs* used for the cure of cuts, stabs, etc :—

"In the sea, in the ocean, on the island, on Buyan, lies the white burning stone Alatuir. On that stone Alatuir there sits a fair maiden, a masterful sewer. She holds a steel needle, threads it with a silken thread, of reddish-yellow hue, and sews together bloody wounds. I charm the servant So-and-so from cuts. Steel, stand aloof, and thou, blood, cease to flow[9].!"

I will not dwell at present on the mystic stone, Alatuir, but it should be mentioned, in order that an allusion in the next *zagovór* may be intelligible, that from the elysian isle of Buyan comes *toská*, grief or longing. This may at first sight appear to be a strange dweller in what is represented as a land of eternal light and life. But the longing here alluded

---

[9] Sakharof, I. ii. 27.

to is that which springs from love, and leads to marriage, and therefore it is that it derives its origin from the same source as beings associated with all that is bright and joyous. Here is—

A ZAGOVÓR TO GIVE A GOOD YOUTH A LONGING FOR A FAIR MAIDEN.

I, the servant of God —— , stand still, uttering a blessing.

I, crossing myself, go from the room to the door, from the courtyard to the gates.

I go out into the open field, to the eastern side. On the eastern side stands an *izbá* [cottage or room], in the middle of the *izbá* lies a plank, under the plank is the LONGING.

The Longing weeps, the Longing sobs, waiting to get at the white light. The white light, the fair sun, waits, enjoys itself, and rejoices.

So may He wait longing to get to me, and [having done so] may he enjoy himself and rejoice! And without me let it not be possible for him to live, nor to be, nor to eat, nor to drink; neither by the morning dawn, nor by the evening glow.

As a fish without water, as a babe without its mother, without its mother's milk, cannot live, so may he, without me, not be able to live, nor to be, nor to eat, nor to drink; neither by the morning dawn, nor by the evening glow; neither every day, not at mid-day, nor under the many stars, nor together with the stormy winds. Neither under the sun by day, nor under the moon by night.

Plunge thyself, O longing! gnaw thy way, O longing, into his breast, into his heart; grow and increase in all his veins, in all his bones, with pain and thirst for me[1]!

---

[1] Sakharof, I. ii. p. 34, No. 62.

In some *zagovórs* the longing is said to spring from underneath the stone Alatuir, whence it is borne on the wings of seventy-seven aerial beings called both birds and winds. In some cases its bearers are styled "The Three Brothers," in others "The Seven Brothers," who are implored "to gather together from all the white world the griefs of widows, of orphans, and of little children." In some of the charms a lover addresses to fire and storm the following appeal: "Take from me my longing; carry it away, and do not drop it, but make it enter into such and such a female heart." In one of the *zagovórs* three mystic smiths are mentioned, who assist in forging hooks, by which one person can be "attached" to another.

In a Siberian *zagovór* a "Fiery Snake" is invoked for the kindling of amorous longing. With this idea may be compared the popular belief, that with the beginning of every January—that is, at the end of the festival in honour of the return of the sun towards summer—the Fiery Snake begins to fly, enters into the *izbá* through the chimney, turns into "a brave youth," and steals by magic the hearts of fair maidens. In one of the Servian songs, a girl who has been carried off by a fiery snake calls herself his "true love."

All this, says a bold mythologist, is explained by the fact that in mythical language the Fiery Snake is one of the forms of the lightning. The blooming Earth, fructified by the rains poured forth during the first spring storms, is turned in the myth into the bride of the Fiery Snake. But the wedder of nature became looked upon at a later period as the patron of weddings among the children of men; and so the inducing of love-pangs naturally became ascribed to the Fiery Snake.

Sometimes the powers of darkness are represented as having to do with the creation of amorous desire. Some of the *zagovórs* begin, "I rise up without uttering a blessing," and they go on to invoke "the demon Sanchak," and sometimes the "longing" is borne on the wings of seventy-seven demons, instead of as many winds. But all this is said to be of a later date. Originally, however, there was opposed to the fiery snake and the vivifying winds a malignant "spirit of the whirlwind" [*dukh-vikhor'*], which congealed instead of melting, and was invoked by evil conjurors in order to produce coldness between man and wife.

Some of the charms are meant to preserve men from drunkenness, which the sun, the moon, and the stars are called upon to keep away; others to gain the good will of a superior, or to ensure safety during a campaign. Here is a specimen of the latter class :—

The red sun has come forth from beyond the Caspian Sea, the moon has gone up into the blue sky, the clouds have drawn together from afar, the dark-blue birds have met in the stone-built city.
Within that stone-built city did my mother bear me, and while bearing me thus did she speak :—
"Be thou, my child, sound and unhurt, whether by guns, or by arquebuses, or by arrows, whether

by wrestlers, or by boxers. May the champions not challenge thee, nor smite thee with weapons of war; neither piercing thee with lance or spear, nor cleaving thee with halbert or hatchet, nor crushing thee with an axe, nor stabbing thee with a knife.

"May the old delude thee not, may the young men do thee no harm; but mayst thou be before them as a hawk, and may they be as thrushes. And may thy body be firmer than stone, thy shirt than iron, thy breast than the stone Alatuir.

"And mayst thou at home be a good father, abroad a brisk youth, in war a brave soldier; in the outer world a source of pleasure, in the upper chamber of the maidens an ornament, at the nuptial feast [a guest] without a trace of guile; and [mayst thou live] with thy father and mother in peace, with thy wife in concord, with thy children in harmony."

But perhaps the most interesting, and certainly the most poetic of the spells, are those which are intended for the relief of sufferers from a longing that is of a different nature from that produced by amorous impulse, for the solace of friends and relatives who have been torn asunder, and especially of parents who have been deprived of children. As a specimen of these may be taken the following

ZAGOVÓR AGAINST THE GRIEF OF A MOTHER ON PARTING WITH A BELOVED CHILD.

I have sobbed away the day—I his own mother, the servant of God—in the lofty parental *terem* [upper chamber], from the red morning dawn, looking out into the open field towards the setting of my red sun, my never-enough-to-be-gazed-on child. There I remained sitting till the late evening glow, till the damp dews, in longing and in woe. But at length

I grew weary of grieving, so I considered by what spells I could charm away that evil, funereal grief.

I went into the open field, I carried with me the marriage cup, I took out the betrothal taper, I fetched the wedding kerchief, I drew water from the well beyond the mountains. I stood in the midst of the thick forest, I traced an unseen line, and I began to cry with a piercing voice,—

"I charm my never-enough-to-be-gazed-on child, over the marriage cup, over the fresh water, over the nuptial kerchief, over the betrothal taper. I bathe my child's pure face with the nuptial kerchief, I wipe his sweet lips, his bright eyes, his thoughtful brow, his rosy cheeks. With the betrothal taper I light up his long kaftan, his sable cap, his figured girdle, his stitched shoes, his ruddy curls, his youthful face, his rapid gait.

"Be thou, O my never-enough-to-be-gazed-on child, brighter than the brilliant sun, softer than a spring day, clearer than fountain water, whiter than virgin wax, firmer than the fiery stone Alatuir.

"I avert from thee the terrible devil, I drive away the fierce whirlwind, I keep thee away from the one-eyed Lyeshy [or wood-spirit], from the stranger Domovoy [i. e. from the house-spirit of another family], from the evil Vodyany [or water-spirit], from the witch of Kief, and from her evil sister of Murom, from the beckoning Rusalka, from the thrice-accursed Baba Yagá, from the flying Fiery Snake. I wave away from thee the prophetic raven and the croaking crow, I screen thee from Koshchei-Yadun, from the wily enchanter, from the spell-weaving wizard, from the daring magician, from the blind soothsayer, from the hoary witch.

"And thou, my child, by night and at midnight, through all hours and at the half-hours, on the highway and the byway, when sleeping and when waking, be thou concealed by my abiding words from hostile powers and from unclean spirits, preserved from untimely death and from misfortune and from woe, saved from drowning when on the water, and kept from burning when amid the flames.

"And should thy hour of death arrive, do thou, my child, remember our caressing love, our unsparing bread-and-salt, and turn towards thy well-loved birth-place, bend thy brow to the ground before it with seven times seven salutations, take leave of thy kith and kin, and fall into a sweet, unbroken slumber.

"And may my words be stronger than water, higher than the mountains, heavier than gold, firmer than the fiery stone Alatuir, more powerful than heroes.

"And he who tries to beguile or to cast a spell over my child, may he be shut up beyond the mountains of Ararat, in the lowest gulfs of hell, in boiling pitch, in burning flame. And may his spells be for him no spells, his deceit be no deceiving, and his guile lead to no beguiling [2]."

We will now return for a time to the "Isle of Buyán," and the "White Stone Alatuir."

Far away amid the ocean waves, according to Slavonic tradition, lies the isle called Buyán, one of the many forms of the *Rai*, or Paradise, of which mention has already been made, the Slavonian counterpart of that happy land which figures in the mythology of all the Aryan nations. In that eastern isle is the home of the sun, which goes there every evening after it has set, to rise from it again with the return of morning. In Buyán are collected, says

[2] Sakharof, I. ii. 19. Every one who is interested in the subject of spells should read Professor Kuhn's excellent article on *Indische und germanische Segenssprüche* in the 13th vol. of the *Zeitschrift für vergleichende Sprachforschung.*

Afanasief, all the mighty forms of the spring-tide storms, all the mythical personifications of thunder, wind, and tempest. There are to be found "the Snake older than all snakes, and the prophetic Raven, elder brother of all ravens," and the Bird, the largest and oldest of all birds, with iron beak and copper claws, and the Mother of Bees, eldest among bees. That is to say, continues Afanasief, there lies the Lightning Snake, and broods the Tempest Bird, and swarm the Thunder Bees who bless the longing earth with the honey of rain [3].

On Buyán, also, stands a dripping oak, under which lies the snake Garafena [perhaps a corruption of *Goruinich*, Son of the Mountain, the name usually borne by the snake of the Russian fable], and there sits the divine maiden, Zaryá [the Dawn, or the Spring-tide Sun, or a Thunder-goddess?]. Thither turned the Old Slavonian with prayers, entreating the gods to preserve him from wounds and from diseases, to inspire him with martial courage, to

[3] The word Buyán was originally, says Afanasief, an epithet only of the fabled isle, but afterwards it became looked upon as its name. Even now, instead of *Buyán-ostrof* is written *buevoi-ostrof*. The root *bui* is synonymous with *yary*, which includes ideas of what is burning, ardent, passionate, fruitful, vernal, etc. The verb *buyat'* means to grow luxuriantly. The adjective *buiny*, when applied to fields, is equivalent to fruitful, etc.; when to the wind, it means stormy, etc. ; and when to a hero's head, it stands for bold, daring, etc. [P. V. S. II. 131]. Some connexion between Buyán and the grave may be suspected from the fact that *bui* and *bui-vishche* mean the fenced-in ground around a church, in which the dead used to be buried, and *buevo* is a name for a cemetery. [P. V. S. II. 140.]

bless him with success in love, in hunting and fishing, and in household affairs.

On Buyán is found the white stone Alatuir, the name and the nature of which have been discussed at some length by various Slavonic scholars, who have not, however, entirely dispelled the mystery which hangs about them. The *zagovórs* generally describe it as lying on the Buyán isle, but sometimes they merely say, " On the sea, on the ocean, lies the fiery stone[4]." From under it flow rivers of healing. On it originally was wont to sit either a " fair maiden who sewed up bleeding wounds "—supposed to be the Dawn, or the bird Stratim, the meaning of whose name has not yet been discovered — or some other mythical being. But under the influence of Christian ideas the locality of the stone was altered, and with it the character of its occupants. Sometimes, for instance, we find a spell in which the stone has been transferred to the neighbourhood of the river Jordan, and over it rises " a golden church," or a throne of gold occupied by " the Lord Himself," or by " the Holy Mother of God," or by one of the Apostles, or by some member of the heavenly host. Or near it stands a sacred grove composed perhaps of cypresses—the cypress having been the tree of which the cross was made—or a golden staircase up which the Archangel Michael is ascending to heaven. But whatever else has been changed, the idea of warm, blazing light is always connected with the stone. " Look, wife,

[4] The epithet *goryuch* means inflammable, easily set on fire.

on the blue sea," says a husband in a national song, when leaving his wife for ever; "when the fiery white stone grows cold, then will I come home;" meaning that he will never return. Sometimes, instead of the epithet "fiery white," the designation *kip* [*kipyet'* = to boil, foam, seethe, etc.] is applied to the stone.

Various suggestions have been made with regard to the etymology of the word Alatuir. One writer compares it with the Greek *élektron*, the Russian *yantar* [amber], and another with *alabastros*, each supporting his argument by the fact that the word he suggests represents something specially bright. The alabaster theory seems to have fallen to the ground, but the identity of the words *alatuir* and *yantar* seems to be generally admitted, though it is difficult to see, as Afanasief remarks, why such magical properties should have been attributed by the Old Slavonians to amber[5]. It may be that, as Buyán seems to have been turned from an epithet into a proper name, so Alatuir may, in the course of time, have changed its meaning, which possibly was at first "amber-like."

And now it is time that we should turn from the spell to its wielder—that having gained some fami-

[5] P.V.S. II. 148, 149. In a note to this passage (III. 800, 801) Afanasief remarks, "The Russian *alatuir* and the Greek ἤλεκτρον are derived from a root which in Sanskrit is found under the form *ark* (= αλκ), to flash, to emit rays (*ark-as* = light, the sun, crystal, etc.: ἠλέκ-τωρ = the sun, i. e. the shining one, ἤλεκτρον = shining metal (a mixture of gold and silver)"—and so = *Alatuir* in its form *latuir* or *lak-tuir*. Dahl in his great dictionary looks on *yantar* as a Tartar form of *élektron*.

liarity with the language of Sorcery, we should make the acquaintance of the Sorcerer himself. And having done so, it may be worth our while to trace his spiritual pedigree, to test his own claims, and those of his predecessors, to magic power, and to attempt to account for the readiness with which, century after century, those claims were admitted. Such an investigation will lead us back to the region whence we started, for if we perseveringly trace backwards up the stream of time the ancestral line of that poor creature, the Sorcerer of to-day, we shall find ourselves at last in the presence of those ill-defined but still majestic shapes of gods, under which the fanciful reverence of the heathen Slavonians seems to have personified the powers of nature.

But a little time ago every Russian village had its wizard, almost as a matter of course, and to this day it is said there is not a hamlet in the Ukraine that is not reported to keep its witch. In the vicinity of the great cities the supernatural, as revealed by the professors of the black art, may have lost its attractive hold upon the popular mind; but out in the open country the *Koldún* still holds his own, the *Vyéd'ma* still retains her power[6]. To him and to her the rustics still have recourse in their troubles, still

---

[6] Of the numerous names for the wizard and the witch, those of *Vyédun* and *Vyéd'ma*, springing as they do from a root *vyed*, answering to the Sanskrit *vid*, mean *people who know*, having exactly the same primary signification as two other terms applied to them, *Znákhar'* and *Znákharka* (*znat'* = to know). Of another like couple of synonyms, *Koldún* and *Koldún'ya*, the root has not

trustfully turn for such advice and aid as may enable them to obtain blessings and ward off evils. They are supposed to be able to look into the future, and to decipher the hidden meaning of omens and auguries; to possess charms which will cure the diseases of the body and calm the troubles of the mind; and even to be capable of controlling the elements, of bestowing the gift of fertilizing rain, or of ruining by the curse of drought or storm. The faith, in short, which was once professed in every European land, and which was the cause in them of so many thousands of terrible deaths, is still held in Russia, where, however, it has seldom assumed the virulent aspect which it used to wear farther west.

In Russia, as in many other lands, the common people look upon diseases as evil spirits, to be driven away by purification with fire and water, and so the

---

yet been satisfactorily made out. Professor Sreznievsky thinks that the *Koldún* was anciently the sacrificer to the gods, for in Croatian *Kaldovati* means to offer a sacrifice, and a *Kaldovants* is a priest.

Besides these names there are those of the *Charóvník* or *Charodyéets* (fem. *Charóvnítsa*, etc.), the dealer in *chárui*, spells or magic; of the *Kudésnik* (fem. *Kudésnitsa*), the worker of wonders, (*chudesá = kudesá*); and finally of the *Volkhv* (fem. *Vlkhva, Volkhvitka*), a term which was used by Nestor as a synonym of *Kudésnik*, and which Professor Buslaef considers as having had the same meaning as *zhrets*, a heathen priest, deriving *Volkhv* from a root akin to the Sanskrit *valg* = to shine, and *zhrets* from *zhryeti*, to burn, and comparing *Vlkhva* with the like-meaning Scandinavian name of *völva, völa, vala.*—See Afanasief, P. V. S. I. 405—409, III. 423—426; and Buslaef, *O Vliyanii Khristianstva*, pp. 21—24.

popular practice of physic is founded on a theory of fumigations, washings, and sprinklings, attended by exorcisms of various kinds. Some of the strangest of the magical practices to which the peasants have recourse are those which they employ as a defence against the attacks of the malignant beings whom they identify with the cholera, the small-pox, and the cattle-plague. Of some of these rites an account will presently be given. Against the evil influence of an angry house-spirit, or of nightmares and other baleful demons, the Wise Men and Women contend in various ways, all highly prized by the peasants: they keep away fevers from a house by washing the lintels of its doorways, and by performing certain magical rites in the fields they prevent insects and other vermin from hurting the crops. For the success of a wedding, the presence of the wizard is in many places considered indispensable[7]. His duty is to preserve the young couple and their friends from the attacks of hostile magicians; and so, in the Government of Perm, the bride is always attended by a *znákharka*, and the bridegroom by a *znákhar'*, who goes in front of the bridal procession, and anxiously pries around, whispering to himself the while. The people imagine that he is contending with the evil spirit which pursues newly-married persons, and attempts to

---

[7] By the peasantry, of course. Their superiors in social rank are said to have been wont in former days to lay equal stress on the presence of a general. Satirists declared that the confectioner who contracted for the wedding-breakfast always asked his customers whether they supplied " their own generals."

ensnare them. In some districts, when a wedding is being celebrated, all the doors and windows are carefully shut, and even the chimney is stopped up, to prevent malicious witches from flying in, and doing the bride or bridegroom an injury.

As in other countries, so in Russia, according to the opinion of the peasants, wizards and witches are greatly addicted to stealing the dew and the rain. These they either hoard or pour forth at their discretion. Thus, for instance, there is a story in South Russia of a wizard who could control the elements. Once, in harvest-time, a storm-cloud was seen moving towards the fields where he and his fellow-villagers were at work. They hurried homewards, but he stopped where he was, saying there would be no rain, though all the sky was black with clouds. Presently there gallops up to him a black rider on a black horse. "Let go!" he cries imploringly to the wizard, who refuses to do so. The clouds take a lighter hue, and the peasants this time look for a hail storm. Up rides a second horseman, "all white and on a white steed," and cries, "Let go, please do!" "No, I won't," replies the wizard. "Do let go; there's no holding out!" exclaims the white rider. At last the wizard sends him on to the other side of the corn-field, where in a little time a hail-storm comes pelting down[8].

With whirlwinds, also, the wizards have a great

---

[8] A Bohemian version of this story is given by Grohmann, *Aberglauben ... aus Böhmen, etc.*, p. 34.

deal to do. The Russian peasant generally attributes such winds to the wild dances in which the devil indulges when celebrating his marriage with a witch; but sometimes, he thinks, a wizard is being whirled about in the "dust-spouts" which may be seen in summer in the open plains. And so if a sharp knife be thrown with good aim at one of them, it will fall to the ground streaming with blood. There is a Little-Russian story of a peasant who flung his hatchet at one of these revolving columns, in which it stuck, "just as if it were in a tree," and by which it was carried off into space. Some little time afterwards the peasant, while making a journey, happened to spend a night in a cottage, the owner of which lay ill in bed, having cut himself, said his family, with a hatchet. As the guest lay down to sleep, he caught sight of something gleaming under a bench, and recognized it as the hatchet he had lost. Immediately he knew that he had wounded a wizard, so in fear of his life he fled from the cottage into the darkness[9]. When our sailors fire cannon at waterspouts they, of course, do so for purely philosophical reasons.

In Little-Russia the witches are reported to steal from the sky its rain and dew, which they carry off in pitchers and bags, and hide in their cottages. A long time ago one of their number, it is said, did this to such an extent that not a single rain-drop fell in a whole summer. Having to go out one day, she

[9] Afanasief, P. V. S. III. 448.

gave strict orders to the girl whom she left in charge of the house not to meddle with the pitcher which stood in the corner. But no sooner had she disappeared, than the girl opened the pitcher and peeped in. Nothing was to be seen inside, only a voice was heard coming from it, "Now there will be rain!" The frightened girl ran to the door, and, sure enough, the rain was coming down "just as if it were rushing out of a tub." The witch came running home, and closed the pitcher, when the rain stopped in a moment. "If the pitcher had stood open a little longer," she said to the girl, "the whole of the village would have been drowned[1]." In some versions of the same story the witch forbids certain tubs to be touched. When they are opened by an inquisitive visitor they are found to be full of frogs, toads, water-snakes, and other vermin, which set up a strange croaking and crawl away in different directions. Immediately the blue sky turns black, and a terrible storm arises, only to be quelled by the return of the witch, and the restoration of the toads and their companions to their prison-tubs.

In some places, and especially in Little-Russia, the witches are supposed to steal and hide away, not only the rain and dew, but even the moon and stars. With particular eagerness they attempt to do so during the festivals of *Kolyáda* and of *Kupála*, [i. e. at the times of the winter and the summer solstice], when the principal gatherings of unclean spirits and

---

[1] Afanasief, P. V. S. III. 450.

their families take place. There was once a village, they say in the Chernigof Government, in which there lived as many as a thousand witches, and they went on clearing the sky of stars until there were none left " to light up our sinful world." Then God sent St. Andrew [one of the Christian successors of Perun], who struck with his mace, and that wicked village sank into the earth, the place it had occupied becoming a swamp[2]. Akin to these witches must have been the heroine of the following spell:—

> The maiden fair
> Through the forest went.
> Evil she muttered,
> Herbs she collected,
> Roots she extracted,
> The moon she stole,
> The sun she ate.
> Aroynt her, hag!
> Aroynt her, witch[3]!

In Russia, as elsewhere, the objects by means of which a sorceress flies through the air are those which are connected with the domestic hearth—the brooms and besoms used for sweeping up ashes, and the equivalents for our tongs, poker, and shovel. A Russian witch always keeps by her a supply of water which has been boiled together with the embers of a kupála pyre, or Midsummer bonfire. When she wants to fly she sprinkles herself with this, or she rubs herself under the armpits and the

---

[2] Afanasief, P. V. S. III. 455.   [3] Afanasief, P. V. S. III. 456.

knees with an ointment, the chief ingredient of which is the magical herb *tirlich*, or gentian. Sometimes witches cleave the air in the cauldrons wherein they prepare their magic broths, or, like the Baba Yagás, they skim along in mortars, sweeping away their traces with a broom.

The witches generally hold their meetings on "bald hills," though in Servia they haunt threshing-floors for this purpose. And their chief gatherings take place three times a year; at springtide, and at the periods of the summer and winter solstice. According to Sakharof the witches begin to seek their trysting-place on the 26th of December. On the 1st of January they wander about with unclean spirits, and on the 3rd, returning from their wanderings, they take to milking cows. In Ruthenia it is believed that on the Feast of the Annunciation [March 25, the day on which spring subdues winter], witches and vampires are born. On St. George's day [April 23], and on the "Kupála night" [June 24—both days originally consecrated to Perun] wizards and witches collect on a bare hill, and there hold diabolical orgies. Sometimes they may be followed thither. In the Ukraine they tell how a certain soldier happened to see a witch, in whose house he lodged, preparing herself for flight. After she had gone he followed her example, and was immediately caught up, through the chimney, into the sky and on to the "bare hill." There he watched the revels for some time. At last his landlady caught sight of him, and immediately told him to be gone, if he valued his life, without a moment's delay. "Here is a good steed," she cried; "mount and be off." Away he was borne home by the good steed, which he tethered at the end of his journey. The next morning he saw that the tether was attached to a log.

It is unnecessary to go into the details of these meetings of witches and wizards, for they differ but little from those of such assemblies as the well-known Walpurgisnacht and other Teutonic gatherings of demons and their earthly associates. In Russia, as in other lands, the connexion between sorcerers and devils is very close, and when a wizard is about to die, evil spirits enter into him, and tear his life out with terrible agonies. With him all nature seems to suffer. The earth shudders, the winds howl, the wild beasts roar, and flocks of crows and ravens, or rather of evil spirits in their forms, throng the roof and chimney of the house, seize the soul of the dying wizard or witch, and, with wild cries, bear it away to the other world.

Among the defensive weapons employed against witchraft, some of the most important are the different objects connected with the domestic hearth, or supposed to refer in some way to the lightning. Thus a *kochergá*, or stove-rake, if suspended at the door of a cottage, will prevent any wizard who may have gained admittance from getting out again. As in Germany, on the first nights in May, so in Russia, on the eve of the Epiphany, says Afanasief, crosses may be seen chalked on every door and window.

These are to keep off witches, who fear every symbol of the Thunder-god's hammer, as, for instance, the sallow, the aspen-stake, and the fern. If any one takes a willow or aspen-twig with him to matins on Easter day, say the peasants in the Poltava Government, and looks at the congregation through it, he will see all the wizards and witches among them turned upside down[4]. In the Chernigof Government it is believed that if, on the last day of the *Máslyanitsa* any one takes a piece of cheese, wraps it up, and carries it about with him during the whole of Lent, then on Easter eve the witches of his village will appear to him, and ask for cheese.

To a wizard who dealt in *náuzui*, or amulets, [*úzui* = ties; *úzel* = a knot; *úzit'* = to tighten], was given in old times the names of *Náuznik* or *Uzol'nik*. These amulets generally consisted of various materials, such as herbs, roots, embers, salt, bats' wings, heads and skins of snakes, etc., which were tied up in small packets, and hung round the neck. Sometimes a spell was written on a piece of paper which was attached to the pectoral cross worn by Russians. After the introduction of Christianity, incense [*ládon*] entered so largely into the composition of these amulets that they received from it the general designation of *ládonki*. These amulets are still in great request among the peasants, especially among those who have to undertake long and hazardous journeys. In olden days it seems to have been customary to

[4] Afanasief, P. V. S. III. 497.

take young children to a witch, who provided them with suitable amulets.

The efficacy of these tied or knotted amulets depended to a great extent upon the magical force of their knots. To these knots frequent reference is made in the spells. Here is one, for instance, intended to guarantee its employer against all risk of being shot:—

"I attach five knots to each hostile, infidel shooter, over arquebuses, bows, and all manner of warlike weapons. Do ye, O knots, bar the shooter from every road and way, lock fast every arquebuse, entangle every bow, involve all warlike weapons, so that the shooters may not reach me with their arquebuses, nor may their arrows attain to me, nor their warlike weapons do me hurt. In my knots lies hid the mighty strength of snakes—from the twelve-headed snake[5]." With such a spell as this it was supposed that the insurgent chief, Stenka Razin, had rendered himself proof against shot and steel.

Sometimes the amulet is merely a knotted thread. A skein of red wool wound round the arms and legs is supposed to ward off agues and fevers; and nine skeins, fastened round a child's neck are deemed a preservative against scarlatina. In the Tver Government a bag called *vyázlo* is fastened round the neck of the cow which walks before the rest of a herd, in order to keep off wolves. Its force binds the maw of the wild beast [*vyazát'* = to bind]. In accordance with a simi-

[5] Afanasief, P. V. S. III. 434.

lar idea, a padlock is carried three times round a herd
of horses, before they are allowed to go afield in the
spring, he who carries it locking and unlocking it as
he goes, while these magical words are being uttered,
"I lock from my herd the mouths of the grey wolves
with this steel lock." After the third round the
padlock is finally locked, and then, when the horses
have gone off, it is hidden away somewhere till late
in the autumn, when the time comes for the herd to
return to winter quarters. In this case the "firm word"
of the spell is supposed to lock up the mouths of
the wolves. The Bulgarians have a similar method
of protecting their cattle against wild beasts. A
woman takes a needle and thread after dark, and
sews together the skirt of her dress. A child asks
her what she is doing, and she tells him she is sewing
up the ears, eyes, and jaws of the wolves, so that they
may not hear, see, or bite the sheep, goats, pigs, and
calves. In the Smolensk Government, when cattle
are being driven afield on St. George's day, the following spell is used:—

"Deaf man, deaf man, dost thou hear us?"
"I hear not."
"God grant that the wolf may not hear our cattle!"
"Cripple, cripple, canst thou catch us?"
"I cannot catch."
"God grant that the wolf may not catch our cattle!"
"Blind man, blind man, dost thou see us?"
"I see not."
"God grant that the wolf may not see our cattle[6]!"

* Afanasief, P. V. S. III. 437.

Sometimes the amulet locks away hurtful things from a man's body. A net, from its affluence of knots, was always considered very efficacious against sorcerers; and therefore, in some places, when a bride is being dressed in her wedding attire, a fishing-net is flung over her, to keep her out of harm's way. With a similar intention the bridegroom and his companions are often girt with pieces of net, or at least with tight-drawn girdles, for before a wizard can begin to injure them he must undo all the knots in the net, or take off the girdles. The girdle, with which the idea of a snake is frequently connected, has some mystic sympathy with its wearer, and therefore the peasants in some parts believe, that if a sick man's girdle be taken off, and thrown on the highway, whoever picks it up and puts it on will have its former wearer's diseases transferred to himself[7]. The knotted surface of a harrow (made of interwoven branches) gives it great power against witchcraft. The best way to catch a witch is to hide under a harrow, and angle for her with a bridle.

Russian cows have always been as liable as those of other countries to be drained of their milk by witches. During the Christmas *Svyatki* the peasants object to letting their cattle leave the cow-sheds, for fear of attacks from the powers of darkness. On the 3rd of January the witches return from their Sabbath in a state of ravenous hunger, and are to be debarred from the cow-sheds only by means of a church taper

[7] A similar belief is said to be still prevalent in England.

attached to the doors. Crosses chalked upon the eve of the Epiphany are also very useful. On St. Vlas's [Blasius's] day [Feb. 11] it is necessary to sprinkle the flocks and herds with holy water, for at that time, in Little-Russia at least, werewolves, in the shape of dogs and black cats, suck the cows, mares, and ewes, and slaughter their male companions. On St. George's day in April, and again during Whitsun and Trinity weeks, the danger is no less to be dreaded. At Midsummer bonfires are made of nettles, etc., and the horned cattle are driven through the flame, in order to keep off wizards and witches, who are then ravenous after milk. On the 30th of July witches frequently milk cows to death, dying themselves afterwards of a surfeit.

A witch can milk a cow from a great distance. In order to do so she sticks a knife into a plough, a post, or a tree: the milk trickles along the edge of the knife, and continues to do so till the cow's udder is emptied. On the eves of St. George's day, Whit-Sunday, and Midsummer day, witches go out at night without clothing, and cut chips from the doors and gates of farmyards. These they boil in a milk-pail, and so charm away the milk from those farms. Careful housewives are in the habit of examining their doors, and of smearing any new gashes they find in them with mud, which frustrates the plans of the milk-stealers. In such cases the witches climb the wooden crosses by the wayside and cut chips from them, or lay their hands on stray wooden wedges. These they stick into a post in the cattle-sheds, and press them with their fingers till milk flows from them freely, as from a cow's udder. As in Germany, so in Russia, witches often bear milk-pails on their heads. In Lusatian Wendish a witch is called *Khodojta* [*doit'* = to milk], from her nefarious dealings with her neighbours' cows.

As a farmer's cows are exposed to the attacks of the witch, so are his crops to those of the wizard, who sometimes takes a handful of ears of corn, bends them down to the ground, and ties them together with a string; or he twists them round toward the west, the quarter with which is connected the idea of death, and fastens them in that position. This ceremony, which is done only with malicious intent, is of course entirely different from the somewhat similar rite styled "the plaiting of the beard of Volos." [See p. 251.] The wizard's proceeding is called making a *zakrút*. [*zakrutít'* = to twist]. The old church books called *trebniki* contain prayers intended to be employed against the *zakrút*. After they had been said, it was formerly the custom to pull it out with a church cross, and so to deprive it of its power to do harm. Now-a-days it is customary to hire the services of a friendly wizard, who cuts an aspen-stake, splits it asunder, and pulls out the enchanted ears with it. Afterwards the *zakrút* is set on fire with a holy taper, and the aspen-stake is driven into the spot it had occupied, the latter proceeding giving rise to terrible pains inside the hostile wizard[8].

[8] Afanasief, P. V. S. III. 516.

Besides destroying crops and cattle, the dealers in magic were supposed to be able to bring disease and death upon mankind. The Kashoubes along the Baltic still attribute most illnesses to sorcery, and in former days such an explanation of plagues, and murrains, and other evils of a like nature, seems to have been generally accepted. The Russian peasants believe that wizards and witches can bring destruction on men as well as beasts, letting loose on their enemies evil spirits, which manifest themselves in hiccoughs, ravings, and fits, or wreaking their vengeance upon them by means of poison. The victim who accepts a beverage from the hands of a witch, will perhaps swallow with it the " Fever-Sisters" or other demons of torment, who will become transformed within him into snakes, toads, or mice, and will suck dry his veins, and bring him, amid prolonged agonies, to the grave. Sometimes, instead of sending evil spirits to torment a man internally, a witch is supposed to change him by night into a horse, and ride him over hill and dale until he is all but dead with fatigue—an idea of which Gogol has made excellent use in his story of the *Vy*. At other times she is believed to ride on his spirit, while his body sleeps. In that case he finds himself utterly exhausted the next day, though he knows nothing about what has been done to him.

As a general rule, however, wizards and witches are supposed to destroy their victims by means of poison distilled from herbs and roots. The girl who poisoned her brother by mistake, when she merely intended to kill the lover who had offended her—as described in a song already quoted—probably belonged to the same class as the wilfully murderous sister of the following weird story :—

> A brave youth splintered chips.
> A fair maiden gathered the chips,
> Gathered and set them on the fire,
> Baked snakes and distilled poison.
> The sister thought her brother to kill.
> Into the midst of the court she went,
> Filled a cup betimes,
> Offered it to her brother dear.
> " Sister, be thou the first to drink."
> " Brother, I drank when pouring forth,
> Wishing good health to thee."
> A drop fell on the horse's mane,
> The horse's mane began to burn.
> Down from his good steed leaped the youth,
> Drew from its sheath his sabre keen,
> Struck off his sister's head.
> " No sister true of mine art thou,
> But a snake from under a log."
> Faggots he piled in the midst of the court,
> And her body white he burnt,
> Till nought but ashes remained.
> Her dust he scattered across the plain;
> No voice would he suffer to mourn [9].

Sometimes the poisoning is supposed to be effected on a large scale, as when an epidemic is introduced by means of unholy science. In that case recourse is had to magic, to counteract the designs of the malicious sorcerer. The rites which are performed by the Russian peasants in order to ward off an attack

---

[9] Sakharof, I. iii. 202.—See also *supra*, p. 23.

of the cattle-plague are very striking, whether they are intended to prove efficacious against an evil spirit invoked by a human will, or one that acts of its own accord. In olden days, it is said, when such a disease broke out in Ruthenia, it was customary to seize some old woman who was suspected of dealing in magic, and to bury her alive, or to fling her into a river, having previously fastened her up in a sack along with a cock, a dog, and a black cat. After that it was expected that the epidemic would disappear. Not long ago, an opinion was expressed by the peasants, that if the first cholera patient were to be buried alive, the disease would lose its power. In some villages a hole is dug in the earth at the precise spot on which the first victim to cattle-plague has fallen, and in it they bury its remains, with a live dog, cat, and cock fastened to its tail. The Commune recompenses the owner of the dead beast for the loss of its hide. In the Nijegorod Government the Siberian Plague is supposed to be kept at a distance by ashen stakes being driven into the ground at crossways, and the remains of a dog, calcined for the purpose, being scattered about the village. Sometimes, when a murrain is dreaded, the assembled peasants drive their herds overnight into some farmyard, and keep watch over them till morn. Then the cattle are counted, and if a beast which no one claims is found among them, it is looked upon as the Cow Death in person, and is immediately burnt alive. Sometimes the popular fancy personifies the Cow Death under the form of a haggard old woman, against whose attacks various precautions of a heathenish kind are taken. When a village is alarmed lest such a murrain should fall upon its herds, the men are all ordered to shut themselves up in their cottages. Then the women meet together, clad only in white shifts, having their hair hanging loose about their shoulders—in striking resemblance to the Prophetesses of heathen times—and provided with the various utensils connected with the hearth, such as brooms, shovels, and the equivalents for pokers and tongs. In some places, also, they carry scythes and sickles, and other instruments used in their daily avocations, but this seems to be an innovation of later date. The oldest woman among them is then yoked to a plough, and she must draw it three times round the whole of the village, the rest of the party following after her, and singing the songs set apart for such occasions. It is supposed that the malignant spirit whom they recognize in the cattle-plague will be unable to cross the lines thus traced by the plough, or to get at the cattle, which, during the ceremony, have been kept shut up within the village. Here is one of their songs, many of which are quite unpresentable :—

> From the ocean—from the deep sea . . .
> There have come out twelve maidens.
> They have gone on their way, by no short road,
> Up to the steep, the high mountains,
> To the three old Elders . . .
> " Get ready the white oak tables . . .
> Sharpen the knives of steel,
> Make hot the boiling cauldrons,

Cleave, cut unto death,
Every life under the heavens!"

The Elders comply with the request of the Twelve Maidens, and all living things are put to death. Then,—

In those boiling cauldrons,
Burns with an inextinguishable fire
Every life beneath the heavens.
Around the boiling cauldrons
Stand the old Elders;
The old Elders sing
About life, about death,
About the whole human race.
The old Elders give
To the whole world long lives.
But on the other, on evil Death,
The old Elders fix
A great curse.
The old Elders promise
Eternal life
To all the human race [1].

The Three Elders, says Orest Miller, are evidently beneficent divinities, but it is not clear who the Twelve Sisters are. They are often mentioned in exorcisms, many of which are intended to be used as a protection against the attacks of these "Evil Shakers," as they are called; shakers of mankind, that is to say. Sometimes each one has her own name, that of some special disease. In the exorcisms preserved in writing, most of which show evident signs of having been submitted to Christian influences, these weird sisters are called the Daughters of Herod.

[1] Orest Miller, *Opuit*, I. 10.

Tereschenko, in his description of the *Opakhivanie*, the ploughing rite [*pakhát'* = to plough] used as a preservative against the cattle-plague, gives a few additional details. In the villages of which he speaks, the procession is headed by a young girl who carries the image of St. Blasius—Vlas, the Christian representative of the old Slavonic deity Volos, the patron-god of cattle[2]. Behind her walk the rest of the female villagers, those in the front row carrying besoms and handfuls of hay and straw. Next comes an old woman, riding on a broomstick, her locks dishevelled, a single shift her only covering; around her are several women and girls with stove-irons. The third row is composed of women who shout, dance, gesticulate, and beat frying-pans. A number of old women, bearing lighted fir-splinters, form a circle around a widow, who wears a horse-collar round her neck and nothing else, and the old woman yoked to the plough. In front of each farmyard the procession halts, while its members knock at the gates, and, amid the din of beaten pots and pans, exclaim "Ai, Ai! cut, hew the Cow Death! Ai, Ai! cut, hew! There she goes! Ai, Ai!" If a dog or a cat happens to rush out it is killed on the spot, being taken for the cattle-plague in person.

Another rite, of an equally heathenish nature, is considered efficacious against various epidemics. The female inhabitants of a village heap up two piles of

---

[2] See *supra*, p. 251.

refuse at midday, one at each end of the street, and set them on fire at midnight. To one of these bonfires the girls, in white shifts, with loosely flowing hair, drag a plough, one of their number following the rest and carrying a holy picture. To the other bonfire a black cock is taken by the older women—who wear black petticoats and dirty shifts—and carried three times round the flames. Then one of the women seizes it, and runs away with it to the other end of the village, the rest following and screeching "Ah! Ai! Atu! disappear, perish, black disease!" When she reaches the glowing heap at the other end, she flings the bird into it. While it is burning, the girls, after heaping dry leaves on the fire, take hands and dance round it, repeating "Perish, disappear, black disease!" The women then drag the plough three times round the village [3].

Near Mtsensk, in the Government of Orel, the Cow Death procession is headed by three girls who carry a picture of St. Vlas, with a taper burning in a lanthorn before him, or a censer containing live coals and incense. After them walk three widows, and in some places three soldiers' wives. As they go round the village they sing,—
    Death, O thou Cow Death!
    Depart from our village,
    From the stable, from the court!
    Through our village
    Goes holy Vlasy,
    With incense, with taper,
    With burning embers.

[3] Tereshchenko, VI. 41.

We will consume thee with fire,
We will rake thee with the stove-rake,
We will sweep thee up with the broom,
And we will stuff thee with ashes.
Come not to our village!
Meddle not[4] with our cows,
Nut-brown, chestnut, star-browed,
White-teated, white uddered,
Crumpled-horned, one-horned!

After them follow the other women, one dragging a plough which another directs, and a third riding on a broomstick, while the others carry, and strike together, various utensils, chiefly of iron. The rest of their proceedings resemble those which have already been described, but their narrator adds that "if a man falls in their way, they set upon him furiously. It has often occurred that the man thus met has not at a cheap rate made good his escape from them[5]."

One of the stories about the Cow Death relates that—

A peasant was driving from a mill, at a late hour. Towards him comes crawling an old woman and says,—

"Give me a lift, grandfather!"

"Where to?"

"There, my own, to the village you're going to yourself."

"And who are you, grandmother?"

"A doctoress, my own; I doctor cows."

---

[4] *Chur*—here translated "meddle not"——is now an exclamation, or a word meaning a border or boundary, but was once the name of a friendly deity resembling the Roman Terminus.

[5] *Etnograf. Sbornik*, VI. Mezhof's article, pp. 63—65.

"And where have you been doctoring?"

"Why I've been doctoring at Istomina's; but they're all dead there. What was to be done? They didn't call me in till a little time ago, and I couldn't manage to stop the thing."

The peasant gave the woman a seat on his cart, and drove off. Coming to a cross road he could not remember the way, and by this time it had begun to grow dark. Uttering a prayer, the peasant took off his hat and crossed himself. In a moment there was no old woman to be seen!

Turning into a black dog, she ran into the village. Next day three cows died in the outside farm; the peasant had brought the Cow Death there[6].

Under such circumstances, according to Tereshchenko, instances of voluntary immolation have been known. In a village attacked by an epidemic, "the men and women have been known to cast lots, and the person on whom the lot fell has been buried alive in a pit, along with a cock and a black cat."

In the month of February, according to the Russian peasants, the Cow Death wanders through the villages in the guise of a hideous old woman, withered and starved in aspect, bearing a rake in her hands. Sometimes, however, as we have seen, she takes the form of a black dog or cow, and, among the Slovenes, of a mottled calf. In the Tomsk Government the Siberian murrain is represented as a tall, shaggy man, with hoofs instead of feet, who usually lives among the hills. The Bulgarians have a tradition that when the cattle-plague, or the small-pox, wishes to depart from a village, she appears to

[6] Tereshchenko, VI. 42.

some one in his sleep, and orders him to convey her to such and such a place. The person thus designated takes bread smeared with honey, salt, and a flask of wine, and leaves them, before sunrise, at the appointed spot. After this the epidemic disappears, having accompanied the bearer of the food out of the village.

The rites which serve to keep away the cattle-plague are supposed to be efficacious against the Cholera also. In Ruthenia that disease is personified as an old woman, with a hideous face disfigured by suffering. In the Vladimir Government she bears the name of the Dog Death. In Little-Russia it is affirmed that "she wears red boots," that she can walk on water, that she is perpetually sighing, and that at night she haunts villages, exclaiming, "Woe was; Evil will be." In whatever house she passes the night, there she leaves not one soul alive. In some villages they think that the Cholera comes "from beyond the sea," and that she is one of three sisters, all clad in white shrouds. Once a peasant, going into a town, gave a lift to two of the sisters in his cart, on which they sat, "holding on their knees bundles of bones. One of them was going to slay in Kharkof, and the other in Kief'."

One of the strangest superstitions about disease is that which is connected with small-pox. In some places the Russian peasants hold that it is sinful to

[7] Afanasief, P. V. S III. 114—116. A number of similar superstitions are given in the *Deutsche Mythologie*, art. *Pest*, pp. 1133—1141.

vaccinate children, such a deed being equivalent to impressing upon them "the seal of Antichrist." Moreover it is believed that whoever dies of small-pox "will walk in the other world in golden robes." For this belief even the professional wizards can give no reason, grounding their faith entirely on tradition. Professor Buslaef accounts for it in the following manner:—The modern Greeks, he says, personify small-pox in the guise of a supernatural female being, and the Servians call her *bogine*, or goddess. And the ancient Greeks knew of a spectral creature called Alphitô (ἀλφιτώ, " a spectre, or bugbear with which nurses frightened children "—*Liddell and Scott*), a name supposed to be akin to that of the German *Elbe*, or the English *Elves*. The kindred word *Alphos* (ἀλφός) also meant a skin disease, apparently a form of leprosy. Professor Buslaef thinks that the small-pox was originally represented as a female being with whom was connected the idea of whiteness or light, and that from that idea arose the notion of her victims being clad, after death, in bright or golden robes.

The power of dealers in magic to transform themselves or their victims into various shapes is widely spread in Russia, and plays an important part in the popular mythology of the country. A person thus changed bears the name of *ôboroten* [*oborotit'* = to turn], or, when changed into a wolf, of *volkodlák* [*volk* = wolf, *dlaka* = a tuft of hair, and so a hide[8]].

* This is Afanasief's explanation (P. V. S. III. 527). Dahl suggests *volk* and *kúdla*, the latter word signifying something shaggy,

Werewolf stories are so well known among all nations[9], that it is unnecessary to give a detailed account of the proceedings of the Russian *volkodlaki*. But it may be as well to mention that the collection of laws, etc. called the *Kormchaya Kniga* states that in these transformed beings the people used to see no mere mortals, but "chasers of the clouds." Afanasief connects them with the *okrutniki*, or maskers disguised as various animals, who used to participate in the religious games of the Old Slavonians, and who still, though their original signification is forgotten, play a part in the rustic festivals at springtide and Christmas. So strong an odour of heathenism still hangs about them, that the peasants think the wearing of a mask at the Christmas *Svyatki* is a sin, one which can be expiated only by bathing in an icehole, after the benediction of the waters.

Connected with the idea of transformation is the belief, common among the Russian peasantry, that all witches have tails, and all wizards have horns, and that a werewolf may be known by the bristles which grow under his tongue. Such dealers in sorcery take various shapes, but generally, says Afanasief, those of the animals known as symbols of the cloud and the storm. In the Ukraine witches

---

a hide, etc. The Great-Russian *volkodlák* becomes, says Afanasief, in Little-Russian *vovkulak*, in Bohemian *wlkodlak*, in Servian *vukodlak* in Dalmatian *vakudluk*, in Bulgarian *vrkodlak*, in Lett *wilkats*.

[9] A long list of references is given by Mr. Tylor in his "Primitive Culture," I. 279—284.

assume a canine form; their long teats trail on the ground, a fact on which Afanasief lays stress, remarking that the bosom, udder, or teat, was a well-known mythological synonym for a rain-cloud. Cats are generally thought uncanny in Slavonic countries, the Russian peasants believing that evil spirits enter into them during storms, and the Bohemians holding that a black cat at the end of seven years becomes either a witch or a devil[1]. The owl is considered to be of a demoniacal nature, while the dove is so pure and holy that no witch is able to assume its form.

Of all living creatures, magpies are those whose shapes witches like best to take. The wife of the false Demetrius, according to popular poetry, escaped from Moscow in the guise of a magpie. As a general rule, no such bird is to be seen in that city, its race having been solemnly cursed by the Metropolitan Alexis, on account of the bad behaviour of the witches who often assumed its plumage. At the present day the peasants often gibbet a dead magpie, just as our gamekeepers do, but it is in order to scare away witches from stables and cow-sheds. Besides changing into the birds and beasts, of which mention has been made, Russian witches often assume the forms of stones, hay-cocks, or balls of thread—that is to say, observes Afanasief, of various objects mythologically connected with clouds.

[1] There is a Bohemian tradition, however, that the devil invented mice in order to destroy "God's corn," whereupon God created the cat.

Here is a specimen of a *zagovór* to be employed by a wizard who desires to turn into a werewolf:—

"In the ocean sea, on the island Buyán, in the open plain, shines the moon upon an aspen stump, into the green wood, into the spreading vale. Around the stump goes a shaggy wolf; under his teeth are all the horned cattle; but into the wood the wolf goes not, in the vale the wolf does not roam. Moon, moon! golden horns! Melt the bullet, blunt the knife, rot the cudgel, strike fear into man, beast, and reptile, so that they may not seize the grey wolf, nor tear from him his warm hide. My word is firm, firmer than sleep or the strength of heroes[2]."

In this spell, says Buslaef[3], the aspen stump is mentioned because a buried werewolf or vampire has to be pierced with an aspen stake. The expression that the wolf has all the horned cattle in or under his teeth resembles the proverb now applied to St. George, "What the wolf has in his teeth, that Yegory gave"—St. George, or Yegory the Brave, having taken the place which was once filled by the heathen god of flocks, the Old Slavonic Volos. And the warm hide of the werewolf is in keeping with his designation *Volkodlak*, from *dlaka*, a shaggy fell.

There is, of course, a great difference between the voluntary and the involuntary undergoers of transformation. Dealers in the black art who have

[2] Sakharof, I. ii. 28. [3] *Istor. Ocherki*, I. 36.

turned themselves into wolves are, for the most part, ravenous destroyers of all that falls in their way, but people who have been made wolves against their will seldom disgrace their human nature. Such gentle werewolves as these attach themselves to men, and by tears and deprecatory pawings attempt to apologize for their brutal appearance. Unless driven beyond endurance by hunger, they never slay and eat, and when they must kill a sheep, they seek one belonging to some other village than that in which they used to live. There once was a youth, says a Polish tradition, who was loved by a witch, but he scorned her affection. One day he drove into the forest to cut firewood, but no sooner had he swung his axe in the air than his hands turned into wolf's paws, and in a short time his whole body bristled with shaggy hair. He ran to his cattle, but they fled in terror; he tried to call them back, but his voice had become a mere howl. In another instance a witch turned one of her neighbours into a wolf, and he stated, after he had regained his former shape, that during the period of his transformation he made friends with a real wolf, and often went out hunting with him, but that he never forgot that he was really a man, though he had lost the faculty of articulate speech. The White-Russians have a tradition that once, when a wedding party were thoroughly enjoying themselves, they were all transformed by some hostile magician—the bridegroom and the other men into wolves, the bride into a cuckoo, and the rest of the women into magpies.

Ever since that time the metamorphosed bride has flown about seeking for and lamenting her lost bridegroom, and moistening the hedges with the "Cuckoo's tears," which we less poetically style "Cuckoo's spittle."

In order to produce such an effect as this on a wedding party, the hostile wizard, it is generally believed, must girdle each member of it with a leather strap or piece of bast, over which unholy spells have been whispered. According to a Ruthenian story, however, a witch once gained her end by simply rolling up her girdle, and hiding it beneath the threshold of the cottage in which the wedding festivities were being held. Every one who stepped across it immediately became a wolf. In order to effect the cure of an involuntary werewolf, it is necessary either to strip off his hide, or to remove the magic girdle or other amulet which has reduced him into his brute state. In one of the Russian stories a black dog behaves in so reasonable a manner, that the people to whom it has attached itself take it to a wizard for relief. Acting upon his advice, they heat a bath as hot as possible, and scald the dog's skin off. No sooner is this done than the dog turns into a young man belonging to a neighbouring village, whom an old sorceress had bewitched[4].

Witches and wizards constantly metamorphose people by the touch of a magic wand, stick, or whip.

---

[4] Afanasief, P. V. S. III. 549—553.

Sometimes, however, even this is not essential. In Ruthenia, at least, it is believed that a wizard, if he only knows a man's baptismal name, can transform him by a mere effort of will, and therefore a man should conceal his real name, and answer to a fictitious one. Such a power as this is supposed by the Russian peasantry to have been employed upon one occasion by the Apostles Peter and Paul. As they were passing over a bridge one day, "a bad woman and her husband," who had agreed to frighten the holy travellers, and had dressed themselves up in sheepskins turned inside out, ran at them, roaring like bears. "Then the Apostles said, 'Go on roaring from this time forward and for ever!' and at that very instant the mockers were turned into bears[5]."

More terrible even than the werewolf, but closely connected with him, as well as with the wizard and the witch, is the dreaded Vampire. It is in the Ukraine and in White-Russia—so far as the Russian Empire is concerned—that traditions are most rife about this ghastly creation of morbid fancy. There vampires are supposed to be such dead persons as in their lifetime were wizards, witches, and werewolves; or people who became outcasts from the Church and its rites, by committing suicide, for instance, or by drinking themselves to death; or heretics and apostates, or victims of a parental curse. The Little-Russians, on the other hand, attribute the birth of a

[5] Afanasief, P. V. S. III. 552.

vampire to an unholy union between a witch and a werewolf or a devil.

The name itself has never been satisfactorily explained. In its form of *vampír* [South-Russian *upuír*, anciently *upír*], it has been compared with the Lithuanian *wempti* = to drink, and *wempti, wampiti* = to growl, to mutter, and it has been derived from a root *pî* [to drink] with the prefix *u* = *av, va*. If this derivation is correct, the characteristic of the vampire is a kind of blood-drunkenness. In accordance with this idea the Croatians call the vampire *pijawica;* the Servians say of a man whose face is coloured by constant drinking, that he is "blood-red as a vampire;" and both the Servians and the Slovaks term a hard drinker a *vlkodlak*. The Slovenes and Kashubes call the vampire *vieszcy*, a name akin to that borne by the *witch* in our own language as well as in Russian. The Poles name him *upior* or *upir*, the latter being his designation among the Czekhs also.

"There is a whole literature of hideous vampire stories, which the student will find elaborately discussed in Calmet," says Mr. Tylor ["Primitive Culture II., 175], who thinks that "vampires are not mere creations of groundless fancy, but causes conceived in spiritual form to account for the specific facts of wasting disease." Some writers, however, of whom Afanasief is one, explain the vampire stories mythologically. Of their explanations some account will presently be given.

In the opinion of the Russian peasant vampires,

as well as witches, exert a very baneful influence on the weather. To them, and to werewolves, are attributed the presence of storms, droughts, famines, cattle-plagues, and similar evils. Where such unholy beings wander, one woe succeeds another. But worse than their evil effect upon the weather—one which they produce in common with the spirits of all persons who have died by violence—worse than their attacks upon cattle, are their terrible dealings with mankind. As a specimen of the Russian vampire stories, the following, heard in the Tambof Government, may be taken:—

A peasant was driving past a grave-yard, after it had grown dark. After him came running a stranger, dressed in a red shirt and a new jacket, who cried,—
"Stop! take me as your companion."
"Pray take a seat."
They enter a village, drive up to this and that house. Though the gates are wide open, yet the stranger says, "Shut tight!" for on those gates crosses have been branded. They drive on to the very last house: the gates are barred, and from them hangs a padlock weighing a score of pounds; but there is no cross there, and the gates open of their own accord.

They go into the house; there on the bench lie two sleepers—an old man and a lad. The stranger takes a pail, places it near the youth, and strikes him on the back; immediately the back opens, and forth flows rosy blood. The stranger fills the pail full, and drinks it dry. Then he fills another pail with blood from the old man, slakes his brutal thirst, and says to the peasant,—

"It begins to grow light! let us go back to my dwelling."

In a twinkling they found themselves at the graveyard. The vampire would have clasped the peasant in its arms, but luckily for him the cocks began to crow, and the corpse disappeared. The next morning, when folks came and looked, the old man and the lad were both dead [6].

According to the Servians and Bulgarians, unclean spirits enter into the corpses of malefactors and other evilly-disposed persons, who then become vampires. Any one, moreover, may become a vampire, if a cat jumps across his dead body while it lies in the cottage before the funeral, for which reason a corpse is always carefully watched at that time. In some places the jumping of a boy over the corpse is considered as fatal as that of a cat. The flight of a bird above the body may also be attended by the same terrible result; and so may—in the Ukraine—the mere breath of the wind from the Steppe [7].

The bodies of vampires, of wizards, and of witches, as well as those of outcasts from the Church, and of people cursed by their parents, are supposed not to decay in the grave, for "moist mother-earth" will not take them to herself. There is a story in the Saratof Government of a mother who cursed her son, and after his death his body remained free from corruption for the space of a hundred years. "At last he was dug up, and his old mother, who was still alive, pronounced his pardon; and at that very moment the corpse crumbled into dust [8]."

[6] Afanasief, P. V. S. III. 558.
[7] Afanasief, P. V. S. III. 559—568. [8] Afanasief, P. V. S. III. 565.

Every one knows that when a vampire's grave is opened no trace of death is found upon its body, its cheek being rosy and its skin soft; and that the best way to destroy the monster is to drive a stake through it, when the blood it has been sucking will pour forth from the wound. The Servian method of discovering its grave may not be so well known. According to Vuk Karadjic[0] it is customary to take an immaculately black colt, and drive it through the churchyard. Over the vampire's grave it will refuse to pass. The whole village then turns out, the vampire is dug up, pierced with a white-thorn stake, and committed to the flames.

It is worthy of remark that the stake with which the vampire's corpse is pierced must be driven into it by a single stroke. A second blow would reanimate it. This idea is frequently referred to in the Russian *skazki* and other Slavonic stories, in which it is customary for the hero to be warned that he must strike his enemy the snake, or other monster, once only. A repetition of the blow would be certain to prove fatal to himself.

Sometimes, instead of blood-sucking vampires, heart-devouring witches trouble the peasant's repose. A Mazovian story relates how a certain hero was long renowned for courage. But at last one night a witch struck him on the breast with an aspen twig as he lay asleep; his breast opened, and out of it she took his heart, and inserted a hare's heart in its

[0] Quoted by Afanasief, P. V. S. III. 576.

place. The hero awoke a trembling coward, and remained one till the day of his death. Another Polish story of a similar nature tells how a witch substituted a cock's heart for that of a peasant. From that time forward the unfortunate man was always crowing[1]. Sometimes the witches did not eat the hearts they stole, but merely exposed them to a magic fire so as to create love-longings in the breasts from which they had been taken. The idea still survives, as Jacob Grimm remarks, in our expressions of "giving" or "stealing one's heart[2]."

A fondness for human flesh is attributed to ogre-like beings all over the world, so there is nothing remarkable in the depraved appetites of the supernatural man-eaters of the Slavonic tales. Somewhat singular, however, is one group of stories in which a dead wizard or witch is described as coming to life at midnight, and desiring to eat the person who is watching beside the bier. The body has generally been enclosed in a coffin, secured with iron bands, and conveyed to the church in which the watcher has to read aloud from Holy Writ above it all night long. As the clock strikes twelve a mighty wind suddenly arises, the iron bands give way with a terrible crash, the coffin-lid falls off, and the corpse leaps forth, and with a screech rushes at the doomed watcher, of whom, as a general rule, nothing remains next morning but bare bones. His only chance of escape is to trace a magic circle around him on the

---

[1] Afanasief, P. V. S. III. 571. [2] *Deutsche Mythologie*, 1035.

floor, and to remain within it, holding in his hand a hammer, the ancient weapon of the thunder-god. Here is one of the stories of this class from the Kharkof Government. " Once, in the days of old, there died a terrible sinner. His body was taken into the church, and the sacristan was told to read psalms over him. The sacristan took the precaution to catch a cock, and carry it with him. At midnight, when the dead man leaped from his coffin, opened his jaws wide, and rushed at his victim, the sacristan gave the bird a pinch. The cock uttered his usual crow, and that very moment the dead man fell backwards to the ground a numb, motionless corpse[3]."

It would be easy to quote many stories of this kind, for Slavonic folk-lore abounds in them, but I will not do so now, preferring to devote such space as remains to me to a brief sketch of the history of Russian witchcraft. What has been said will probably give some idea of the wizards and witches of modern times; the following remarks may serve to convey a similar idea of those of a remoter period.

In very distant times, it is supposed, the Slavonians, like many other peoples, placed great faith in the power of certain spells to rule the elements, to turn away storms, and to provide sunlight or rain according as either might be requisite; they even deemed such utterances necessary in order that the day might succeed to the night, and the summer follow the winter. These charms were then known only to

[3] Afanasief, P. V. S. III. 584.

professed seers. At first the persons who were acquainted with them were looked upon merely as exceptionally wise people. A *koldún*—afterwards a wizard in the bad sense of the word—was originally, as we have seen, a kind of priest. For even if the Old Slavonians recognized no separate caste of priests, at all events, as time passed by, there arose a special class of men and women who preserved the secret of composing such charms and incantations as were held to sway the seen and the unseen world. The hoarders of this mystical lore were generally old men, but the gift of divination was usually ascribed to women, and especially to young maidens, the volition of whose fresh, pure minds was supposed to exercise a magic influence over the forces of nature.

But when Christianity drove out the Slavonic deities, all the old dealings with the spirit-world were declared illicit, and those who were versed in them fell into dishonour. The *Koldún* became a mere conjuror or wizard, who by his spells realized unholy gains, and the *Vyeshchaya Zhená*, the Divining Woman or Prophetess, turned into the feared and hated *Vyéd'ma*, or witch. Their nature and their occupation became equally degraded: the witches, for instance, for private gain milking their neighbours' cows; whereas, in old times, they milked the heavenly cows—i.e. they drew down rain from the clouds—for the general good. As in pagan days many sacrifices were offered up on high places, especially at three fixed times in the year, so in after-days it was supposed that often on mountain tops, and especially at those very times, the wizards and witches held unholy revels, characterized by just such music, dancing, and feasting as used to accompany the heathen festivals[4]; as the smoke of other sacrifices formerly rose to heaven from the domestic hearth, so witches came to be associated with the various implements connected with the hearth, and were supposed to ride on the broom or the ovenfork, and to soar into the air through the stovepipe or the chimney[5].

It has been mentioned already, that although the wizard and the wise woman were generally respected in heathen times, yet there were occasions when they sank in the estimation of the people, who sometimes even carried their disrespect so far as to bury them alive in sacks, each attended by a dog, a cat, and a cock. But if they were liable to such treatment, it seems to have been only at times when the popular judgment was unhinged by some great calamity, such as a drought or a pestilence. As a general rule they stood high in the opinion of the masses, and their exaltation was attended by material advantages, so that it is scarcely to be wondered at that they watched the progress of the new religion with particularly unfavourable eyes, and did all that they could to impede it. On the other hand, the Christian hierarchy set them down as "devilish vessels," by the aid of which Satan was enabled to prolong his unwelcome resistance.

[4] Afanasief, P. V. S. 483.
[5] Orest Miller, *Opuit*, etc. т. 67—69.

The introduction of Christianity by St. Vladímir was not allowed to take place without a struggle. The inhabitants of Novgorod, for instance, broke into revolt, and those of Rostof, about the year 1070, put St. Leontius to death, and forced the Bishops Theodore and Hilarion to fly for their lives. Still more closely connected with the subject of the present chapter is the fact that, during the eleventh century, several risings against Christianity were instigated by dealers in magic. Thus in 1071 a wizard appeared in Kief, and prophesied that at the end of five years the Dnieper would flow backwards, and that the Russian and the Grecian lands would change places. Certain "ignorant persons," says the chronicler, gave heed to his words, but "the faithful" laughed at him, saying, "the devil plays with thee for thy ruin;" and in truth the wizard disappeared one night and left no trace behind. Another wizard, also, who appeared at Rostof in 1091, soon perished, and at Byeloozero two warlocks were seized by an armed force, and put to death, their corpses being left a prey to the beasts of the forest. At Novgorod, during the rule of Prince Glyeb, an insurrection was stirred up by a wizard, who gave out that he would publicly walk across the river Volkhof. Many of the townspeople took his side, and wanted to kill their bishop; but that courageous prelate put on his robes, seized a cross, and called upon the faithful to follow him. So the people were divided into two bodies, the Prince and his *drujina*, or military companions, following the bishop, while the common herd sided with the wizard. Then the Prince hid an axe under his dress, and drew near to the wizard, and asked him—

"Knowest thou what will happen in the morning, and in the evening?"

"I know all things," answered the wizard.

"Knowest thou what is going to take place now?"

"I shall perform great wonders."

At this point of the argument the Prince drew out his axe, and struck the wizard with such force that he immediately fell dead. Whereupon the people gave up all faith in him, and went quietly home [6].

Even after the adherents of heathenism had given up what they saw was a hopeless struggle, and Christianity had become the recognized religion of the Russian people, the old gods retained a hold, if not upon the affections, at least upon the fears of those "ignorant persons" who formed the great mass of the rural population. What had occurred at an earlier period in many other European lands was now repeated in Russia. Many a peasant who went publicly to church, privately worshipped the ancient objects of his allegiance, the old pagan rites being long kept up in sequestered nooks within dense forests, or by the side of lonely streams. At the same time, in Russia, as in other countries, even the "faithful" proselytes of the new religion could not at once forget the teaching of the old, so they retained a mass of familiar traditions, chiefly of a mythical nature, but they substituted in them for the names of

---

[6] Afanasief, P. V. S. III. 596—599.

their elementary gods and demigods, others which they took from the calendar of the Church. The consequence was a confusion of ideas which justified the epithet " two-faithed " which an old ecclesiastical writer bestowed upon the Russian people.

The superior clergy did all they could to remedy what they naturally considered a serious evil, levelling from time to time severe denunciations against the believers in " conjurors, witches, and wizards," and the performers of " demoniacal rites." In the twelfth century, the Metropolitan Ioann ordered that no practiser of magic should be allowed to participate in the sacraments of the church. The book of laws called the *Kormchaya Kniga*, according to a copy dated 1282, inflicted a six years' exile from church on persons addicted to " pagan practices," such as dealings in witchcraft and the like, and similar restrictions were laid on the indulgence of a leaning towards spiritualism by a series of ecclesiastical ordinances. But it was in vain that St. Cyril rebuked his flock for having recourse in illness to "accursed women," and that the Metropolitan Photius, in 1410, besought his clergy to " induce their congregations to abstain from " listening to fables, and frequenting wicked women." The wizards and witches held their own, just as the people, in spite of the remonstrances of their pastors, continued the " satanic games," attended by dance and song, which had come down to them from their heathen ancestors.

The clergy were more successful in their attacks on the books of a superstitious nature, mostly of

Byzantine origin, which they placed upon their Index. Many of these, of which Afanasief gives a full account, extending over six pages, were destroyed by orthodox fire, and with them not a few of the persons whose property they were. In 1227, for instance, a chronicler relates how four wizards were burnt to death at Novgorod. In 1411 the people of Pskoff burnt " twelve divining women," probably because a deadly epidemic was then ravaging the country. Sometimes, however, witches were only beheaded, or, as we have already seen, buried alive in a sack with various animals. Iván the Terrible greatly harassed the dealers in magic, but, if tradition is to be believed, they had their revenge. In the winter of 1584 a comet appeared which the Tsar, whose health was fast failing, took to be a sign of his approaching death. In order to obtain more certain information on this point, he appealed to the sorcery which he had tried to exterminate, sixty wizards from the north of Russia being brought together for his convenience in Moscow. There every attention was paid them, but in spite of this they prophesied that he would die on the 18th of March. On the morning of that day he felt himself stronger than usual, so he sent to tell the wizards that he intended to put them to death as false prophets. But they, probably remembering the celebrated Ides of March, received his message with contempt; and their behaviour was justified by the fact that the Tsar was soon afterwards seized by a fit in the middle of a game of chess, and died before he had time to carry out his intention.

This story is an evident fable, but the sufferings of persons accused of witchcraft in Russia are proved by incontestable evidence. The number of such victims to the superstitious terror of the civil and religious authorities seems to have been small, compared with that of the multitudes who perished in other lands, but the story of their martyrdom is sufficiently sad. At one time we find Iván the Terrible slowly roasting one of his generals, Prince Mikhail Vorotuinsky, in order to extort from him a confession of having attacked the royal health through the agency of "whispering women." In vain did the unfortunate sufferer protest his innocence. The Tsar listened to his agonized expressions, and then raked the coals nearer to his victim with his curved staff. At another time we read of cruel sufferings undergone by persons charged with having bewitched members of the royal family by means of magic practices brought to bear upon the traces of their footsteps. At various times we meet with accounts of the executions of men and women from whom confessions of dealing in magic had been wrung by torture. One of these, a woman named Fedosia who was put to death in 1674, declared her innocence on the scaffold, saying that she had accused herself only because she could not endure her torments. The annals of the law courts contain numerous cases of persons accused of having thrown others into convulsions, or at least of having afflicted them with hiccoughs. These convulsions were sometimes fictitious, being assumed for the

purpose of ruining an enemy by a charge of witchcraft. Even at the present day in the north of Russia, says Afanasief, the hiccough is supposed to be a demon inflicted on the sufferer by means of sorcery, and persons afflicted with epilepsy and St. Vitus's dance are regarded as the victims of hostile enchantments, and are called *klikushi*. As late as the year 1815 a charge of this kind was brought before a legal tribunal in the Pinejsk district. A peasant named Mikhail Chukharef was accused of afflicting his cousin, Ofimiya Lobanova, with "an evil spirit" in the shape of a hiccough. The accused pleaded guilty, stating that he had, after removing the cross he wore round his neck, whispered a certain spell over salt. The formula he used was as follows:—
"Lodge in such and such a person, ye hiccough-pains! tear and torture him to the end of time! As this salt shall dry up, so may that man also dry up!" and the salt thus enchanted was to be scattered on the road along which the intended victim had to pass. The court sentenced Chukharef to undergo thirty-five blows of the knout, as well as "a public church penance'."

. In 1715 Peter the Great gave orders that in future *klikushi*, or "possessed people," should be subjected to an examination, so as to find out whether they were really "possessed," or were only feigning "possession" (*klikushestvo*)—as did a certain Varvara Loginova, a carpenter's wife in St. Peters-

' Quoted from Maksímof's "Year in Siberia," by Afanasief, P. V. S. III. 66.

burg, who, after accusing a number of persons of having bewitched her, ultimately confessed, in 1714, to having been an impostor throughout. In 1770, in the Yarensk district of the Government of Vologda, several persons were accused of having bewitched certain girls and women, and were flogged till they confessed their guilt. One of the women of their number stated in her confession how she had acted on her victims—namely, by means of worms which the devil had given her. Some of these worms she produced, and her judges forwarded them to the Senate. On examination these diabolical worms turned out to be simple maggots, whereupon the Senate ordered the "possessed woman" to be flogged, turned the provincial judges out of their seats, and gave orders that in future similar complaints were not to be listened to [8].

But though the law has long ceased to examine such charges, they still command attention among the peasantry. The belief in vampires, also, retains its hold upon the popular mind, and the old custom of digging up those among the dead who are suspected of unfavourably affecting the weather is to this day observed, it is said, in remote localities. While the Slavonians were heathens they all seem to have been in the habit of resorting to this practice, and even after they had accepted Christianity they retained their original theories with respect to the influence of the dead upon the elements.

[8] Afanasief, P. V. S. III. 637.

In the thirteenth century Serapion, Bishop of Vladímir, was obliged to utter sharp reproofs of those superstitious men who would not allow the bodies of drowned or suffocated persons to rest in their graves, but exhumed them on the ground that they caused drought and scarcity; and in the sixteenth century a similar reprimand was considered necessary by Maxim the Greek. The false Demetrius was suspected by the people of dealing in witchcraft, and when, after his burial in the early part of May, 1606, a strong frost set in, hurtful to cornfields, gardens and orchards, they attributed it to his demoniacal influence. His dead body had been exposed for three days to public view, stretched on a table along with a reed-pipe, a mask, and a bagpipe, objects generally associated with jugglers and "transformers;" and it had afterwards been buried in one of the " poor-houses," the winter receptacles of the bodies of the unknown and friendless dead. Thence the populace tore his remains, and having consumed them with fire, mingled his ashes with gunpowder, and shot them from guns into the air. It is but a little time ago, if common report may be believed, that the peasants of any district in which a drought had long prevailed were in the habit of digging up the corpse of some person who had died from excess of drink, and of sinking it in the nearest swamp or lake, with the full belief that this proceeding would ensure the fall of rain. About three years ago the prospect of a bad harvest, caused by continual drought, induced the peasants of a village in the Tarashchansk district to have recourse to the following means of procuring better weather. They dug up the body of a Raskolnik, or Dissenter, who had died in the previous December, and had been buried in the village graveyard. Some of the party then beat it about the head, exclaiming, "Give us rain!" while others poured water upon it through a sieve. Then they put it back into the coffin and restored it to its resting-place[9]. All that can be said in excuse of such a practice as this is, that it is not as bad as that which so long prevailed in England, as well as in other lands, of testing a woman suspected of witchcraft by flinging her into a pond or river. The Servians are said still to keep up the practice, and it is asserted that among the Ruthenians bordering on Hungary a witch was drowned in this manner as late as 1827. But, as has already been remarked, sad as are the records of the sufferings inflicted among Slavonic nations upon the victims of a fear of witchcraft, they are far less tragic than those which tell of the thousands upon thousands of innocent persons whom a similar fear, in lands tenanted by Teutonic and Latin races, condemned to torture and to death. The Russian peasant sometimes murdered in his blind wrath; the legal tribunals of his country too often behaved with dull cruelty; but neither among the populace nor on the bench does there ever seem to have been found so persistent a murderer as our own Hopkins

[9] Afanasief, P. V. S. III. 572—574.

the Witchfinder, nor can any Russian laws on the subject of witchcraft be fairly charged with the cold-blooded malignity which characterizes the pages of the " Malleus Maleficarum."

From the dreary picture of fanaticism and superstition offered by the records of trials for witchcraft—always so monstrously terrible, whether they took place in Russia or in any other land—it is a relief to turn to the speculations in which some comparative mythologists have indulged, while endeavouring to account for the belief which gave rise to those trials; a belief of world-wide extent and of the most venerable antiquity. Disinclined to accept such theories as that supported by Mr. Tylor, who considers that "witchcraft is part and parcel of savage life[1]," and apparently looks upon the belief in it rather as the rank growth of an untilled soil than as the decayed form of one of the results of ancient mythological culture—preferring to trace back such stories as those of witches who feloniously milk their neighbours' cows to the poetic ideas of the primeval Aryans about storms and clouds, rather than to explain them by a partnership in the superstitions of the most degraded of African and American savages—these writers have applied to witchcraft traditions another system of explanation, a similar one to that which has restored to order and meaning so many of the apparently wild and irrational myths of old religion.

[1] "Primitive Culture," I. 125.

A considerable part of the twenty-sixth chapter of that work of Afanasief's which has been so frequently quoted in these pages, is devoted to an attempt to prove that the wizards and witches of modern days are, as a general rule, the representatives of the priests and the priestesses, or the "wise men" and "wise women," of pagan times; and also that the greater part of the superstitious ideas now connected with them are remnants or survivals of a mythical system, in which were expressed, in figurative language, the views of the ancient Slavonians about the forces of nature, the strife of the elements. Whether his arguments are or are not conclusive, I leave to more competent critics to decide. It will be sufficient here to mention a few of their most striking points.

The *Koldún* and *Vyéd'ma* he considers—whether in their modern forms of wizard and witch, or in their old capacities of priest and prophetess—as types of certain atmospheric forces or phenomena, and as the human inheritors of a reverence originally paid to the demons of cloud-land. Therefore it is, in his opinion, that they are supposed to direct the storm-cloud, to guide the whirlwind, to dispense the rain and hail, to be able to steal the dew or to hide the lights of heaven, to love to glide above the surface of the earth, to gather on the bare hill-side, to whirl to and fro in a wild dance, and to change at will from one form to another; therefore it is that dealers in magic are mentioned in old Slavonic documents as "cloud-compellers" — *oblakoprogon-*

niki [*óblako* = cloud, *gonyát'* = to chase], a word closely associated with the epithet of Zeus, *nephelêgeretês*[2].

The steeds on which wizards and witches make their aerial journeys are of a nature to suggest some connexion with the element of fire, either as burning on the domestic hearth or as flashing across the vault of heaven. Such are, according to Russian traditions—closely akin in this respect to those of Teutonic or Lettic extraction—the broom (in its different forms of *metlá*, *pomeló*, and *vyénik*), the poker (*kochergá*), the tongs (*ukhvát* = oven-fork), the shovel (*lopáta*), and the rake (*grábli*). On these the wizard or witch flies fast, resembling in rapid course the swift winds which sweep the clouds from the sky, or rake them together in masses which at times are rent by the fiery dart of the lightning. So closely are some of these implements still associated in parts of Russia with the storm, that the peasants often try to frighten away an ominous cloud by flinging a frying-pan out of doors, together with a broom, a shovel, or a poker.

Sometimes Russian traditions represent witches as riding to the Midsummer festival, not only on wooden or metal instruments, but also on actual horses. These, as well as all the other animals with which the popular fancy associated dealers in magic, are supposed to have been meant, in mythical language, for types of the cloud and the storm. The

[2] The word occurs in the *Kormchaya Kniga*—in a copy dated A.D. 1282—and in the *Domostroi*.

wolf, the cat, and the snake constantly figure in Russian stories as the associates of the witch or the Yagá Baba, and the cock, the well-known symbol of fire, plays in them an important part.

The wizards of Russian storyland are usually represented as old men with long beards and flashing eyes, and the witches—like the German *Hexen*—either as hideous old hags, or as young and fair damsels; just as in ancient times the clouds were depicted, in the language of poetry, as bearded demons, or as female forms, whether nymph-like or haggard. According to Russian tradition, a witch, when she gathers dew, or milks cows, or performs any other unholy deed, is always clothed in a long white shift, and has her hair loosely flowing over her shoulders. In this array she strongly resembles the Vilas, Rusalkas, and other fairy beings of aqueous nature, whose occupation it so often is to spin and weave, producing filmy textures which seem not unlike the clouds which now veil, and now melt away before the sunlight. As not only by spinning and by weaving, but also by other womanly employments, such as washing, milking, and the like, were the actions of the elementary forces of nature represented in ancient mythical language; so at last it became usual to associate women rather than men with the idea of commanding the elements; and thus it was more usually a witch than a wizard who was supposed to be on terms of familiarity with the inhabitants of the invisible world[3].

[3] Afanasief, P. V. S. III. 466—469.

Of all these womanly employments that of milking is the most prominent, and, according to some commentators, the most evidently mythical. The vulgar witch of to-day steals the milk from the earthly cows of her neighbour; her prototype was wont to milk the heavenly cows, that is to say, to draw the rain from the clouds. In the Government of Kief, it is affirmed that witches by night, when good folks sleep, "go out of doors, wearing long shifts and with dishevelled hair, trace a line with their hands round the starry sky, and eclipse the moon with clouds (or steal it); then, on the approach of a storm, they betake themselves to milking the cloud-cows themselves, and milk them so violently that from their teats, together with milk, there begins to flow blood (another metaphor for rain)[4]." In some villages, also, the witches are said to chase the moon into a cow-shed, and there to milk cows by her light; and the Bulgarians have a tradition to the effect that sorceresses can take the moon (*luná*) out of the sky, which accounts for lunar eclipses, and that she is then turned into a cow, which they milk, thus eventually obtaining such butter as heals otherwise incurable wounds.

In a similar manner, according to Afanasief, the stories about werewolves and other transformed creatures, and also about vampires, may be accounted for. As the clouds shift their plastic shapes, now "backed like a weasel," and now resembling a

[4] P. V. S. III. 488.

whale, so the mythical beings, under whose forms the philosophy of our ancestors personified the forces of nature, were originally supposed to undergo rapid metamorphoses, and the power of similar transformation was eventually attributed to the human beings who, in many respects, replaced them in popular belief. Thus, in the Ukraine, there lingers a tradition that a werewolf who is touched with a pitchfork or a flail immediately resumes his human form: this is explained as meaning that the thunder-god strikes a blow with his mace [the lightning], which tears the wolf's hide from his opponent [or disperses the cloud][5].

In the case of vampires, their sucking of blood is explained by Afanasief in the same manner as the draining of milk by witches. When winter condemns all nature to a temporary death, the thunder-god and the spirits of the storm sleep a sleep like that of death in their cloud-coffins. But with the return of spring they assume renewed life, and draw rain from the clouds, or, in mythical language, suck blood from sleepers[6]. According to this sytem of interpretation, some glimmering may be obtained, he thinks, of the original meaning of what, if taken literally, seems a needlessly improbable story—that of the vampire father who eats all his daughters but one; her escape being effected by her throwing off, as she runs, various portions of her dress, each of which her too fond parent has to tear up and then restore to its

[5] Afanasief, P. V. S. III. 556. [6] Afanasief, P. V. S. III. 564.

original form, before he can recommence his furious pursuit.

Whether these explanations are sound or not, they have at least the merit of ingenuity. Moreover, it would be a relief to our feelings if we could succeed in resolving the werewolves, vampires, and other demoniacal creatures, who have so long made night hideous, into not only harmless, but even beneficent elements—recognizing in their laidly lineaments the shapely features of the mythical beings under whose forms our Aryan ancestors personified the powers of nature. But before indulging in the pleasure of a belief in such desirable transformations, it may be as well at least to remember the existence of very different hypotheses on the subject. Even if we do not altogether agree with Mr. Fergusson[7], that none of the serpents and dragons, none of the dwarfs and magicians and such like creatures, are of Aryan extraction,—that "all the fairy mythology, in fact, of the East and West, belongs to the Turanian races,"—yet we may find, in his and in similar arguments, reason enough to make us pause before considering the opposite theory conclusively made out.

And if it would be hazardous to form rapid conclusions with respect to our own familiar fairies, still more dangerous would it be to decide hastily in the case of foreign demigods and demons. Great caution is requisite on the part of every one who undertakes to evolve a mythological system from a mass of

[7] Tree and Serpent Worship, p 73.

popular traditions. In no case is such caution more urgently demanded than in that of a student who has to deal with materials of so mixed a nature, and of so doubtful an extraction, as are the songs and stories of the Russian people.

Of that people I trust I have not conveyed an unfavourable idea. The nature of my work has led me to speak frequently of their foibles, to dwell at length upon their superstitions. But it is not by such weaknesses as these, which are to some extent common to all mankind, that we ought to judge of a peasantry who have always been signally remarkable for family affection, for reverence towards age, for sympathy with misfortune—who have retained for centuries, even under the pressure of that system of slavery which has but recently been overthrown, so keen a sense of loyalty, so warm a love for their native land.

In one of the most popular of the Russian stories —a Slavonic variant of a world-wide tale—the hero sits for thirty years beside his father's hearth, a helpless cripple, incapable of active life. But, at the end of that time, he is not only cured by two mystic personages, disguised as beggars, to whom he has given a draught of water, but he is endowed by them with gigantic strength. So, when he has risen from his lowly couch, he goes forth into the world, a noble conqueror, overcoming infidels, and slaying monsters, and freeing Christian prisoners, and in all ways succouring the needy and the oppressed. In the career of Ivan Muromets—this Slavonic counterpart of the Norse *Askepot*—the Russian people are said to have long recognized, in accordance with a vague tradition, a symbol of their own national life. For centuries, the story ran, they were doomed to remain inactive and despised. But the time would come, it proceeded to say (if reliance can be placed upon a somewhat improbable report), when they would shake off their lethargy, and put on irresistible might, and enter upon a warlike progress through the world, conquering and to conquer.

It may be that the prophecy is destined to receive a fulfilment, but one of a peaceful nature. The common people of Russia may figuratively be said to have lain long among the ashes. For nearly ten times the thirty years of the tale the great mass of the population was "fastened to the soil," debarred by law from anything like continuous progress. Now, at last, thanks to the unwearied efforts of what was once but a small body of statesmen, thanks, above all, to the forethought and the courage of the present Emperor, the land has been freed from the plague of slavery, and the millions whom its deadening influence had benumbed have the prospect opened out before them of a wider and a higher existence. They may be destined, like the long crippled Ivan Muromets, to mighty struggles terminating in decisive victories. But the struggles may perhaps be of the nature of those by which the labourer and the artisan work out their honest livelihood; the victories may prove of that priceless order by which men, having overcome their own besetting sins, emancipate themselves from a moral thraldom which is by no means less degrading than a physical servitude.

APPENDIX A.

The following are the Russian books to which I am principally indebted. In alluding to them in the foot-notes to the present volume I have frequently given only the initials of their titles, just as I have often represented the words *Deutsche Mythologie* by the letters *D. M.*

AFANASIEF. *Poeticheskiya Vozzryeniya Slavyan na Prirodu.* [Poetic Views of the Slavonians about Nature.] 3 vols. Moscow, 1865-69. 8vo.

――― *Narodnuiya Russkiya Skazki.* [Popular Russian Tales.] Third edition. 8 Pts. Moscow, 1863. 8vo.

BEZSONOF. *Kalyeki Perekhozhie.* [Wandering Psalm-singers. A collection of their songs.] 6 pts. Moscow. 1860-62. 8vo.

BUSLAEF. *Istoricheskie Ocherki, etc.* [Historical Sketches of National Literature and Art.] 2 vols. St. Petersburg, 1861. fol.

――― *O Vliyanii Khristianstva na Slavyansky Yazuik.* [On the Influence of Christianity on Slavonic Language.] Moscow, 1848. 8vo.

DAHL. *Poslovitsui Russkago Naroda.* [Proverbs of the Russian People.] Moscow, 1862. fol.

ERLENBEIN. *Narodnuiya Skazki.* [Popular Tales collected by village Schoolmasters.] Moscow, 1863. 8vo.

KASTORSKY. *Nachertanie Slovanskoi Mithologii.* [Outline of Slavonic Mythology.] St. Petersburg, 1841. 8vo.

KAVELIN. *Sochineniya.* [Collected works.] 4 vols. Moscow, 1859.

KHUDYAKOF. *Velikorusskiya Skazki.* [Great-Russian Popular Tales.] 3 pts. Moscow, 1860-62.

KIRYEEVSKY. *Pyesni sobrannuiya P. V. Kiryeevskim, etc.* [Songs collected by P. V. Kiryeevsky. Edited by P. A. Bezsonof and others.] Second edition. Parts 1—8. Moscow, 1868, etc. 8vo.

KOTLYAREVSKY. *O Pogrebal'nuikh Obuichayakh Yazuicheskikh Slavyan.* [On the Funeral Customs of the heathen Slavonians.] Moscow, 1868. 8vo.

MAIKOF. *O Builinakh Vladimirova Tsikla.* [On the Builinas of the Vladimir Cycle.] St. Petersburg, 1863. 8vo.

—————— *Velikorusskiya Zaklinaniya.* [Great-Russian Spells.] St. Petersburg, 1869. 8vo.

OREST MILLER. *Opuit Istoricheskago Obozryeniya Russkoi Slovesnosti.* [Attempt at an Historical Survey of Russian Literature Part 1. Section 1. Second edition.] St. Petersburg, 1866. 8vo.

—————— *Khristomatiya, etc.* [Chrestomathy, appended to the "Attempt, etc."] Part 1. Section 1. Second edition. St. Petersburg, 1866. 8vo.

—————— *Ilya Muromets.* [Ilya of Murom and the Heroes of Kief.] St. Petersburg, 1869. Royal 8vo.

RUIBNIKOF. *Pyesni sobrannuiya P. N. Ruibnikovuim.* [Songs collected by P. N. Ruibnikof. Edited by P. A. Bezsonof, etc.] 4 vols. Moscow, 1861-67. 8vo.

SAKHAROF. *Skazaniya Russkago Naroda.* [Utterances of the Russian People. Third edition.] 2 vols.[1] St. Petersburg, 1841. Royal 8vo.

—————— *Pyesni Russkago Naroda.* [Songs of the Russian People]. 5 vols. St. Petersburg, 1838-39. 12mo.

SCHOEPPING (or Shepping). *Mithui Slavyanskago Yazuichestva.* [Myths of Slavonic Heathendom.] Moscow, 1849. 8vo.

—————— *Russkaya Narodnost', etc.* [Russian Nationality in its Superstitions, Rites, and Popular Stories.] Moscow, 1862. 8vo.

SHCHEPKIN. *Ob Istochnikakh i formakh Russkago Basnosloviya.* [On the Sources and Forms of Russian Mythology.] 2 pts. Moscow, 1859-61.

---

[1] I possess, unfortunately, only the first volume. The second I have never even so much as seen, so rare has the book become.

APPENDIX A. 439

SHEIN. *Russkiya Narodnuiya Pyesni.* [Russian Popular Songs, collected and arranged by P. V. Shein.] Vol. I. Moscow, 1870. Royal 8vo.

SNEGIREF. *Russkie Prostonarodnuie Prazdniki, etc.* [Russian Popular Festivals and Superstitious Rites.] 4 vols. Moscow, 1837-39. 8vo.

SNEGIREF. *Russkie v svoikh Poslovitsakh.* [The Russians in their Proverbs.] 4 vols. Moscow, 1832. 12mo.

SOLOVIEF. *Istoriya Rossii.* [History of Russia.[2]] Fourth edition. Moscow, 1856, etc. 8vo.

TERESHCHENKO. *Buit Russkago Naroda.* [Manners and Customs of the Russian People.] 7 vols. St. Petersburg, 1848. 8vo.[3]

---

[2] In progress; only about twenty-one volumes have as yet been published.

[3] Students who wish to compare the folk-songs of the Russians with those of the other Slavonic peoples will find the following books of great service. To avoid typographical difficulties I have translated their titles:—

KOLBERG. "Songs of the Polish People." Warsaw, 1857. 8vo.
WOJCICKI. "Songs of the White-Croatians, Masures, etc." 2 vols. Warsaw, 1836. 8vo.
KARAJIC. "Servian Popular Songs." 5 vols. Vienna, 1841-65. 8vo.
SUSIL. "Moravian Popular Songs." Brunn, 1860. 8vo.
HAUPT AND SCHMALER. "Folk-Songs of the Wends in Upper and Lower Lusatia" [in Wendish and German.] Grimma, 1841-43. 4to.
ZEGOTA PAULI. "Songs of the Ruthenians in Galicia." 2 vols. Lwow, 1839-40. 12mo.

APPENDIX B.

A few words about the measures of the songs may be considered useful. The following specimens are given by Sakharof in his *Pyesni Russkago Naroda*[1].

The Khorovod Songs are as follows:—

(1) Ā мы̆ | про̄со̆ | сѣ̆я̄лй.
Ā mŭi | prōsŏ | sy̆ēyā̆lĭ.
But we | millet | have sown.

(2) Зӑпле̄тй | ся̆ | пле̄тӗнь | зӑпле̄тйся̆.
zăplētĭ | syă | plētĕn' | zăplētĭsyă.
Become woven | | fence | become woven.

(3) Ăй во̄ по̆лѣ̄ | Ăй во̄ по̆лѣ̄.
Ăй во̄ по̆лѣ̄ | Лӣпйнькӑ.

Ăȳ vō pŏlȳē | Ăȳ vō pŏlȳē.
Ăȳ vō pŏlȳē | Lĭpĭn'kă.

Ah, afield, | Ah, afield.
Ah, afield, | Lindenling.

The "Dance Songs" are usually in one of the following metres;—

(1) Во̄ по̆лѣ̄ бӗ | рӗза̄ | сто̆ | я̄лӑ.
Vō pŏlȳē bĕ | rĕzā | stŏ | yā̆lă.
Afield, a | birch-tree | | stood.

---
[1] II. 51—53.

(2) Пойду млада | по Дунаю.
Poydŭ mladă | po Dunayu.
I will go, the young one | by the Danube.

(3) Ахъ, утушка | луговая.
Akh, utushka | lugovaya.
Ah, duckie | meadowy.

(4) Какъ у насъ | во садочку.
Kak u nas | vo sadochku.
How with us | in the gardenling.

Of the Svyatki songs, sung at Christmas, Sakharof gives the following specimens in his *Skazaniya Russkago Naroda*[1], the work to which such frequent reference has already been made:—

(1) Щука шла | изъ Нова | города.
Она хвостъ | волокла | изъ Бѣлаозера.
Какъ на щу | къ чешуй | ка серебраная.

Shchuka shla | iz Nova | goroda.
Ona khvost | volokla | iz Byelaozera.
Kak na shchu | kye cheshuy | ka serebranaya.

A Pike came | out of | Novogorod.
She [her] tail | trailed | from Byeloozero.
How on the Pike | [are] scales | silvery.

---

[1] I. iii. 10.

(2) Растворю | я квашон | ку на донышкѣ.
Rastvoryu | ya kvashon | ku na donuishkye.
I knead | the dough | on the *donuishka*.

(3) Ахъ ты сѣй | мати, мучи | цу, пеки | пироги;
Къ тебѣ бу——дутъ го | сти неча | янные:
Къ тебѣ бу | дутъ въ лаптяхъ | ко мнѣ въ сапогахъ,
Akh tui cyey | mati, muchi | tsu, peki | pirogi:
K tebye bu——dut go | sti necha | yannuie:
K tebye bu | dut v laptyakh | ko mnye v sapogakh.

Ah [do] thou sift | mother, flour, | bake | pies:
To thee will be guests | not | expected:
To thee will be | in lapti | to me in boots.

(4) И я золото | хороню, | хороню,
Чисто серебро | хороню, | хороню.
I ya zoloto | khoronyu, | khoronyu,
Chisto serebro | khoronyu, | khoronyu.
And I gold | bury, | bury,
Pure silver | bury, | bury.

(5) Жемчужина | окатная,
До чего тебѣ | докатитися?
Zhemchuzhina | okatnaya.
Do chego tebye | Dokatitisya?
O Pearl | round [and able to roll.]
Whither to thee | to roll thyself.

INDEX.

Alatuir, the White Stone, 37.
Amulets, 387.
Ancestral Worship, 260.

Bába Yagá, ogress or witch, 161—164.
Bab'e Lyeto, or women's summer, 254.
Bear King, story of the, 182.
Beauty song, 275.
Besyéda, or social gathering, description of, 36.
Betrothal customs, 267—271; rings, 297.
Bratchina, or brotherly feast, 258.
Bread, superstitions concerning, 247.
Bride, purchase of, 290, 291.
Builinas, or metrical romances, cycles of, 57; story of Svyatogor, 58—63; collections of, 63: Ruibnikof's journey in quest of, 64—76.
Burial of the Gold, game and song of, 200.
Burning of Corpses, 325—330.
Buyan, the Happy Isle of, 37.
Byelbog, the White God, 103.

Capture of Bride, 283—286.
Cattle-plague, spells against, etc., 395—402.

Christening of Cuckoos, 215—217.
Christening of Rusalkas, 144.
Christmas songs, 186.
Coffins, 317.
Corn, superstitions concerning, 247: leading ears of, 248.
Cossack songs, 42—44.
Cuckoos, traditions about, 214; christening of, 215—217.

Danilof, Kirsha, 55.
Dawn, 188, 190, 349.
Dazhbog, the Day-god, 85.
Dead, commemoration of the, 260, 310—313; funeral rites, 313—320; banquet to the, 321.
Dmitry Saturday, commemoration of souls on, 260.
Dodola, 227—229.
Domovoy, or House-spirit, 120—139.
Dyevíchnik, or Girls' party, 271.

Easter, 219.
Elijah's Day, 247.
Epiphany, Eve of the, 207.
Expulsion of Tarakáns, 255.

Fern, traditions about the, 98.
Fire-worship, 257.
Foundations, sacrifices at, 127.

Funerals:—of Kostroma, 244; of Yarilo, 245; wedding-funerals, 309; modern funeral customs, 313—320; funeral banquets, 320; feast to ghosts, 321; ancient funeral rites, 323—327; human sacrifices at, 328, 329; the Strava and Trizna, 331, 332; burial of strangers, 333; songs about the dead, 334—344.

Gadániya, or guessings, 195.
Glory song, 198.
Guessings, 195.

Harvest, opening of the, 249; harvest-home feast, 250, 251.
Hell, Slavonic ideas about, 113.
Historical songs, 54.
House, ceremonies attendant on a change of, 137.
House-spirit, *see* Domovoy.

Ibn Fozlan, account of a burial by, 328.
Ilya's, or Elijah's Day, 247.
Ilya Muromets, 59—63.
Insect burial, 255.

James, Richard; his collection of Russian historical poems, 55.

Kásha, or stewed grain, 205.
Khorovods, or circling dances to songs, 2, 6—13; 223—226.
Kikimora, or Nightmare, 133.
Kirsha Danilof, 55.
Kolyáda Songs, 186—201.
Koshchei the Immortal, 165—167.

Kosá, or maiden braid of hair, 272—275, 288.
Kostroma, funeral of, 244.
Kostrubonko, 222.
Krasnaya Gorka, or Red Hill, 222, 223.
Kupalo, Midsummer feast of, 239—246.
Kulikovo, battle of, 259.

Laume, story of a, 101.
Lado and Lada, the deities of the Spring and of Love, 105, 241.
Leading ears of corn, rite of, 248.
Love-spells, 369.
Lyeshy, or Wood-demon, 153—160.

Malchik-s-Palchik, or Tom Thumb, 181, 183.
Magpies, 405.
Marriage:—list of the *dramatis personæ* at a, 263; the proposal and striking of hands, 265; the betrothal, 267—271; the girls' party, 271—275; the wedding day, 276—280; expenses of a peasant wedding, 281; ancient Slavonic ideas about marriage, 282; capture or purchase of bride, 283—286; her sorrow at leaving her home, 287—292; her feelings towards her parents, 292—295; freedom of choice, 295—301; wife's family position, 302; a bride's lament, 303, 304; songs about a happy marriage, 305; mythical wedding guests, 306—308.

Máslyanitsa, or "Butter-week," 208, 209.
Mavkas, or Little-Russian fairies or water-nymphs, 142, 143.
Midsummer Customs, 239—246.
Mythology: — Old Slavonic Deities, 80—84, 102; Svarog, 85; Dazhbog and Ogon', 85, 86; Perun, 86—102: Byelbog, 103; Lado and Lada, 105; spirit-world, 106; ideas about the soul, 107—118; Paradise, 111; the Rakhmane, 112; the Domovoy, or House-spirit, 120—139; the Rusalka, or Naiad, 139—146; the Vila and Poludnitsa, 147; the Vodyany, or Water-sprite, 148; the Lyeshy, or Wood-demon, 153—160; the Bába Yagá, or Ogress, 161—164; Koshchei the Immortal, 165—167; the Vyed'ma, or Witch, 168—172; the Snake, 173—177; the Water-king, 178: Swan Maidens, 179; Tom Thumb, 183; Kolyáda rites, 186—201; Ovsen, 202—204; New Year, 205—207; the "Butter Week," 209; the death of Winter, 210; reception of Spring, 211—213; Cuckoo christening, 214—218; Tree-worship, 219; Easter and the Krasnaya Gorka, 220—227; Dodola, 228; St. George songs, 229—233; Semík and Whitsuntide, 233—239; Kupalo and Midsummer, 239—243; funeral of Kostroma, or Yarilo, 244—246: traditions about corn, 247; leading cars of corn, 248, 249; the harvest, 250, 251; plaiting Volos's beard, 251; Volos's name, 252; St. Vlas, 253; the Women's Summer, 254; expulsion of Tarakáns, 255; the Ovín, or corn-kiln, 257; Dmitry Saturday and ancestral worship, 259, 260; mythological riddles, 348—350; the Isle of Buyan, 37; the White Stone Alatuir, 37; witchcraft, 37; personification of cattle-plague, cholera, small-pox, etc., 395—403; werewolves and vampires, 403—415, 428—433.

New Year songs and customs, 203—207.
Nightmare, 133.

Ogon', or Fire, 85.
Orphans, songs about, 293, 334.
Ovín, or corn-kiln, respect paid to, 257.
Ovsén songs, 202—204.

Paradise, Slavonic ideas about, 111—113.
Parjanya and Perun, 86.
Perun the Thunder-god, compared with Parjanya, 86; Lettic songs about, 88—91; his statues, 93; myths about, 74—102.
Perkunas, 88—91, 101.
Pigeons, traditions about, 181.
Plakal'shchitsa, or Wailer, 342.
Poludnitsa, 147.
Posidyelka, or social gathering, 32.
Potters' Field, near Moscow, 333.

446　INDEX.

Prichitaniya, or laments, 343, 344.
Pripyevka, prelude or refrain, 303.
Purchase of a bride, 273, 274, 283—286, 290, 291.
Purification, rite of, after a funeral, 319.

Rádunitsa, or commemoration of the dead, 222, 310—313.
Rain, effect of witchcraft on, 383.
Rakhmane, or Brahmans, legend of the, 113.
Riddles, 346—356.
Robber songs, 45—47.
Rukobitie, or striking of hands before marriage, 265.
Rusalkas, or Water-nymphs, 139—146, 216.

Semík, feast of, 233.
September customs, 253—256.
Small-pox, Russian ideas about, 403.
Snakes, stories about, 173—176.
Soul, Slavonic ideas about the, 107—118.
Soldier songs, 51—54.
Songs:—general sketch of Russian songs, 1; their influence on the people, 4: their age, 5; their themes, 14; classes of, 39; Cossack songs, 42; Robber songs, 45; Soldiers' songs, 51; historical songs, 54; metres of, 77—79.
Mythic and Ritual songs, 186; Kolyádki, or Christmas songs, 187—201; Ovsén and New Year songs, 202—207; Spring songs, 212; Krasnaya Gorka Khorovods, 223—226; songs about St. George, 230; Semík and Whitsuntide songs, 236—238; Midsummer songs, 239—246; Harvest songs, 249—251; Autumn songs, 256, 259.
Marriage songs, 262; Betrothal songs, 266—271; Kosá, or Maiden-tresses songs, 272—275, 288; Bridal-benediction songs, 278; the "Sowing of the Millet," 283; bargaining for a bride songs, 286, 287, 220, 291; love songs, 295—302; a bride's lament, 303; happy-marriage songs, 305; songs about Cosmas and Demian, 307.
Funeral Songs; Lament of orphans, 334—337; of widows, 338—340; wailings above graves, 343, 344; a riddle-song, 356; a witchcraft song, 394; cattle-plague songs, 396, 399.
Sowing of the Millet, song of the, 213.
Spells, see Zagovórs.
Spring songs, 212.
Stars, song to the, 207.
Stenka Razin, songs about, 45.
St. George, traditions about, 229—233.
St. John's Day, 240—242.
St. Peter's Day, 246.
St. Philip's Fast, 255.
Strava, or funeral feast, 331.
St. Simeon, 253.
St. Vlas, 253.
Sun, stories about the, 242.

INDEX. 447

Sun's Sister, story of the, 169.
Svarog, or Ouranos, 85.
Svarozhich, or the Sun, 85, 86.
Swan-maidens, 148, 179.

Tarakáns, expulsion of insects called, 255.
Threshold, traditions about, 136.
Tom Thumb, Slavonic counterpart of, 177, 183.
Toothache, spells against, 367.
Tree-Worship, 219, 238.
Trizna, or funeral feast, 331.
Tsar Morskoi, or Sea-king, 178—180.
Tur, 236—238.

Vampires, 409—415, 432.
Vasíly's, or New-Year's Day, 203—207.
Vodyany, or Water-sprite, 148—153.
Vii, a Servian mythical being, 100.
Vilas, Servian mythical beings, 147—181.
Volos, the Cattle-god, 251, 252.
Voplenitsa, or Wailer, 342.
Vyed'ma, or Witch, 168—170.

Water of Life and Death, 97.
Water-sprite, see Vodyany.
Water-nymph, see Rusalka.
Werewolves, 403—409, 432.

Whirlwinds, connexion of witchcraft with, 382.
Whitsuntide customs, 233—235.
Widow's lament, 338.
Widow-sacrifice, 327—330.
Winter, death of, 211.
Witchcraft : — stories about witches, 168—170; Russian names for wizards and witches, 378; their power and functions, 380; dealers in amulets, etc., 387; milking of cows by witches, 390; destruction of crops by wizards, 392; poisoning, 393; werewolves, 403—408; vampires, 409—415; history of witchcraft in Russia, 417—427; mythological explanation, 428—433.
Wood-demon, see Lyeshy.

Yarilo, funeral of, 245.
Yegory, or St. George songs, 229.

Zagádkas, or Riddles, 346—356.
Zakrút, or twisting of ears of corn by a wizard, 392.
Zagovórs, or spells, 357; against toothache, 367; against cuts, 368; to produce love, 369; against a mother's grief, 372; against wild beasts, 388.

LONDON:
GILBERT AND RIVINGTON, PRINTERS,
ST. JOHN'S SQUARE.

www.ingramcontent.com/pod-product-compliance
Lightning Source LLC
Chambersburg PA
CBHW031955300426
44117CB00008B/774